Computational Geometry and Computer Graphics in C++

Michael J. Laszlo

School of Computer and Information Sciences
Nova Southeastern University

Prentice Hall
Upper Saddle River, NJ 07458

Library of Congress Cataloging-in-Publication Data

Laszlo, Michael Jay.
   Computational geometry and computer graphics in C++ / by Michael
J. Laszlo.
      p.   cm.
   Includes bibliographical references and index.
   ISBN 0-13-290842-5
   1. C++ (Computer program language)   2. Computer graphics.
I. Title.
QA76.73.C153L38   1996
006.6'6—dc20

95–38141
CIP

Acquisitions editor: **Alan Apt**
Production editor: **Rose Kernan**
Copy editor: **Patricia Daly**
Cover designer: **Bruce Kenselaar**
Buyer: **Donna Sullivan**
Editorial assistant: **Shirley McGuire**

©1996 by Prentice-Hall, Inc.
Simon & Schuster / A Viacom Company
Upper Saddle River, NJ 07458

The author and publisher of this book have used their best efforts in preparing this book. These efforts include the development, research, and testing of the theories and programs to determine their effectiveness. The author and publisher make no warranty of any kind, expressed or implied, with regard to these programs or the documentation contained in this book. The author and publisher shall not be liable in any event for incidental or consequential damages in connection with, or arising out of, the furnishing, performance, or use of these programs.

Printed in the United States of America

10 9 8 7 6 5 4 3 2 1

ISBN   0-13-290842-5

Prentice-Hall International (UK) Limited, London
Prentice-Hall of Australia Pty. Limited, Sydney
Prentice-Hall Canada Inc., Toronto
Prentice-Hall Hispanoamericana, S.A., Mexico
Prentice-Hall of India Private Limited, New Delhi
Prentice-Hall of Japan, Inc., Tokyo
Simon & Schuster Asia Pte. Ltd., Singapore
Editora Prentice-Hall do Brasil, Ltda., Rio de Janeiro

**To my parents
Maurice and Phyllis**

Contents

Preface

Our principal objective in this book is to describe some basic problems that arise in computer graphics and computational geometry and to present some practical and relatively simple methods for solving them. In these pages we will not attempt a comprehensive survey of these fields. Rather, we will cover a number of core problems and solutions that may serve as an introduction to these fields and at the same time prove both interesting and accessible to the reader.

Another goal of this book is to introduce the reader to the design and analysis of algorithms (an algorithm is a recipe or method for solving a computational problem). This will provide the framework for studying the algorithms we will cover. Themes discussed include elementary data structures such as lists and search trees, algorithmic paradigms such as divide and conquer, and methods for analyzing the performance of algorithms and data structures.

The problems we will cover are culled from the fields of computer graphics and computational geometry. Spurred on by pressures from the marketplace and by advances in computer technology (not least being the introduction of the personal computer), computer graphics has developed rapidly since its inception in the 1950s. By contrast, computational geometry is ancient, with roots in the straightedge-and-compass constructions of Euclid. Yet it too has undergone tremendous growth in the last several decades, encouraged by (and encouraging) advances in algorithmic science and by growing recognition of its wide applicability.

Computer graphics encompasses methods for modeling and rendering scenes. *Modeling* is used to construct a scene description, and the nature of the scene may be varied: ordinary objects in two or three dimensions, natural phenomena such as clouds or trees, pages of text, oceans of numbers obtained from imaging devices or simulation studies, and many others. *Rendering* is used to transform the scene description into a picture or animation.

The computer graphics problems we will consider in this book involve rendering. *Clipping* is used to determine that portion of a geometric object that lies outside a region (or window) so it can be discarded prior to image formation. *Hidden surface removal* is used to identify those objects (and portions of objects) in space which are hidden from view by other objects that lie even closer to the viewing position, so they too can be discarded prior to image formation.

Computational geometry encompasses algorithms for solving geometry problems. The problems we will cover are easy to formulate and involve simple geometric objects: points, lines, polygons, and circles in the plane; and points, lines, and triangles in space. Some of the problems we will consider include decomposing polygons into triangles, finding shapes—polygons, decompositions, and convex hulls—that are "hidden" among finite sets of points, forming the intersection of various geometric objects, and searching in the plane for geometric objects satisfying certain conditions.

The connection between computer graphics and computational geometry does not end with the fact that both involve geometric objects. Although some methods clearly belong to one field or the other, many methods can be claimed by both. Moreover, certain methods in computational geometry have been motivated by or fruitfully applied to problems arising in computer graphics. Hidden surface removal is a case in point. Although central to computer graphics and solved in numerous ways by researchers in the computer graphics community, in recent years the problem has been subjected to the more exacting methods of computational geometry.

Prerequisites

The material we cover assumes only a modest background. Some trigonometry and linear algebra is used when classes for geometrical objects are defined in Chapter 4. However, what little mathematics is required will be explained to the extent needed for the nonmathematical reader to appreciate the material. Prior experience with basic data structures, such as linked lists and binary trees, is helpful but not necessary. In Chapter 3 we address the role of data structures and develop from scratch those we will require through the remainder of the book: lists, stacks, and binary trees.

In this book we provide working C++ programs for every algorithm and data structure we cover. There are two main advantages in integrating working code into a book about algorithms. First, each implementation complements the prose account of how the underlying algorithm works, reinforcing the key ideas, providing a formal perspective of the algorithm, and supplying details that the prose account omits. Second, the reader can execute, modify, and experiment with a program to understand better how the underlying algorithm behaves in practice. The program is a launching pad for creativity and exploration.

Those readers familiar with C++ will, of course, benefit most from the programs in the text. However, readers with experience in the C language will also be in a position to gain from the programs since C++ is a superset of C; and they will be all the more so if willing to study C++ while reading this book. Even those with no programming experience can skip over the implementations and still enjoy the text.

Outline of Topics

This book consists of two parts. Part I, "Basics" (Chapters 1 to 4), presents background—the fundamentals of data structures and algorithms and the necessary geometrical concepts and tools. Part II, "Applications" (Chapters 5 to 9), poses problems and presents solutions.

Chapter 1 provides a broad framework, which includes the definition of such essential terms as *algorithm*, *data structure*, and *analysis*. The chapter also addresses our use of the C++ language and the issue of robustness in our implementations. Chapter 2, which concerns the analysis of algorithms, provides the concepts and methods needed to analyze the performance of the algorithms and data structures to follow. Chapter 3 presents C++ classes which embody both the abstract data types we will need later and the data structures for their implementation: linked lists, stacks, and several versions of binary search trees. Chapter 4 presents classes for representing and manipulating basic geometric objects in the plane and in space. Among other things, these classes provide functions for computing the point at which two skew lines in the plane intersect and for classifying a point relative to a line in the plane or a triangle in space.

Part II is organized by algorithmic paradigm—each of its chapters presents algorithms conforming to a given paradigm. Chapter 5 covers *incremental insertion* methods, which process the input one item at a time without first scanning the input in its entirety. Algorithms to be covered include an insertion method for finding the convex hull of a finite point set, an algorithm for clipping a line to a convex polygon (the Cyrus-Beck method), an algorithm for clipping an arbitrary polygon to a convex polygon (the Sutherland-Hodgman method), and an algorithm for decomposing into triangles a special class of polygons known as *monotone* polygons.

Chapter 6 covers *incremental selection* methods, which are incremental methods that scan the input in its entirety before proceeding. Algorithms to be covered include two more methods for finding the convex hull of a finite point set (the gift-wrapping method and the Graham scan), a linear-time algorithm for computing the intersection of two convex polygons, and an incremental method for triangulating a set of points in the plane.

Chapter 7 covers *plane-sweep* algorithms, which work by sweeping a line from left to right across the plane while constructing a solution to the subproblem that lies to the left of the sweepline. One of the plane-sweep algorithms we cover finds the union of a collection of rectangles in the plane; another decomposes an arbitrary polygon into monotone pieces.

Chapter 8 covers *divide-and-conquer* algorithms, which solve a problem by splitting it into two subproblems each half the size of the original, solving these, and then combining their solutions into a solution for the original problem. Algorithms to be covered include yet another method for finding the convex hull of a finite set of points (the merge hull method), a method for decomposing an arbitrary polygon into triangles, and a method for partitioning the plane into polygonal cells known as *Voronoi regions*.

Chapter 9 presents methods based on *spatial subdivisions*. We will present three subdivisions—*grids*, *quadtrees*, and *2D trees*—for solving the *range searching* problem in the plane: Given a finite set of points in the plane and an axes-parallel rectangle, report those points which lie in the rectangle. We will also cover the use of *binary space partition trees* for performing hidden surface removal in space.

Acknowledgments

I would like to thank a number of people who read portions of this text at various stages and provided useful suggestions: David Dobkin, Erik Brisson, Burt Rosenburg, Deborah Silver, and Shai Simonson, as well as several anonymous reviewers. I am also thankful to the Department of Mathematics and Computer Science of the University of Miami (Coral Gables, Florida) for the time and resources to write this book, and to the School of Computer and Information Sciences of Nova Southeastern University (Ft. Lauderdale) for its support during the production phase of this project. For their enthusiasm and encouragement, I thank Prentice Hall editors Bill Zobrist (during the writing phase of this project), Rose Kernan and Alan Apt (production phase) and their assistants, Phyllis Morgan and Shirley McGuire.

I am grateful for the love and encouragement of my wife, Elisa, without whose support I would not have attempted, much less completed, this book. I also wish to thank our young daughter, Arianna, whose "terrible twos" are if anything a joy, and my parents, Maurice and Phyllis.

I
Basics

1

Introduction

In this chapter we present a framework for the study of algorithms, geometrical or otherwise. We address such questions as, What are algorithms? What are data structures? What does it mean to analyze an algorithm? Our concern is to orient the reader, to introduce the basic concepts and raise the relevant questions. The answers and definitions we supply in this chapter are intended to be concise and skeletal. They will be fleshed out in later chapters, where we encounter more detailed explanations and many examples.

We also address this book's use of the C++ language, as well as how robust its implementations are.

1.1 Framework

Let us briefly survey the terrain. A *computational problem* is a problem to be solved by a method employing an agreed-upon set of instructions. A computational problem is framed by a problem statement, which both characterizes all legal inputs and expresses the output as a function of these legal inputs. For example, consider the problem we will name BOUNDARY-INTERSECTION: Given two polygons in the plane, report whether their boundaries intersect. A legal input consists of two polygons in some specified format. Given two legal input polygons, the output is yes if their boundaries intersect, and no otherwise.

An *algorithm* is a method for solving a computational problem. Algorithms are abstract— a given algorithm can be expressed in many ways, implemented as a computer program in different programming languages, and executed on different computers. Every computer program embodies an algorithm and, if the program is well written, the underlying algorithm can be discerned in the program. As an example of an algorithm, the following algorithm solves the BOUNDARY-INTERSECTION problem: Given two input polygons, compare each edge of the first polygon with every edge of the second. Report that the boundaries intersect if some pair of edges intersect, and report that the boundaries do not intersect otherwise. Note that another algorithm is needed to decide whether any two edges intersect.

An *algorithmic paradigm* is a design after which an algorithm is patterned. Just as different programs can be based on the same algorithm, so can different algorithms be based on the same paradigm. Familiarity with paradigms helps us understand and explain an algorithm whose form we have encountered before and helps in the design of new algorithms. The algorithm we have sketched for the BOUNDARY-INTERSECTION problem iteratively applies the *incremental insertion* paradigm: In each stage, an edge of the first polygon is selected and then compared to each edge of the second polygon in turn. This and other algorithmic paradigms will be explored in this book.

Algorithms employ objects for organizing data called *data structures*. Algorithms and data structures go hand in hand: Algorithms motivate the design and study of data structures, and data structures serve as the building blocks from which algorithms are constructed. Our algorithm for BOUNDARY-INTERSECTION relies on a data structure for representing polygons and one for representing edges.

An *abstract data type*, or *ADT*, is the public view of a data structure, separate from its implementation. The ADT comprises the set of operations which the data structure supports, and it serves as the interface between an algorithm and its data structures: The algorithm executes the operations supported by the ADT, and the data structure implements these operations. Viewed differently, each ADT represents a computational problem (a set of operations), and each data structure that supports the operations represents a solution to the ADT. Our BOUNDARY-INTERSECTION algorithm requires the use of two ADTs: A *polygon* ADT, which includes operations for accessing a polygon's edges, and an *edge* ADT, which includes an operation for deciding whether a given pair of edges intersect.

For most problems, there exist several competing algorithms, and for most abstract data types, there are several competing data structures. How can we identify the most efficient solutions? *Algorithm analysis* encompasses methods for describing and measuring the performance of algorithms and data structures. Analysis provides a basis for choosing the best solution to a given problem and for deciding whether a more efficient solution is possible. Analysis reveals, for instance, that our BOUNDARY-INTERSECTION algorithm runs in time proportional to the product of the polygons' sizes (where the size of a polygon equals the number of edges it contains). The algorithm is not optimal; indeed, in Chapter 6 we will present a solution which runs in time proportional to the *sum* of the polygons' sizes.

1.2   Our Use of the C++ Language

In this book we provide working C++ programs for every algorithm and data structure we cover. There are two main advantages to dovetailing working code and text. First, each program complements the prose account of how the underlying algorithm works, reinforcing the key ideas, providing a formal perspective of the algorithm, and supplying details that the prose account omits. Second, the reader can execute, modify, and experiment with a program to understand better how the underlying algorithm behaves in practice.

We will be using a number of features specific to C++, which are not a part of C. We will employ classes, member functions, access control, constructors and destructors, operator functions, overloaded functions, and reference types. We will also derive new classes from other (base) classes, whereby a new class inherits the attributes and behavior of its base classes. Class templates and function templates will also be used. A template defines a type-independent class or function from which can be obtained a family of classes or functions, which operate on different types but which otherwise behave alike.

This book makes no attempt to teach C++. We will occasionally explain our use of certain language features to account for some design decision or to jog the reader's memory, but not to teach the language. Good introductions to C++ are provided by [23, 79], and an annotated reference manual by [26].

Nor does this book intend to teach object-oriented programming (OOP). The programs we present are designed to be easily understood and followed. While intelligibility usually follows from rigorous OOP practices, we will sometimes depart from this practice for the sake of simplicity or conciseness (without sacrificing intelligibility). In OOP, one typically spends a great deal of time, effort, and code in the design of classes so time may be saved later when developing application programs in which the classes are used. However, many of the classes we will be defining are "throw-away," intended for use in only one or two applications. In such cases, it would take us too far afield to define the class for fullest generality and integrity. Object-oriented programming is treated by the texts [11, 13, 15, 32].

A note concerning efficiency is in order. Our programs are generally efficient. However, we willingly compromise efficiency in little ways for the sake of clarity, our main concern. This may entail, for example, adding an unneeded local variable to correspond to a concept explained in the text, or making a redundant procedure call to avoid saving the results of a previous call, or calling an already-defined function instead of a more specialized function that we do not wish to take the trouble to define. You are, of course, welcome to fine-tune these programs.

All of the programs in this book were implemented on a Macintosh LCIII using Symantec C++. This development program implements the C++ language as defined in *The Annotated C++ Reference Manual* by Ellis and Stroustrup [26]. The programs were implemented verbatim, as given in this book, with one exception: The class names `Point` and `Polygon` used in the book were changed to `Point2D` and `Polygon2D` in the implementation. This was necessary to avoid name conflicts.

1.3   Robustness

An algorithm is robust if it always works right, even when the input embodies degeneracies and special cases. Of course, one possible source of failure is that the algorithm simply is not correct. Yet even if the algorithm is correct, it may fail due to round-off during floating-point calculations. Round-off error occurs because real numbers are represented using only a limited amount of memory, such as the 8 bytes commonly used for type `double`. Thus all real numbers, of which there are infinitely many, are represented in only a finite number of ways. The round-off error equals the difference between the real number and its floating-point approximation.

Round-off error can be troublesome for geometric algorithms like those covered in this book, which operate in a continuous space such as the plane or three-dimensional space. Ideal points can only be approximated because their components are real numbers; ideal line segments can only be approximated because they are represented by their endpoints; and so forth. Round-off error is most problematic when the input embodies, or gives rise to, special cases, for in such borderline cases it may lead the algorithm to make faulty decisions. For example, given an ideal line and an ideal point through which the line passes, a computer program may determine that the point lies to the left of the line, to the right of the line, or on the line, depending on how the program represents both the line and the point. When special cases arise, the solution produced by a program can be wrong due to round-off error, even though the underlying algorithm—operating on ideal geometric objects—may be correct.

We have taken two approaches to ensure—or at least to try to ensure—that the programs in this book are robust. For some programs, we have restricted input to the program in order to exclude certain special cases. Although such programs are less general than they might be, little harm is done. It is the general cases that *are* handled that usually prove the most interesting. Moreover, handling special cases often requires extra code, which obscures the main ideas.

The special cases that are excluded tend to occur only rarely in practice. Nonetheless, some of the programs we will cover specifically give rise to special cases, which must be handled by other programs in this book; the latter programs must handle these special cases correctly if the former programs which depend on them are to work. Our second approach to robustness allows special cases and attempts to remove them when they arise by perturbing the problem in small ways: extending the length of a line segment by a slight amount, shifting a line to the left an infinitesimal distance, moving a point that is very close to a line onto the line, and so forth. The goal in all cases is to transform a decision that can go either way into one that is black and white, whose outcome is independent of how we choose to represent geometric objects.

The problem of ensuring robust computation has gained considerable attention in recent years. Although the approaches we have adopted in this book are in common use, they are by no means the final word. Other approaches leading to greater robustness exist, though they lie beyond the scope of this book.

2

Analysis of Algorithms

To analyze an algorithm is to measure and describe its performance. Understanding how well an algorithm performs indicates whether the algorithm is practical, given the resources that are available. Moreover, algorithm analysis provides a basis for comparing different algorithmic solutions to the same problem, ranking them by performance, and identifying which are most efficient.

Algorithm analysis generally concentrates on the resources of space (memory cells) and time required by algorithms. In this chapter we will focus on the time it takes for an algorithm to execute. Time is often the critical resource. Real-time systems like those used for flight control or robot vision must execute in the blink of an eye if (often catastrophic) failure is to be avoided. Even more tolerant systems like text editors are expected to respond to the user's commands on the order of seconds, and off-line programs like those for tallying payrolls or analyzing medical imaging data should execute in no more than a few hours or at most a few days. It is sometimes imagined that running time will become less critical as faster computers are developed. This is simply not the case. The problems posed to computers today are more difficult than ever, and their difficulty seems to outpace the computer technology on which fast solutions too often depend.

Space is generally less critical than time. Many algorithms encountered in practice, as well as nearly every algorithm covered in this book, use space proportional to input length; thus if there is enough memory to pose the problem, there is usually enough memory to solve it. In any case, much of what follows can be applied in analyses of space requirements.

Space and time are by no means independent resources. It is often possible to conserve one of the resources by spending more of the other, in what is sometimes referred to as a *space/time tradeoff*. This is, of course, advantageous when one of the resources is especially scarce or costly.

In this chapter we will present three established approaches that simplify the task of analysis without compromising the usefulness of its results. The first approach is to adopt an abstract model of computation; the second to express running time as a function of input size; and the third to express running time as a simple growth rate function. In the last section we will discuss problem complexity, which concerns how much time is both necessary and sufficient to solve a given problem.

2.1   Models of Computation

To analyze an algorithm, we must first identify the operations it uses and what each one costs. This is specified by a *model of computation*. Ideally, we choose a model of computation that abstracts the algorithm's essential operations. For instance, to analyze an algorithm involving polygons, we might count the number of times vertices are visited. Numerical algorithms are typically analyzed by counting arithmetic operations. Sorting and searching algorithms are usually analyzed by counting the number of times pairs of items are compared.

The cost of each operation encompassed by a model of computation is given in abstract units of time called *steps*. In some models of computation, every operation costs a constant number of steps; in others, the cost of some operations may depend on the arguments with which the operation is called. The *running time* of an algorithm for a given input is the total number of steps it executes.

Although adopting an abstract model of computation simplifies analysis, the model must not be so abstract that it ignores significant amounts of work performed by the algorithm. Ideally, the time between successive operations counted by the model of computation is constant and so can be ignored. Then running time—the total cost of the operations covered by the model of computation—is proportional to actual execution time.

Since running time depends on the model of computation, it is natural to adopt the same model of computation for different solutions to the same problem. Then by comparing their running times, we can identify the most efficient solutions (were models of computation to vary, we would be comparing apples and oranges). For this reason we generally adopt—though often only implicitly—a model of computation as part of a problem statement. To make these ideas more concrete, let us work with the problem of finding a given integer x in a sorted array of integers. We will call this problem SEARCH:

Given an integer x and a sorted array a of distinct integers, report the index of x within a; if x does not occur in a, report -1.

Integer x is referred to as the *search key*.

The model of computation we will adopt for SEARCH includes only the *probe* operation: comparing the search key x to some integer in the array. Assuming integers of bounded size, a single probe can be performed in constant time. So we will say that a probe costs one step.

The simplest solution to SEARCH is given by *sequential search*: Step through array *a* while probing each integer. If *x* is found (the search succeeds), then return its index in *a*; otherwise return -1, indicating that the search failed. A reasonable implementation is as follows:

```
int sequentialSearch(int x, int a[], int n)
{
    for (int i = 0; i < n; i++)
        if (a[i] == x)
            return i;
    return -1;
}
```

Where $f(x, a, n)$ denotes the running time of `sequentialSearch` as a function of input, we have

$$f(x, a, n) = \begin{cases} k + 1 & \text{if } x \text{ occurs in position } k \text{ of } a \\ n & \text{otherwise (the search fails)} \end{cases} \qquad [2.1]$$

Observe that Equation 2.1 expresses running time—the total number of probes, or steps—as a function of all legal inputs. Observe also that, because `sequentialSearch` spends only constant time between successive probes, the equation is a good measure of the program's actual performance.

2.2 Complexity Measures

Choice of a sufficiently abstract model of computation simplifies the task of analysis. To simplify analysis even further, we usually express running time as a function of input size, rather than as a function of all legal inputs. There are two main reasons for this. First, the simpler the expression of running time, the easier it is to compare the running times of different algorithms. Descriptions of running time as a function of all legal inputs can be awkward and complex. Even Equation 2.1 is a bit unwieldy, and few algorithms are as simple as sequential search. Second, it can be difficult to analyze running time in terms of all legal inputs. The behavior of many algorithms is highly sensitive to input, and it can be all but impossible to trace the myriad paths that computation follows as input varies.

Input size characterizes the space used to store input. How input size is measured usually depends on the problem in a natural way and can be regarded as an implicit part of the problem statement. If the input consists of an array, input size is taken to be the length of the array; if input consists of a polygon, input size is taken to be the number of vertices the polygon possesses. Any reasonable scheme will do as long as it is applied consistently to all solutions to a given problem.

Expressing running time as a function of input size reduces all legal inputs of a given size to a single value. Since this can be done in many ways, it is no longer clear what running time measures. We pin it down by specifying a *complexity measure*, which describes what aspect of performance is to be measured. The complexity measures in most common use are *worst case*, *average case*, and *amortized case*.

2.2.1 Worst-Case Running Time

Worst-case running time describes the longest running time for any input of each input size. It is a useful measure since it captures the program's running time at its worst. For example, since `sequentialSearch` performs n probes in the worst case (when it fails), its worst-case running time $T(n)$ is $T(n) = n$.

Calculating the worst-case running time is sometimes relatively easy since it is not necessary to consider every legal input, but only some worst-case input of each size. Moreover, worst-case running time often represents a tight bound since worst performance is realized by the input used in the analysis.

2.2.2 Average-Case Running Time

Average-case running time describes running time averaged over all inputs of each input size. The average-case running time of `sequentialSearch` is $\frac{n+1}{2}$ under the assumptions that each of the n items is equally likely to be sought and that the search succeeds. If the second assumption is dropped, the average-case running time lies in the range $[\frac{n+1}{2}, n]$, depending on the likelihood of failure.

Average-case analysis is usually more difficult to carry out than worst-case analysis since it depends on what is meant by typical input. Even if we adopt some relatively simple assumptions (e.g., that every input of a given size is equally likely to occur), the calculation often remains difficult; furthermore, if the program runs in a setting in which the assumption does not hold, the analysis may be a poor predictor of actual performance.

2.2.3 Amortized-Case Running Time

The operations carried out by an algorithm are typically interdependent. The performance of each operation—its cost, in particular—depends on what was achieved by all previous operations. In some algorithms, it is not possible for all operations to achieve worst-case behavior simultaneously. More generally, the cost of relatively expensive operations may be offset by numerous inexpensive operations. Amortized analysis attempts to take this into account: It measures the average cost of each operation, in the worst case.

Consider an algorithm that executes n operations of a *multidelete stack* s. (Stacks are covered more thoroughly in Section 3.4.) This data structure supports these two operations:

- `s.push(x)`—Push item x onto the top of s.
- `s.pop(i)`—Pop the i topmost items from s. The operation is not defined if stack s contains fewer than i items.

As part of our model of computation, let us assume that operation `s.push(x)` takes constant time (or one step), and that `s.pop(i)` takes time proportional to i (or i steps).

Amortized analysis can be carried out in several ways. We will consider an approach based on an accounting metaphor which assigns "charges" to the different operations. Called the *amortized cost* of an operation, each such charge may be greater or less than the actual cost of the operation. Inexpensive operations are generally assigned amortized costs that exceed their actual costs, and expensive operations are assigned amortized costs that are less than their actual costs. When the amortized cost of an operation exceeds the actual cost of the operation, the difference represents credit that can be used to help defray the cost of subsequent expensive operations. The idea is to assign amortized costs to operations so that the credit accumulated through inexpensive operations offsets the cost of expensive operations.

With regard to the multidelete stack, the actual cost and amortized cost of each operation is as follows:

Operation	Actual cost	Amortized cost
s.push(x)	1	2
s.pop(i)	i	0

The table indicates that the amortized cost of each push operation is two steps and the amortized cost of each pop operation is zero steps. Whenever an item is pushed onto the stack, the operation is paid for with one of the two steps, and the second step is held in reserve. Whenever i items are popped from the stack, the operation is paid for with the i steps that had been held in reserve, one step for each of the items popped. At all times, the total credit available in reserve equals the number of items in the stack.

Total amortized cost is maximized by a sequence of n push operations, at a total cost of $2n$ steps. Therefore, each operation runs in two steps on average, in the worst case. That is, each operation runs in constant time in the amortized sense.

The key to this accounting-based approach lies in the choice of amortized costs, and, notwithstanding the previous example, this is the hard part. Several concerns must be balanced. First, the total amortized cost of every sequence of operations should be an upper bound on the total actual cost of the sequence. This ensures that the analysis shows something meaningful about total actual cost. In our example, total available credit is initially zero and never drops below zero, so the total amortized cost is never less than the total actual cost. Second, to ensure that what is shown is as strong as possible, amortized costs should be chosen so the upper bound is as tight as possible. In our example, total amortized cost exceeds total actual cost by the number of items in the stack and so is never more than twice the actual cost. Third, the total credit must be nonnegative at all times, for otherwise there would exist a sequence of operations that cannot pay for itself.

Amortized analysis is often used to obtain an upper bound on the worst-case running time of an algorithm: We bound the number of operations the algorithm performs as a function of input size and then calculate the amortized cost of each operation. If constant time is spent between successive operations, then the algorithm's worst-case running time is bounded above by the total amortized cost. This sort of analysis often produces a tighter bound for worst-case running time than does a more simplistic analysis. Regarding our multidelete stack example, we might naively argue thus: Since a pop operation takes up to n steps in the worst case, a sequence of n operations can take as many as n^2 steps. However, amortized analysis reveals that no such sequence of operations is possible and that a sequence of n operations executes in at most $2n$ steps.

2.3 Asymptotic Analysis

2.3.1 Growth Rate Functions

So far we have introduced two established approaches for simplifying analysis: adopting an abstract model of computation and expressing running time as a function of input size. A third approach focuses on the *asymptotic efficiency* of algorithms: how running time grows as input size increases to infinity. If the running time (e.g., worst-case) of an algorithm is expressed by the function $f(n)$, we are interested in the *growth rate* of f and capture this in a simple growth rate function $T(n)$.

For example, suppose that $f(n) = an^2 + bn + c$ for some constants a, b, and c. As input size grows large, the lower-order terms become insignificant and so can be ignored—we can treat $f(n)$ as an^2. Moreover, even coefficient a of the leading term becomes relatively insignificant as input size grows large, so we can replace $f(n)$ by the simple growth rate function $T(n) = n^2$.

It is not hard to see why the leading coefficient can be ignored. If we let $T(n) = an^2$, every doubling of input size n increases running time by a function that depends on $T(n)$ but not on a. Indeed we have

$$T(2n) = a(2n)^2$$
$$= 4an^2$$
$$= 4T(n)$$

Thus running time quadruples when input size doubles, regardless of the value of a.

More generally, where $T(n)$ is a growth rate function composed of a leading term with coefficient a, $T(2n)$ is a function of $T(n)$ and possibly a lower-order component which depends on n and a. This is exhibited by the following table, which orders functions by increasing rate of growth:

$T(n)$	$T(2n)$
a	$T(n)$
$a \log n$	$T(n) + a$
an	$2T(n)$
$an \log n$	$2T(n) + 2an$
an^2	$4T(n)$
an^3	$8T(n)$
2^n	$[T(n)]^2$

The various functions $T(n)$ are graphed to logarithmic scale in Figure 2.1, for $a = 1$ and $\log n$ taken with base 2.

The worst-case running time of most of the algorithms we will cover in this book is proportional to one of the following simple growth rate functions. The following list also indicates the most common reason why algorithms of each performance class perform as they do:

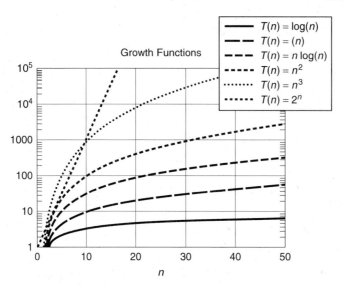

Figure 2.1:   Common growth rate functions (logarithmic scale).

1 (constant time)   Such algorithms run in time independent of input size.

$\log n$ (logarithmic time)   Algorithms in this class often work by repeatedly reducing a problem to a subproblem a fixed fraction of the size.

n (linear time)   Such algorithms generally perform constant-time processing for each input item.

$n \log n$ ($n \log n$ time)   Divide-and-conquer algorithms belong to this class and work by decomposing the original problem into smaller subproblems, solving these, and then combining the results.

n^2 (quadratic time)   Most such algorithms spend constant time processing all pairs of input items.

n^3 (cubic time)   Most such algorithms spend linear time processing all pairs of input items.

2.3.2 Asymptotic Notation

Asymptotic notation provides a convenient language for discussing the growth rate of functions. Among its many uses, the notation is used to express the running time of algorithms and the complexity of problems, and it is often employed in proofs designed to bound the quantity or size of things. We briefly discuss the basic elements of this notation.

O-Notation

O-notation (pronounced *big-oh notation*) is used to describe upper bounds on the growth rate of functions. Where $f(n)$ is a function, $O(f(n))$ denotes the class of functions that grow no faster than $f(n)$. A function $g(n)$ belongs to $O(f(n))$ if $g(n)$ is no larger than some constant times $f(n)$ as n grows sufficiently large. More formally, $g(n) \in O(f(n))$ if for some real number $c > 0$ there exists an integer $n_0 \geq 1$ such that $g(n) \leq cf(n)$ for all $n \geq n_0$.

For example, $an + b \in O(n)$ for all constants a and b. To see why, choose $c = a + 1$ and $n_0 = b$. We then have

$$
\begin{aligned}
an + b &= (a + 1)n + b - n \\
&= cn + n_0 - n \\
&\leq cn
\end{aligned}
$$

for all $n \geq n_0$.

We often express running time using O-notation without specifying a complexity measure. When we say, for instance, that an algorithm runs in $O(f(n))$ time, we mean that its running time is bounded above by $O(f(n))$ for all inputs of size n. This implies, of course, that its worst-case running time is also bounded above by $O(f(n))$.

o-Notation

o-Notation (or *little-oh notation*) is used to describe *strict* upper bounds. Given function $f(n)$, $o(f(n))$ is the class of functions that grow strictly slower than $f(n)$. More formally, a function $g(n)$ belongs to $o(f(n))$ if for *every* constant $c > 0$ there exists an integer $n_0 \geq 1$ such that $g(n) \leq cf(n)$ for all $n \geq n_0$. It is easy to see that $o(f(n)) \subset O(f(n))$ for every function f.

o-Notation provides a way to focus on the leading term of a function. For example, to emphasize the leading term of $f(n) = an \log_2 n + bn + c$, we would rewrite the function as $f(n) = an \log_2 n + o(n \log n)$. This indicates that lower-order terms exist but can be dismissed.

Ω-Notation

Ω-Notation (pronounced *omega notation*) is used to describe lower bounds on the growth rate of functions. Where $f(n)$ is a function, $\Omega(f(n))$ denotes the class of functions that grow no more slowly than $f(n)$. The definition of $\Omega(f(n))$ is symmetric to that of $O(f(n))$: A function $g(n)$ belongs to $\Omega(f(n))$ if for some real number $c > 0$ there exists an integer $n_0 \geq 1$ such that $g(n) \geq cf(n)$ for all $n \geq n_0$.

Θ-Notation

O-Notation and Ω-notation can be used together to define classes of functions whose growth rate lies between two bounds. For instance, $O(n^2) \cap \Omega(n)$ denotes the class of functions which grow at least as fast as n and no faster than n^2. Θ-Notation (or *theta notation*) is used when the gap between the two bounds collapses and the growth rate can be described precisely. Where $f(n)$ is a function, $\Theta(f(n))$ denotes the class of all functions that grow at the same rate as $f(n)$. It is defined more formally by $\Theta(f(n)) = O(f(n)) \cap \Omega(f(n))$.

2.4   Analysis of Recursive Algorithms

Many algorithms solve a large problem by decomposing it into smaller subproblems of the same kind, solving them, and then combining their solutions into a solution to the original problem. Since the subproblems are of the same kind as the original problem, they are solved recursively by the same algorithm. To ensure that the process eventually terminates, a subproblem that is small or simple enough is solved directly. This general approach is known as *recursive decomposition*.

Algorithms based on this approach can be analyzed using *recurrence relations* (or simply *recurrences*). A recurrence is a function that takes integer arguments and is defined in terms of itself. An example is the familiar factorial function $n! = n*(n-1)*\cdots*2*1*1$, defined by the recurrence

$$n! = \begin{cases} n*(n-1)! & \text{if } n \geq 1 \\ 1 & \text{otherwise } (n=0) \end{cases}$$

To analyze an algorithm based on recursive decomposition, we express its running time for input size n as a recurrence relation. For example, consider *selection sort*, which sorts n integers by first extracting the smallest integer from the set and then applying itself recursively to the remaining $n-1$ integers:

```
void selectionSort(int a[], int n)
{
   if (n > 0) {
      int i = positionOfSmallest(a, n);
      swap(a[0], a[i]);
      selectionSort(a+1, n-1);
   }
}
```

Here the function call `positionOfSmallest(a,n)` returns the index of the smallest integer in array a of length n. It works by scanning the array while keeping track of the position of the smallest integer seen so far, and it runs in $\Theta(n)$ time. Function `swap` exchanges two integers in constant time.

The running time of selection sort, a function $T(n)$ of input size n, is expressed by the recurrence

$$T(n) = \begin{cases} T(n-1) + an & \text{if } n > 0 \\ b & \text{otherwise } (n=0) \end{cases} \qquad [2.2]$$

where a and b are constants. In Equation 2.2, $T(n-1)$ corresponds to the cost of the recursive call, an to the cost of finding the smallest integer and exchanging it with `a[0]`, and b to the cost of returning if `n==0`.

For the purpose of comparing selection sort with other sorting algorithms, it is preferable to recast Equation 2.2 in *closed form*—expressing $T(n)$ in terms of n, a, and b only. We briefly consider two methods for obtaining closed-form solutions to recurrence relations: the *telescoping sums method* and the *substitution method*.

2.4.1 Telescoping Sums

The idea of the telescoping sums method is to expand the recurrence relation repeatedly until it is expressed as a summation of terms that depend only on n and the initial conditions. In practice we expand only a few times, until a pattern becomes apparent. For example, Equation 2.2 is solved as follows:

$$
\begin{aligned}
T(n) &= T(n-1) + an \\
&= T(n-2) + a(n-1) + an \\
&= T(n-3) + a(n-2) + a(n-1) + an \\
&= T(0) + a + 2a + \cdots + na \\
&= b + a(1 + 2 + \cdots + n) \\
&= b + a[n(n+1)/2] \\
&= \frac{a}{2}n^2 + \frac{a}{2}n + b
\end{aligned}
$$

Hence $T(n) \in O(n^2)$. It follows that selection sort—indeed all algorithms described by Equation 2.2—runs in $O(n^2)$ time.

Note that the preceding derivation uses the fact that $\sum_{i=1}^{n} i = \frac{n(n+1)}{2}$. Summations are not always so easy to solve. In some cases we are able to do no better than bound a summation from above, which leads to an upper bound for $T(n)$.

2.4.2 The Substitution Method

An algorithm based on the *divide-and-conquer* approach employs a special form of recursive decomposition. In its most simple form, divide and conquer decomposes the original problem into two subproblems, each about half the size of the original. Let us suppose that the process of decomposing the original problem of size n into two subproblems, and the process of combining their solutions to solve the original problem, each take $O(n)$ time. An example is *merge sort*. To sort an array of length n, merge sort recursively sorts the left subarray and the right subarray and then merges the two sorted subarrays:

```
void mergeSort(int a[], int n)
{
    if (n > 1) {
        int m = n / 2;
        mergeSort(a, m);
        mergeSort(a+m, n-m);
        merge(a, m, n);
    }
}
```

The merge step is performed by the function call merge(a,m,n), which merges the two sorted subarrays a[0..m-1] and a[m..n-1] into a[0..n-1]. (Here we use a[1..u] to denote the subarray a between lower index 1 and upper index u inclusive.) Function merge works by maintaining a pointer to the smallest item not yet merged, in each of the two sorted subarrays. The pointers are iteratively moved from left to right until the merge is complete. The merge step, which takes linear time, works much as one would merge two sorted stacks of playing cards into a single sorted stack. (Merge sort will be covered more thoroughly in Chapter 8.)

The running time $T(n)$ of merge sort is described by the following recurrence, in which we assume for simplicity that n is a power of 2:

$$T(n) = \begin{cases} 2T(\frac{n}{2}) + an & \text{if } n > 1 \\ b & \text{otherwise } (n = 1) \end{cases} \qquad [2.3]$$

We use the substitution method to solve Equation 2.3. The idea is to guess a closed-form solution for the recurrence and then use mathematical induction to show that the solution holds.[1] To solve Equation 2.3, we will show by induction that

$$T(n) \leq c_1 n \log n + c_2 \qquad [2.4]$$

for suitably chosen constants c_1 and c_2. Letting

$$c_1 = a + b$$
$$c_2 = b$$

works fine.

For the inductive step, let us assume as the inductive hypothesis that Equation 2.4 solves Equation 2.3 for all powers of 2 less than n. We then have

$$T(n) = 2T\left(\frac{n}{2}\right) + an$$

$$\leq 2\left(\frac{c_1 n}{2} \log \frac{n}{2} + c_2\right) + an$$

$$= c_1 n \log \frac{n}{2} + 2c_2 + an$$

$$= c_1 n \log n - c_1 n + 2c_2 + an$$

$$= c_1 n \log n + c_2 + b - bn$$

$$\leq c_1 n \log n + c_2$$

This establishes the inductive step.

The basis step of the induction also follows from our choice of c_1 and c_2. The following shows that Equation 2.4 holds for $n = 1$:

$$T(1) = b$$

$$= c_2$$

$$\leq c_1(1 \cdot \log 1) + c_2$$

It follows from this discussion that merge sort has worst-case running time $O(n \log n)$.

2.5 Problem Complexity

If we know the performance of an algorithm, we can compare it to other algorithms for the same problem. But suppose we wish to determine whether an algorithm is optimal— whether a more efficient solution is possible. One way to decide if an algorithm is optimal

---

[1] Mathematical induction is a two-step method for proving true an infinite sequence of statements $P(1), P(2), \cdots, P(n), \cdots$. The *basis step* is to prove the first statement $P(1)$. The *inductive step* is to show that for any statement $P(n)$, if $P(n)$ is true, then statement $P(n + 1)$ must be true. Here $P(n)$ of the inductive step is called the *inductive hypothesis*.

is to compare it to a second algorithm known (somehow) to be optimal, but this works only if the latter algorithm can be shown to be optimal. Another approach is needed if we are to escape this infinite regress. How can we determine whether an algorithm is optimal? More generally, how can we determine how much time *any* solution to a given problem is bound to require?

Problem complexity expresses the amount of time that is both necessary and sufficient to solve a problem. Knowing how much time is necessary to solve a problem informs us that any approach that takes less time is bound to fail. And knowing how much time is sufficient indicates how efficient a particular solution is and to what extent it can be improved on.

When the complexity of a problem is known exactly, it is expressed in the form $\Theta(f(n))$. The complexity of many problems that arise as a matter of course is in fact known exactly. However, for some problems the best we can do is establish lower and upper bounds on complexity and then work toward collapsing the gap—bringing the upper bound downward and the lower bound upward until the two bounds meet.

2.5.1 Upper Bounds

Any solution to a given problem bounds its complexity from above: If the solution has worst-case running time $O(f(n))$, then $O(f(n))$ time is sufficient to solve the problem. If no faster solution is possible, implying that the given solution is optimal, then the upper bound is tight. Alternatively, if the solution is suboptimal, then the upper bound is brought downward as more efficient solutions are discovered.

Recall problem SEARCH, that of probe-based searching in a sorted array of n distinct integers. Since sequential search runs in $O(n)$ time in the worst case, $O(n)$ represents an upper bound for the problem. However, $O(n)$ is not a *tight* bound since a more efficient solution exists. *Binary search* takes advantage of the fact that the array is sorted. Given subarray a[l..u], binary search compares the search key x to item a[m] occurring in position m about halfway between positions l and u. If x is no greater than a[m], binary search is applied recursively to the left subarray a[l..m]; otherwise (x is greater than a[m]) binary search is applied recursively to the right subarray a[m+1..u]. In the base case (l==u), we solve the problem directly. The following function returns the index of x in subarray a[l..u], or -1 if the search fails:

```
int binarySearch(int x, int a[], int l, int u)
{
   if (l == u)
      return (x == a[u]) ? u : -1;
   int m = (l + u) / 2;
   if (x <= a[m])
      return binarySearch(x, a, l, m);
   else
      return binarySearch(x, a, m+1, u);
}
```

To find x in array a of length n, use the top-level call binarySearch(x,a,0,n-1).

The worst-case running time of binary search is expressed by the recurrence

$$T(n) = \begin{cases} T(\frac{n}{2}) + a & \text{if } n > 1 \\ b & \text{otherwise } (n = 1) \end{cases} \qquad [2.5]$$

It is not hard to show using either of the methods described earlier that $T(n) \in O(\log n)$.

It follows from our discussion that $O(\log n)$ is an upper bound for problem SEARCH. Is this bound tight, or does there exist a solution even more efficient than binary search? The bound is in fact tight—binary search is optimal. To see why, we now turn our attention to lower bounds on problem complexity.

2.5.2 Lower Bounds

Finding good lower bounds can be difficult. A lower bound of $\Omega(g(n))$ on the complexity of some problem implies that at least $\Omega(g(n))$ time is needed to solve the problem. How can we ever be certain that *every* solution requires at least $\Omega(g(n))$ time, that there does not exist some (perhaps unknown) solution that takes less time?

We will consider two approaches to showing lower bounds: proof by *decision tree*, and proof by *reduction*.

DECISION TREES

Consider problem SEARCH. Any algorithm based on its model of computation (constant-time probes) can be viewed as a *decision tree*. The decision tree represents all possible computations for all inputs of a given size (there is a different decision tree for every input size). Each node of the decision tree corresponds to a probe. The pair of edges that leaves each node corresponds to a branching instruction—based on the outcome of the probe, a given computation follows one of the two edges to the next node. The external nodes of the decision tree—the terminating nodes which no edges exit—correspond to so-lutions. Figure 2.2 shows the decision tree for program binarySearch when applied to a sorted array of length three. The decision tree is in fact a binary tree with a probe associated with each (circular) internal node and a final outcome associated with each (square) external node. (See Section 3.5 for more about binary trees.)

The decision tree can be used to show a lower bound for problem SEARCH. Each path from the topmost node (or *root*) down to some external node represents a possible computation, and the path's length equals the number of probes performed by the computation. (Here the length of a path equals the number of edges it contains.) Hence the length of the longest such path in the decision tree represents the number of probes performed in the worst case. What is the shortest this largest path can be?

For problem SEARCH with array length n, the decision tree must possess at least n external nodes: Each of the n distinct solutions—$n + 1$ if we include failed search—is associated with at least one unique external node. Let us show that in *any* binary tree containing n external nodes, there exists some path with length at least $\log n$. Where the *height* of a binary tree is defined as the length of some longest path from root to external node, we can state what we wish to show as follows:

Theorem 1   *A binary tree containing n external nodes has height at least* $\log_2 n$.

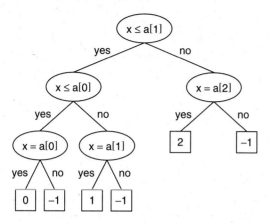

Figure 2.2:   The decision tree for program `binarySearch` applied to a sorted array of length three.

We can show Theorem 1 by induction on n. For the basis of the induction, $n = 1$ and the binary tree consists of a single external node. In this case the length of the only path is $0 = \log_2 1$, so the basis is satisfied.

For the inductive step, assume as the inductive hypothesis that the theorem holds for all binary trees with fewer than n external nodes. We must show that it holds for every binary tree T containing n external nodes. The root node of T attaches to two smaller binary trees T_1 and T_2 containing n_1 and n_2 external nodes, respectively. Since $n_1 + n_2 = n$, either n_1 or n_2 (or both) is greater than or equal to $\frac{n}{2}$; assume without loss of generality that $n_1 \geq \frac{n}{2}$. Furthermore, since $n_2 > 0$ (why?), we have $n_1 < n$, so we can apply the inductive hypothesis. Where *height(T)* denotes the length of some longest path in binary tree T, we have

$$
\begin{aligned}
\text{height}(T) &= 1 + \max\{\text{height}(T_1), \text{height}(T_2)\} \\
&\geq 1 + \text{height}(T_1) \\
&\geq 1 + \log_2 n_1 \\
&\geq 1 + \log_2 \frac{n}{2} \\
&= \log n
\end{aligned}
$$

Let us connect this result to our discussion of lower bounds. Any algorithm for problem SEARCH corresponds, on input size n, to a decision tree which contains at least n external nodes. Theorem 1 informs us that the decision tree has height not less than $\log_2 n$. Hence the algorithm performs at least $\log_2 n$ probes for some inputs of size n. Since this holds for all possible algorithms for SEARCH, $\Omega(\log n)$ is a lower bound for the problem. Binary search is indeed an optimal solution to the problem.

REDUCTIONS

A second way to establish a lower bound for some problem P_B makes use of the known lower bound for some other problem P_A. The idea is to show that P_B can be solved no faster than P_A, thereby transfering P_A's lower bound to P_B. To show that the two problems are related in this way, we exhibit an efficient algorithm A for P_A which calls a procedure solving problem P_B no more than a constant number of times. Algorithm A is called a *reduction* from P_A to P_B.

Let us consider an example before formalizing these ideas. Consider the problem ELEMENT UNIQUENESS:

Given an unordered set of n integers, decide whether any two are equal.

We will construct an efficient reduction from ELEMENT UNIQUENESS to the problem SORT:

Given an unordered set of n integers, arrange the integers in nondecreasing order.

For both problems we will assume a *comparison-based* model of computation: The only operations we count are comparisons, in which we compare two integers in constant time (one step).

A simple reduction A from ELEMENT UNIQUENESS to SORT works as follows. To decide whether some integer occurs more than once in a given array of n integers, first sort the array and then step down the array while comparing all pairs of consecutive integers. An integer occurs twice in the original array if and only if it occupies consecutive positions in the now-sorted array.

That such a reduction exists demonstrates that ELEMENT UNIQUENESS's known lower bound of $\Omega(n \log n)$ transfers to SORT. Suppose there were to exist some algorithm B for SORT with running time $o(n \log n)$. Then reduction A would solve ELEMENT UNIQUENESS in $o(n \log n)$ time if it used algorithm B to sort: Sorting would take $o(n \log n)$ time, and checking consecutive integers in the now-sorted array would take $O(n) \subset o(n \log n)$ time. But this leads to contradiction, since the lower bound of $\Omega(n \log n)$ for ELEMENT UNIQUENESS implies that no solution with running time $o(n \log n)$ is possible.

Let us formalize these ideas. An algorithm A for problem P_A is a $\tau(n)$-*time reduction* from P_A to P_B if

1. A uses some (hypothetical) algorithm B for P_B as a function call some constant number of times, and

2. A runs in $O(\tau(n))$ time, where each call to B costs one step.

In effect, we are augmenting the model of computation for problem P_A by a constant-time operation B which solves problem P_B. We are free to assume operation B without specifying (or even having knowledge of) a particular solution for problem P_B. In our example, problem P_A is ELEMENT UNIQUENESS, problem P_B is SORT, A is an n-time (or linear-time) reduction from ELEMENT UNIQUENESS to SORT, and B is a hypothetical algorithm for SORT.

Let us suppose that problem P_A has known lower bound $\Omega(f(n))$ and that we can devise a $\tau(n)$-time reduction A from P_A to P_B. Then, assuming that $\tau(n) \in o(f(n))$, problem P_B must also have lower bound $\Omega(f(n))$. Were there to exist some algorithm B for P_B which runs in $o(f(n))$ time, algorithm A would also run in $o(f(n))$ time if it used algorithm B, and A would then violate the lower bound on problem P_A. This argument

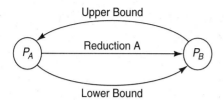

Figure 2.3: A $\tau(n)$-time reduction from problem P_A to problem P_B.

depends on the assumption that $\tau(n) \in o(f(n))$. Were this assumption not to hold, algorithm A would run in $\Omega(f(n))$ time regardless of algorithm B's performance, and P_A's known lower bound would not be violated. This is the sense in which the reduction must be efficient to be useful (see Figure 2.3).

An efficient reduction from problem P_A to problem P_B can also be used to transfer a known upper bound for P_B to P_A. Let us return to our example. SORT has an upper bound of $O(n \log n)$; merge sort is but one algorithm which solves the problem in $O(n \log n)$ time. By relying on any $O(n \log n)$-time sorting algorithm, reduction A solves ELEMENT UNIQUENESS in $O(n \log n)$ time. Hence ELEMENT UNIQUENESS inherits SORT's upper bound of $O(n \log n)$.

More generally, suppose that problem P_B has known upper bound $O(g(n))$ and we can exhibit a $\tau(n)$-time reduction from problem P_A to problem P_B. Then, assuming $\tau(n) \in O(g(n))$, problem P_A must have the same upper bound $O(g(n))$.

2.6   Chapter Notes

The texts [2, 20, 56, 73, 83, 89, 90] discuss algorithm analysis as well as analyze the algorithms they present. Also recommended is the paper [82], which explores amortized analysis and presents several examples.

Knuth employed O-notation and asymptotic analysis of algorithms as early as 1973 [48] and endorsed conscientious use of O-, Ω-, Θ-, and o-notations three years later in [49]. Both references discuss the history of asymptotic notation.

Mathematical induction is defined and discussed in [57] and is made the basis for algorithm design and analysis in [56].

2.7   Exercises

1. Use mathematical induction to show that $\sum_{i=1}^{n} i = \frac{n(n+1)}{2}$.

2. Use mathematical induction to show that a binary tree with n internal nodes must have $n + 1$ external nodes (see Section 3.5 for more about binary trees).

3. Discuss the advantages and disadvantages of measuring the running time of a program by timing it while it executes on a computer. Is this a reliable performance measure?

4. Implement sequentialSearch and binarySearch and graph their execution times as input grows large. Since both programs realize worst-case performance when search fails, you will probably want to use search keys that do not occur in the input

array. Does your graph bear out the worst-case running time of $O(n)$ for sequential search and $O(\log n)$ for binary search?

5. Implement the sorting algorithms `insertionSort` [which runs in $O(n^2)$ time], `selectionSort` [$O(n^2)$ time], and `mergeSort` [$O(n \log n)$ time], and graph their execution times as input grows large. Does your graph bear out their running times? (These programs are discussed at the beginning of Chapters 5, 6, and 8.)

6. Solve the recurrence

$$T(n) = \begin{cases} T(n-1) + a & \text{if } n > 0 \\ b & \text{otherwise } (n = 0) \end{cases}$$

   for constants a and b.

7. Solve the recurrence

$$T(n) = \begin{cases} T(\frac{n}{2}) + a & \text{if } n > 1 \\ b & \text{otherwise } (n = 1) \end{cases}$$

   for constants a and b.

8. Solve the recurrence

$$T(n) = \begin{cases} 2T(n-2) + a & \text{if } n > 1 \\ b & \text{otherwise } (n = 0 \text{ or } n = 1) \end{cases}$$

   for constants a and b.

9. Show that $f_1 \in O(g(n))$ and $f_2 \in O(g(n))$ imply $(f_1 + f_2)(n) \in O(g(n))$, where $(f_1 + f_2)(n) = f_1(n) + f_2(n)$.

10. Show that $f_1 \in O(g_1(n))$ and $f_2 \in O(g_2(n))$ imply $(f_1 \cdot f_2)(n) \in O((g_1 \cdot g_2)(n))$, where $(f_1 \cdot f_2)(n) = f_1(n) f_2(n)$.

11. Show that $f(n) \in O(g(n))$ and $g(n) \in O(h(n))$ imply $f(n) \in O(h(n))$.

12. Show that $\log_b n \in \Theta(\log_c n)$ for all $b, c > 1$.

13. Show that $a_m n^m + a_{m-1} n^{m-1} + \cdots + a_0 \in O(n^m)$ for any constants a_i.

14. Show that $\log n \in O(n^k)$ for all $k > 0$.

15. Show that $n^k \in O(2^n)$ for all $k > 0$.

16. Show that $f(n) \in O(g(n))$ implies $g(n) \in \Omega(f(n))$.

17. Use decision trees to show that comparison-based sorting (problem SORT) has lower bound $\Omega(n \log n)$. [Hint: Use the fact that $\log(n!) \in \Omega(n \log n)$.]

18. Use decision trees to show a lower bound of $\Omega(\log n)$ for the yes/no version of problem SEARCH: Given a sorted array a of n distinct integers and a search key x, report whether or not x occurs in a. (Hint: Although only two outcomes are possible, argue that the decision tree must nonetheless contain at least n external nodes.)

3

Data Structures

Data structures—methods for organizing data—are the principal building blocks from which algorithms are pieced together. The data structures an algorithm uses affect the algorithm's efficiency, as well as the ease with which it can be programmed and understood. This is what makes the study of data structures so important.

C++ provides a number of predefined data structures. One example is the integers, together with the operations for manipulating them: arithmetic operators such as addition and multiplication, relational operators, assignment operators, and so forth. Other examples include floating-point numbers, characters, pointer types, and reference types. The predefined data structures can be used "as is" in programs, or combined through such devices as classes and arrays to form data structures of greater complexity.

In this chapter we present and implement the data structures we will use: lists, stacks, and binary search trees. These data structures are elementary yet powerful, and the implementations we provide are standard and practical. We will not attempt a comprehensive treatment of data structures in this chapter; rather, our primary motivation is to provide the data structures needed for the programs to follow.

3.1 What Are Data Structures?

A data structure consists of a storage structure to hold the data, and methods for creating, modifying, and accessing the data. More formally, a *data structure* consists of these three components:

1. A set of operations for manipulating specific types of abstract objects

2. A storage structure in which the abstract objects are stored

3. An implementation of each of the operations in terms of the storage structure.

Component 1 of the definition—a set of operations on abstract objects—is called an *abstract data type*, or *ADT*. Components 2 and 3 together make up the data structure's *implementation*. For example, the array ADT supports the manipulation of a set of values of the same type, through operations for accessing and modifying values specified by an index. The implementation employed by C++ stores the array in a contiguous block of memory (the storage structure) and uses pointer arithmetic to convert an index to an address within the block (the implementation of the operations).

An abstract data type specifies what a data structure does—what operations it supports—without revealing how it does it. While crafting a program, the programmer is thereby free to think in terms of what abstract data types the program requires and can postpone the work of implementing them. This programming practice of separating an algorithm from its data structures so they can be considered separately is called *data abstraction*. Data abstraction distinguishes different levels of abstract thought. Thus integer arithmetic, an abstract data type provided by most programming languages (including C++), permits us to think at the level of adding, multiplying, and comparing integers, without also having to consider *how* integers are represented, added, multiplied, and so forth. The stack ADT encourages thought at the level of stack operations while postponing the (lower-level) question of how to implement stacks.

Use of abstract data types also encourages *modular programming*, the practice of breaking programs into separate modules with well-defined interfaces. Modularity has numerous advantages. Modules can be written and debugged apart from the rest of the program, by another programmer or at another time. Modules are reusable, so they can often be loaded from a library or copied from another program. In addition, a module can be replaced by another module that is functionally equivalent to, but more efficient, robust, or, in some other sense, better than the original.

Despite these advantages, not every data structure should be treated as an abstract data type. An array ADT provides index-based access and update operations for manipulating sets, but there is often no advantage to formulating arrays this abstractly: Doing so circumvents the familiar view of an array as a contiguous block of memory and introduces an often unnecessary level of abstraction. It is also inefficient, since the additional function calls may incur an overhead cost, and efficient pointer methods that exploit the close tie between pointers and arrays are forfeited.

Our primary goal in this chapter will be to present the abstract data types used by the algorithms in this book and to implement them efficiently. Familiarity with these ADTs will enable us to describe our algorithms at a higher, more abstract level, in terms of abstract operations. Familiarity with how these ADTs are implemented—besides being of interest in its own right—will enable us to implement and run the algorithms which employ them. Moreover, knowing how an ADT is implemented will allow us to tinker with a data structure when it only approximately meets our needs.

3.2   Linked Lists

The linked list, like the array, is used to manipulate lists of items. The items are stored in the *nodes* of the linked list, ordered sequentially in list order. Each node possesses a pointer—often known as a *link*—to the next node. The last node is distinguished by a special value in its link field (the null link in Figure 3.1) or by the fact that it links to itself.

For handling lists, the linked list has two advantages over the array. First, rearranging the order of items in a linked list is easy and fast, usually accomplished by updating a small number of links (e.g., to insert a new node *b* after some node *a*, link *a* to *b*, and link *b* to whatever node *a* had just linked to). Contrast this with insertion of an item into an array a representing a list of n items. To insert the item into position i, each of the items in a[i] through a[n-1] must be shifted one position to the right to make a "hole" for the new item in position i.

Unlike arrays, linked lists are *dynamic*—they are able to shrink and grow in size during their lifetime. With linked lists it is unnecessary to safeguard against running out of space by preallocating an excessive amount of memory.

There are several kinds of linked lists. Each node of a *singly linked* list links to the next node, called its *successor*. Each node of a *doubly linked* list links both to the next node and to the previous node, its *predecessor*. In a *circular* linked list, the last node links to the first node; if the circular linked list is doubly linked, the first node also links to the last node. For example, Figure 3.1 depicts a (noncircular) singly linked list, and Figure 3.2 a circular doubly linked list. We will concentrate on circular doubly linked lists since they are best suited for the algorithms covered in this book; for brevity, we will usually refer to them simply as *linked lists*. We will often use them, for instance, to represent polygons, where each node of the linked list corresponds to a vertex of the polygon, and the nodes are ordered as the vertices around the polygon.

In a pointer-based implementation of the linked list, a node is an object of class Node:

```
class Node {
 protected:
    Node *_next;    // link to successor node
    Node *_prev;    // link to predecessor node
 public:
    Node(void);
    virtual ~Node(void);
    Node *next(void);
    Node *prev(void);
    Node *insert(Node*);
    Node *remove(void);
    void splice(Node*);
};
```

Class Node's constructor creates a new node which doubly links to itself: The new node represents a single-node linked list.

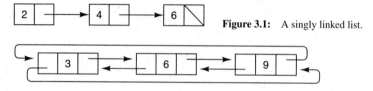

Figure 3.1:   A singly linked list.

Figure 3.2:   A circular doubly linked list.

```
Node::Node(void) :
    _next(this), _prev(this)
{
}
```

Within a member function, the variable `this` automatically points to the receiver object, the object whose member function is invoked. In a constructor, `this` points to the object being allocated. Accordingly, in discussions about member functions, we will often refer the receiver object as *this* object. The destructor ~Node is responsible for deallocating this object. It is declared `virtual` within the class definition so that derived objects—objects of classes derived from class Node—are correctly deallocated:

```
Node::~Node(void)
{
}
```

Member functions `next` and `prev` are used to move from this node to its successor or predecessor:

```
Node *Node::next(void)
{
    return _next;
}
```

```
Node *Node::prev(void)
{
    return _prev;
}
```

Member function `insert` inserts node b just after this node (Figure 3.3):

```
Node *Node::insert(Node *b)
{
    Node *c = _next;
    b->_next = c;
    b->_prev = this;
    _next = b;
    c->_prev = b;
    return b;
}
```

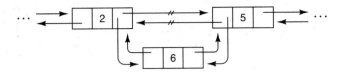

Figure 3.3:   Inserting a node into a linked list.

Nodes can also be removed from linked lists. Member function `remove` removes this node from its linked list (Figure 3.4). It returns a pointer to this node so it can later be deallocated:

```
Node *Node::remove(void)
{
    _prev->_next = _next;
    _next->_prev = _prev;
    _next = _prev = this;
    return this;
}
```

Member function `splice` is used to *splice* two nodes a and b. Splicing achieves different results depending on whether a and b belong to the same linked list. If they do, the linked list is split into two smaller linked lists. Alternatively, if a and b belong to different linked lists, the two linked lists are joined into one larger linked list.

To splice nodes a and b, we link a to `b->_next` (node b's successor) and link b to `a->_next` (a's successor). We must also update the appropriate predecessor links: We link the new successor to a back to a, and the new successor to b back to b. The operation is depicted in Figure 3.5. The figure indicates that `splice` is its own inverse: Splicing nodes a and b in the left diagram yields the right diagram, and splicing a and b once again (in the right diagram) produces the left diagram.

In the following implementation of member function `splice`, this node plays the role of node a, and the function's argument that of node b. We introduce variable a into the

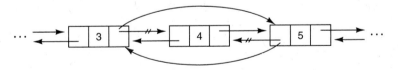

Figure 3.4:   Removing a node from its linked list.

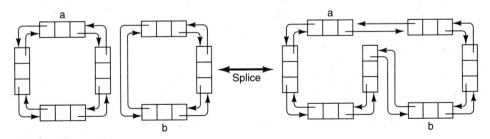

Figure 3.5:   Splicing nodes a and b.

code to reflect the operation's symmetry: Given node pointers a and b, a->splice(b) and b->splice(a) achieve the same net result.

```
void Node::splice(Node *b)
{
    Node *a = this;
    Node *an = a->_next;
    Node *bn = b->_next;
    a->_next = bn;
    b->_next = an;
    an->_prev = b;
    bn->_prev = a;
}
```

Observe that if node a precedes node b in the linked list, then splicing them has the net effect of removing b. Furthermore, splicing a single-node linked list b to node a of some other linked list effectively inserts b after a. This suggests that inserting a node into a linked list and removing a node from a linked list are actually special cases of splice. Indeed this is the case—member functions insert and remove are provided for convenience.

Finally we note that splicing a node to itself, as in the call a->splice(a), has no net effect. This is easily verified by examining the implementation of splice.

3.3   Lists

In this section we define a new class List for representing lists. A *list* is an ordered set of finitely many items. The *length* of a list equals the number of items it contains; a list of length zero is called an *empty list*.

In our view of a list, every item in a list occupies one position—the first item is in the first position, the second item is in the second position, and so forth. There is in addition a *head position* which simultaneously occurs before the first position and after the last position. A List object provides access to its items through a *window*, which at any given time is located over some position in the list. Most list operations refer to either the window or the item in the window. For instance, we can obtain the item in the window, advance the window to the next or previous position, or move the window to the first position or last position in the list. We can also do such things as remove from the list the item in the window or insert a new item into the list, just after the window. Figure 3.6 depicts our view of a list.

We will use linked lists to implement class List. Each node corresponds to a position in the list and contains the item stored at that position (the node corresponding to the head position is called the *header node*). A node is represented by an object of class ListNode, which is derived from class Node. Class ListNode possesses a data member _val, which points to the actual item.

A list is a collection of items of some given type. Yet there is no need to build a specific item type into the definitions of classes ListNode or List, for the list operations behave the same regardless of item type. For this reason we define these classes as class templates. The item type is made a parameter of the class template. Later, when we need

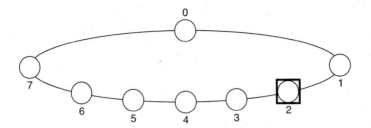

Figure 3.6: The structure of a list of length seven. The items in the list occur in positions 1 through 7; the head position 0 occurs between the first and last positions. The window, indicated by the square, is currently over position 2.

a list of some specific item type, the class template is invoked with the item type; the class template is used to construct an actual class for that item type.

Class template `ListNode` is defined as follows:

```
template<class T> class ListNode : public Node {
 public:
   T _val;
   ListNode(T val);
   friend class List<T>;
};
```

Here T is the type parameter. To declare an instance of `ListNode`, we supply a type for parameter T. For instance, the declaration

```
ListNode<int*> a, b;
```

declares a and b as `ListNode` objects each containing a pointer-to-`int`.

The constructor `ListNode` is defined like this:

```
template<class T> ListNode::ListNode(T val) :
   _val(val)
{
}
```

The constructor `ListNode` implicitly invokes the constructor for base class `Node`, since the latter constructor takes no arguments.

We will not define a destructor for class `ListNode`. Whenever a `ListNode` object is deleted, the base class's destructor `Node::~Node`, which has been declared virtual, is automatically invoked. Note that the item pointed to by data member `ListNode::_val` is not deallocted. It would be safe to deallocate the item only if it were known to have been allocated with `new`, and there is no guarantee of this.

Let us turn to the definition of class template `List`. Class `List` contains three data members: `header` points to the header node corresponding to the head position; `win` points to the node that the list's window is currently positioned over; and `_length` contains the length of the list. The class template is defined as follows:

```
template<class T> class List {
 private:
   ListNode<T> *header;
   ListNode<T> *win;
   int _length;
 public:
   List(void);
   ~List(void);
   T insert(T);
   T append(T);
   List *append(List*);
   T prepend(T);
   T remove(void);
   void val(T);
   T val(void);
   T next(void);
   T prev(void);
   T first(void);
   T last(void);
   int length(void);
   bool isFirst(void);
   bool isLast(void);
   bool isHead(void);
};
```

To simplify our implementation, we will assume that the items in a list are *pointers* to objects of a given type. Thus the declaration

```
List<Polygon*> p;
```

declares p to be a list of pointer-to-Polygons, whereas the declaration

```
List<Polygon> q;
```

is illegal.

3.3.1 Constructors and Destructors

The constructor List creates and initializes an empty list, represented by a single header node linked to itself:

```
template<class T> List<T>::List(void) :
   _length(0)
{
   header = new ListNode<T>(NULL);
   win = header;
}
```

The class destructor deallocates the linked list's nodes:

```
template<class T> List<T>::~List(void)
{
    while (length() > 0) {
        first();
        remove();
    }
    delete header;
}
```

Note that the data items in the list are not deallocated by the destructor.

3.3.2 Modifying Lists

Member functions insert, prepend, and append are used to insert new items into a list. None of the three functions moves the window. Function insert inserts a new item after the window and returns the item:

```
template<class T> T List<T>::insert(T val)
{
    win->insert(new ListNode<T>(val));
    ++_length;
    return val;
}
```

Member functions prepend and append insert a new item at the beginning and end of the list, respectively, and return the new item:

```
template<class T> T List<T>::prepend(T val)
{
    header->insert(new ListNode<T>(val));
    ++_length;
    return val;
}
```

```
template<class T> T List<T>::append(T val)
{
    header->prev()->insert(new ListNode<T>(val));
    ++_length;
    return val;
}
```

The second version of member function append is used to append a list l to the end of this list—the first item of list l is placed after the last item of this list. List l is made empty in the process. This list is returned:

```
template<class T> List<T>* List<T>::append(List<T> *l)
{
    ListNode<T> *a = (ListNode<T>*)header->prev();
    a->splice(l->header);
    _length += l->_length;
    l->header->remove();
    l->_length = 0;
    l->win = header;
    return this;
}
```

Member function `remove` removes the item in the window, moves the window to the previous position, and returns the just-removed item. The operation does nothing if the window is in the head position:

```
template<class T> T List<T>::remove(void)
{
    if (win == header)
        return NULL;
    void *val = win->_val;
    win = (ListNode<T>*)win->prev();
    delete (ListNode<T>*)win->next()->remove();
    --_length;
    return val;
}
```

When member function `val` is called with some item v, it replaces the item currently in the window by v. The function does nothing if the window is in the head position.

```
void List<T>::val(T v)
{
    if (win != header)
        win->_val = v;
}
```

3.3.3 Accessing List Elements

When member function `val` is called with no arguments, it returns the item in the window, or NULL if the window is in the head position:

```
template<class T> T List<T>::val(void)
{
    return win->_val;
}
```

Member functions `next` and `prev` move the window to the next or previous position, respectively. Each returns the item stored in the window's new position. Note that class

List supports "wraparound." For instance, if the window is in the last position, performing next advances the window to the head position, and then performing next once again advances the window to the first position.

```
template<class T> T List<T>::next(void)
{
   win = (ListNode<T>*)win->next();
   return win->_val;
}


template<class T> T List<T>::prev(void)
{
   win = (ListNode<T>*)win->prev();
   return win->_val;
}
```

Member functions first and last reset the window to the first and last positions, respectively; they have no effect if the list is empty. Each returns the item stored in the window's new position:

```
template<class T> T List<T>::first(void)
{
   win = (ListNode<T>*)header->next();
   return win->_val;
}


template<class T> T List<T>::last(void)
{
   win = (ListNode<T>*)header->prev();
   return win->_val;
}
```

Member function length returns the length of this list:

```
template<class T> int List<T>::length(void)
{
   return _length;
}
```

Member functions isFirst, isLast, and isHead return TRUE just if the window is in the first, last, or head position, respectively:

```
template<class T> bool List<T>::isFirst(void)
{
   return ((win == header->next()) && (_length > 0));
}
```

```
template<class T> bool List<T>::isLast(void)
{
    return ((win == header->prev()) && (_length > 0));
}

template<class T> bool List<T>::isHead(void)
{
    return (win == header);
}
```

3.3.4 List Examples

Two simple examples illustrate the use of lists. The first example, function template arrayToList, loads the n items in array a into a list, which it then returns:

```
template<class T> List<T> *arrayToList(T a[], int n)
{
    List<T> *s = new List<T>;
    for (int i = 0; i < n; i++)
        s->append(a[i]);
    return s;
}
```

For example, if a is an array of strings, the following fragment converts a to a list s of strings:

```
char *a[20];
   .
   .
   .
// initialize array a here
   .
   .
   .
List<char*> *s = arrayToList(a, 20);
```

Function template arrayToList is a utility we will use later in some of the programs.

For the second example, function template leastItem returns the smallest item in list s. Two elements are compared using the comparison function cmp, which returns −1, 0, or 1 if its first argument is less than, equal to, or greater than its second argument:

```
template<class T> T leastItem(List<T> &s, int(*cmp)(T,T))
{
    int i;
    if (s.length() == 0)
        return NULL;
    T v = s.first();
    for (s.next(); !s.isHead(); s.next())
        if (cmp(s.val(), v) < 0)
            v = s.val();
    return v;
}
```

To find which of a list of strings occurs first in dictionary order, we would call `leastItem` with the comparison function `strcmp`. This is the standard C++ library function which, when passed two strings, returns −1, 0, or 1 depending on whether the first string is less than, equal to, or greater than the second string in dictionary order. For instance, the following fragment prints the string *ant*:

```
List<char*> s;
s.append("bat");
s.append("ant");
s.append("cat");
cout << leastItem(s, strcmp);
```

3.4 Stacks

Lists are unrestricted in that any item can be accessed. There are also list-oriented data structures that restrict access to items, and one of the most important is the *pushdown stack*, or simply *stack*. The stack limits access to that item most recently inserted. For this reason, stacks are also known as *last-in-first-out lists*, or *LIFO lists*.

The two basic stack operations are `push` and `pop`. The operation `push` inserts an item into the stack, and `pop` removes from the stack the last item pushed. The words *stack*, *push*, and *pop* suggest a helpful picture, that of objects stacked one on top of the next in which only the topmost object is accessible. The `push` operation pushes (inserts) a new item onto the top, and the `pop` operation pops (removes) and returns the top object. Other stack operations include `empty`, which returns TRUE just if the stack is empty, and operations for peeking at select items on the stack without removing them (see Figure 3.7).

One simple implementation of a stack uses an array. A stack of n items is stored in elements `s[0]` through `s[n-1]` of some array `s`, and the number of items (n) is stored in some integer variable `top`. Array element `s[0]` contains the bottom item, and `s[top-1]` the top item. The list of items grows toward higher indices as `push`es are performed and shrinks toward lower indices as `pop`s are performed. Specifically, to push item x we perform `s[top++] = x`, and to pop we return `s[--top]`. The only problem with this implementation is that it is not dynamic—the length of the array limits the size of the stack. We will pursue an implementation of stacks based on the `List` class template of the previous section. Our stacks will then be dynamic since `List` objects are dynamic.

The class template `Stack` contains a private data member s which points to the `List` object representing the stack. The list is ordered from the top of the stack to the bottom; in particular, the top item of the stack is in the first position of the list, and the bottom item of the stack is in the last position of the list.

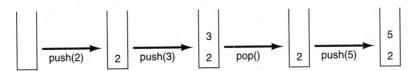

Figure 3.7:   The stack in action.

```
template<class T> class Stack {
 private:
    List<T> *s;
 public:
    Stack(void);
    ~Stack(void);
    void push(T v);
    T pop(void);
    bool empty(void);
    int size(void);
    T top(void);
    T nextToTop(void);
    T bottom(void);
};
```

Implementation of the member functions is straightforward. The constructor `Stack` allocates a `List` object and assigns it to data member `s`:

```
template<class T> Stack<T>::Stack(void) :
    s(new List<T>)
{
}
```

The destructor `~Stack` deallocates the `List` object pointed to by data member `s`:

```
template<class T> Stack<T>::~Stack(void)
{
    delete s;
}
```

Member function `push` pushes item `v` onto this stack, and `pop` pops the topmost item from this stack and returns it:

```
template<class T> void Stack<T>::push(T v)
{
    s->prepend(v);
}
```

```
template<class T> T Stack<T>::pop(void)
{
    s->first();
    return s->remove();
}
```

Member function `empty` returns TRUE if and only if this stack is empty, and `size` returns the number of items on this stack:

```
template<class T> bool Stack<T>::empty(void)
{
    return (s->length() == 0);
}

template<class T> int Stack<T>::size(void)
{
    return s->length();
}
```

Three "peek" operations will prove useful in later chapters: top returns the stack's top item, nextToTop returns the item just below the top item, and bottom returns the bottom item. None of the three peek operations changes the state of the stack (nothing is popped or pushed).

```
template<class T> T Stack::top(void)
{
    return s->first();
}

template<class T> T Stack::nextToTop(void)
{
    s->first();
    return s->next();
}

template<class T> T Stack::bottom(void)
{
    return s->last();
}
```

By way of a simple example involving stacks, the following function uses a stack to reverse the order of strings in array a:

```
void reverse(char *a[], int n)
{
    Stack<char*> s;
    for (int i = 0; i < n; i++)
        s.push(a[i]);
    for (i = 0; i < n; i++)
        a[i] = s.pop();
}
```

Class Stack is a good example of an abstract data type. The class provides a public interface consisting of accessible operations: push, pop, empty, the class's constructor and destructor, and peek operations. A stack is manipulated only through this public interface. The storage structure (the list) is hidden in the private part of the class definition and cannot be modified or otherwise accessed except through the interface. Programs using stacks do not need to know anything about how the stacks are implemented; for example, function `reverse` works whether its stack is implemented using a list or an array.

Observe that we have implemented the stack ADT in terms of the list ADT. This implementation is much simpler than one based directly on lower-level building blocks such as linked lists or arrays. The danger in implementing an ADT in terms of a second ADT is that the first ADT inherits the performance characteristics of the second, whose implementation may be inefficient. But in this case, having implemented the list ADT ourselves, we understand its performance and can show easily that each of the operations supported by `Stack` runs in constant time.

3.5   Binary Search Trees

3.5.1 Binary Trees

Although lists are efficient for inserting and removing items and for rearranging their order, they are not efficient for searching. Searching for a particular item x requires stepping down the list while deciding at each item whether it matches x. A search may require visiting many items or, if the list does not contain x, every item to determine that this is the case. Even if the list is sorted, a search must visit every item preceding the position where x belongs.

Binary trees provide a more efficient way to search. A binary tree is a structured collection of nodes. The collection can be empty, in which case we have an *empty binary tree*. If the collection is not empty, it is partitioned into three disjoint sets of nodes: a *root* node n, a binary tree called the *left subtree* of n, and a binary tree called *right subtree* of n. In Figure 3.8a, the node labeled A is the root; node B, called the *left child* of A, is the root of A's left subtree; and node C, the *right child* of A, is the root of A's right subtree.

The binary tree of Figure 3.8a consists of four *internal nodes* (the labeled circular nodes in the figure) and five *external nodes* (the square nodes). The *size* of a binary tree is the number of internal nodes it contains. The external nodes correspond to empty binary

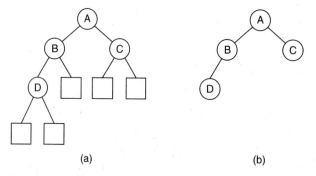

(a)   (b)

Figure 3.8:   A binary tree with external nodes (a) shown and (b) not shown.

trees; for instance, the left child of node B is nonempty (node D), whereas the right child of B is empty. In some contexts the external nodes are labeled, and in others they are not referred to at all and are thought of as empty binary trees (in Figure 3.8b the external nodes are not drawn).

A metaphor based on genealogy provides a convenient way to refer to specific nodes within a binary tree. Node p is the *parent* of node n just if n is a child of p. Two nodes are *siblings* if they share the same parent. Given two nodes n_1 and n_k such that n_k belongs to the subtree rooted at n_1, node n_k is said to be a *descendant* of n_1, and n_1 an *ancestor* of n_k. There exists a unique *path* from n_1 down to each of its descendants n_k: a sequence of nodes $n_1, n_2, \ldots, n_k$ such that n_i is the parent of n_{i+1} for $i = 1, 2, \ldots, k - 1$. The *length* of the path is the number of edges it contains $(k - 1)$. For example, in Figure 3.8a the unique path from node A to node D consists of the sequence A, B, D and has length 2.

The *depth* of a node n is defined recursively:

$$\text{depth}(n) = \begin{cases} 0 & \text{if } n \text{ is the root node} \\ 1 + \text{depth(parent}(n)) & \text{otherwise} \end{cases}$$

The depth of a node equals the length of the unique path from the root to the node. In Figure 3.8a, node A has depth 0 and node D has depth 2.

The *height* of a node n is also defined recursively:

$$\text{height(n)} = \begin{cases} 0 & \text{if } n \text{ is an external node} \\ 1 + \max(\text{height(lchild}(n)), \text{height(rchild}(n))) & \text{otherwise} \end{cases}$$

where *lchild(n)* denotes the left child of node n, and *rchild(n)* the right child of n. The height of node n equals the length of some longest path from n down to an external node in n's subtree. The height of a binary tree is defined as the height of its root node. For example, the binary tree of Figure 3.8 has height 3, and node D has height 1.

In a pointer-based implementation of binary trees, nodes are objects of class `TreeNode`:

```
template<class T> class TreeNode {
 protected:
   TreeNode *_lchild;
   TreeNode *_rchild;
   T val;
 public:
   TreeNode(T);
   virtual ~TreeNode(void);
   friend class SearchTree<T>;
   friend class BraidedSearchTree<T>;
};
```

Data members `_lchild` and `_rchild` link to this node's left child and right child, respectively, and data member `val` contains the item.

The class constructor creates a binary tree of size one—the sole internal node has two empty children, each represented by `NULL`:

```
template<class T> TreeNode<T>::TreeNode(T v) :
    val(v), _lchild(NULL), _rchild(NULL)
{
}
```

The destructor `~TreeNode` recursively deletes this node's left and right children (if they exist) before deallocating this node itself:

```
template<class T> TreeNode<T>::~TreeNode(void)
{
    if (_lchild) delete _lchild;
    if (_rchild) delete _rchild;
}
```

3.5.2 Binary Search Trees

One of the primary uses of binary trees is for efficient searching. Searching encompasses such operations as finding a given item in a set of distinct items, locating the smallest or largest item in the set, and deciding whether the set contains a given item. To search within a binary tree efficiently, its items must be arranged in a particular way. Specifically, a binary tree is called a *binary search tree* if its items are organized as follows: For each item n, all the items in the left subtree of n are less than n, and all the items in the right subtree of n are greater than n. Figure 3.9 depicts three binary search trees, each containing the same set of integer items. In general, there exist numerous binary search trees (of different shape) for any given set of items.

It is implicit that items belong to a *linear order* and, consequently, that any two can be compared. Examples of linear orders include the integers and the real numbers under <, and words and character strings under lexicographic (dictionary) ordering. Searching is accomplished by means of a comparison function for comparing any two items with respect to the linear order. (Recall from Section 3.3 that a comparison function is passed two items and returns -1, 0, or 1 depending on whether the first item is less than, equal to, or greater than the second item.) In our version of search trees, a comparison function is bound to a search tree object when the object is defined.

A function for "visiting" or operating on the items in a search tree is also useful. Such a *visit function* may be used to print, update, or access an item, or operate on it in some

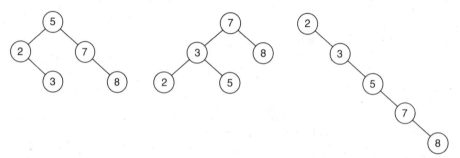

Figure 3.9: Three binary search trees over the same set of items.

other way. Visit functions are not bound to search trees; different visit functions can be applied to the items in the same search tree.

3.5.3 The `SearchTree` Class

Let us define a new class template `SearchTree` for representing binary search trees. The class contains data member `root`, which points to the root of the binary search tree (a `TreeNode` object), and data member `cmp`, which points to a comparison function:

```
template<class T> class SearchTree {
 private:
    TreeNode<T> *root;
    int (*)(T,T) cmp;
    TreeNode<T> *_findMin(TreeNode<T>*);
    void _remove(T, TreeNode<T>* &);
    void _inorder(TreeNode<T>*, void (*)(T));
 public:
    SearchTree(int(*)(T,T));
    ~SearchTree(void);
    int isEmpty(void);
    T find(T);
    T findMin(void);
    void inorder(void(*)(T));
    void insert(T);
    void remove(T);
    T removeMin(void);
};
```

To simplify the implementation, we will assume that the items in a search tree are *pointers* to objects of a given type; when class template `SearchTree` is used to construct an actual class, type parameter `T` is passed a pointer type.

3.5.4 Constructors and Destructors

The constructor `SearchTree` initializes the data member `cmp` to a comparison function, and `root` to the empty search tree:

```
template<class T> SearchTree<T>::SearchTree(int(*c)(T,T)) :
    cmp(c), root(NULL)
{
}
```

A search tree is empty just if data member `root` contains `NULL` instead of a valid pointer:

```
template<class T> int SearchTree<T>::isEmpty(void)
{
    return (root == NULL);
}
```

Chap. 3: Data Structures

The class destructor deletes the entire tree by invoking the root's destructor:

```
template<class T> SearchTree<T>::~SearchTree(void)
{
    if (root) delete root;
}
```

3.5.5 Searching

To find a given item `val`, we start at the root and then zigzag along the unique path down to the node containing `val`. At each node n along the way, we use the tree's comparison function to compare `val` to the item `n->val` stored in n. If `val` is less than `n->val`, we continue searching from n's left child; if `val` is greater than `n->val`, we continue searching from n's right child; otherwise we return `n->val` (we are done). The path from the root node down to `val` is called the *search path* for `val`.

Member function `find` implements this search algorithm, returning a pointer to the item that is sought, or NULL if no such item exists in the search tree:

```
template<class T> T SearchTree::find(T val)
{
    TreeNode<T> *n = root;
    while (n) {
        int result = (*cmp)(val, n->val);
        if (result < 0)
            n = n->_lchild;
        else if (result > 0)
            n = n->_rchild;
        else
            return n->val;
    }
return NULL;
}
```

This search algorithm can be likened to a tournament involving a field of candidates. Initially, when we start at the root, the field includes every item in the search tree. In general, when at node n, the field consists of the descendants of n. At each stage, we compare `val` to `n->val`. If `val` is less than `n->val`, the field is narrowed to the items in n's left subtree; the items in n's right subtree, as well as `n->val` itself, are eliminated from contention. Similarly, if `val` is greater than `n->val`, the field is narrowed to the items in n's right subtree. The process continues until either `val` is located or no candidates remain, implying that `val` does not occur in the search tree.

To find the smallest item in a search tree, we start at the root and repeatedly follow left-child links until reaching a node n whose left child is empty—node n contains the smallest item. We can also view this process as a tournament. When at node n, the field of candidates consists of the descendants of n. In each stage, those items greater than or equal to `n->val` are eliminated from the field, and n's left child serves as the new n. The process continues until some node n with empty left child is reached, implying that no remaining candidate is smaller than `n->val`; we return `n->val`.

Member function `findMin` returns the smallest item in this search tree. It invokes private member function `_findMin`, which implements the search algorithm described earlier, starting at node n:

```
template<class T> T SearchTree<T>::findMin(void)
{
    TreeNode<T> *n = _findMin(root);
    return (n ? n->val : NULL);
}

template<class T>
TreeNode<T> *SearchTree<T>::_findMin(TreeNode<T> *n)
{
    if (n == NULL)
        return NULL;
    while (n->_lchild)
        n = n->_lchild;
    return n;
}
```

The largest item in a search tree can be found analogously, where right-child links are followed instead of left-child links.

3.5.6 Inorder Traversal

A *traversal* of a binary tree is a process that visits every node exactly once. Member function `inorder` performs a special kind of traversal known as an *inorder traversal*. The strategy is to first inorder traverse the left subtree, then visit the root, and finally inorder traverse the right subtree. We visit a node by applying a visit function to the item stored in the node.

Member function `inorder` serves as the driver function. It invokes private member function `_inorder`, which performs an inorder traversal from node n and applies function `visit` to each item reached.

```
template<class T> void SearchTree<T>::inorder(void(*visit)(T))
{
    _inorder(root, visit);
}

template<class T>
void SearchTree::_inorder(TreeNode<T> *n, void(*visit)(T))
{
    if (n) {
        _inorder(n->_lchild, visit);
        (*visit)(n->val);
        _inorder(n->_rchild, visit);
    }
}
```

Inorder traversal of each of the binary search trees of Figure 3.9 visits the nodes in increasing order: 2, 3, 5, 7, 8. Indeed, inorder traversal of *any* binary search tree visits its items in increasing order. To see why, observe that when we perform inorder traversal at some node n, the items smaller than n->val are visited before n since they belong to n's left subtree, and the items larger than n->val are visited after n since they belong to n's right subtree. Therefore, n is visited in the correct position. Since n is an arbitrary node, the same holds for *every* node.

Member function `inorder` provides a way to list the items stored in a binary search tree in sorted order. For example, if a is a `SearchTree` of strings, we can print the strings in lexicographic order with the instruction a.inorder(printString). Here the visit function printString might be defined like this:

```
void printString(char *s)
{
    cout << s << "\n";
}
```

Under inorder traversal of a binary tree, the node visited just after some node *n* is called the *successor* of *n*, and the node visited just before *n* is the *predecessor* of *n*. Neither the predecessor of the first node visited nor the successor of the last node visited are defined (in a binary *search* tree, these nodes hold the smallest and largest items in the tree, respectively).

3.5.7 Inserting Items

To insert a new item into a binary search tree, we first locate its proper position—the external node it is to replace—by zigzagging down the item's search path from the root. In addition to maintaining a pointer n to the current node, we maintain a pointer p to n's parent. Thus when n reaches some external node, p points to the node that is to become the new item's parent. To perform the insertion, we allocate a new node to hold the new item and then link parent p to this new node (Figure 3.10).

Member function `insert` inserts item val into this binary search tree:

```
template<class T> void SearchTree<T>::insert(T val)
{
    if (root == NULL) {
        root = new TreeNode<T>(val);
        return;
    } else {
        int result;
        TreeNode<T> *p, *n = root;
        while (n) {
            p = n;
            result = (*cmp)(val, p->val);
            if (result < 0)
                n = p->_lchild;
            else if (result > 0)
                n = p->_rchild;
```

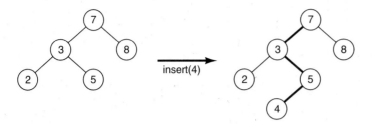

Figure 3.10:   Inserting an item into a binary search tree.

```
        else
            return;
    }
    if (result < 0)
        p->_lchild = new TreeNode<T>(val);
    else
        p->_rchild = new TreeNode<T>(val);
    }
}
```

3.5.8 Removing Items

Removing an item from a binary search tree is trickier than inserting one because the tree can change shape in more complicated ways. Removing a node that has at most one nonempty child is easy: We link the node's parent to this child. However, things are more difficult if the node to be removed has two nonempty children: The node's parent can link to one of the children, but what do we do with the other child? The solution is not to remove the node from the tree; rather, we replace the item it contains by the item's successor and then remove the node containing this successor.

   To remove an item from a search tree, we first zigzag along the item's search path, from the root down to the node n that contains the item. At this point, three cases (illustrated in Figure 3.11) can occur:

1. *Node n has an empty left child.* In this case replace the link down to n (stored in n's parent, if any) by a link to n's right child.
2. *Node n has a nonempty left child but an empty right child.* Replace the link down to n by a link to n's left child.
3. *Node n has two nonempty children.* Find the successor to n (call it m), copy the data item stored in m into node n, and then recursively remove node m from the search tree.

   It is important to observe that a binary search tree results in each case. Consider case 1. If node n (to be removed) is a left child, the items stored in n's right subtree are less than the item in n's parent p. When n is removed and its right subtree is linked to p, the items stored in p's new left subtree are, of course, still less than the item in p. Since no other links are changed, the tree remains a binary search tree. The argument is symmetric if node n is a right child, and trivial if n is the root. Case 2 is argued similarly. In case 3, the item v stored in node n is overwritten by the next-larger item stored in node m (call it w), and then w is removed from the tree. In the binary tree that results, the values in n's left

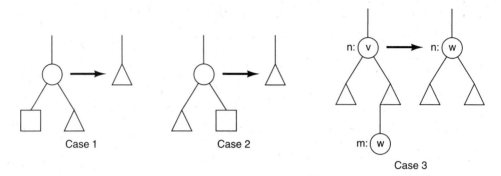

Figure 3.11:   The three cases that can arise when removing an item from a binary search tree.

subtree are less than w since they are less than v. Moreover, the items in n's right subtree are greater than w since (1) they are greater than v, (2) no item in the binary search tree lies between v and w, and (3) w was removed from among them.

Observe that in case 3, node m must exist since n's right subtree is nonempty. Furthermore, the recursive call to remove m cannot lead to a regress of recursive calls—since node m has no left child, case 1 applies when it gets removed.

Figure 3.12 illustrates a sequence of remove operations in which each of the three cases occurs. Observe that inorder traversal of each successive binary tree visits the nodes in increasing order, verifying that each is in fact a binary search tree.

Member function remove is the public member function for removing the node containing a given item. It calls private member function _remove, which does the actual work:

```
template<class T> void SearchTree<T>::remove(T val);
{
    _remove(val, root);
}


template<class T>
void SearchTree<T>::_remove(T val, TreeNode<T>* &n)
{
    if (n == NULL)
        return;
    int result = (*cmp)(val, n->val);
```

```
          7                  7                  7                  7
        /   \              /   \              /   \              /
       3     8            3     9            3     9            4
      / \     \          / \   /            / \                /
     2   5     9        2   5             2   4             2
          \                  \
           4                  4
         (a)                (b)                (c)                (d)
```

Figure 3.12:   A sequence of item removals. (a) and (b) Case 1: Remove 8 from the binary tree. (b) and (c) Case 2: Remove 5. (c) and (d) Case 3: Remove 3.

```
   if (result < 0)
      _remove(val, n->_lchild);
   else if (result > 0)
      _remove(val, n->_rchild);
   else {    // case 1
      if (n->_lchild == NULL) {
         TreeNode<T> *old = n;
         n = old->_rchild;
         delete old;
      }
      else if (n->_rchild == NULL) {    // case 2
         TreeNode<T> *old = n;
         n = old->_lchild;
         delete old;
      }
      else {    // case 3
         TreeNode<T> *m = _findMin(n->_rchild);
         n->val = m->val;
         _remove(m->val, n->_rchild);
      }
   }
}
```

Parameter n, a reference type, serves as an alias for the link field that contains the link down to the current node. When the node to be deleted (old) is reached, n names the link field (in old's parent) which contains the link down to old. Hence the instruction n=old->_rchild replaces the link to old by a link to old's right child.

Member function removeMin removes the smallest item from this search tree and returns it:

```
template<class T> T SearchTree<T>::removeMin(void)
{
   T v = findMin();
   remove(v);
   return v;
}
```

Heap sort, a method for sorting an array of items, is a simple program which employs search trees. The idea is to insert all the items into a search tree and then iteratively remove the smallest item until all items have been removed. Program heapSort sorts an array s of n items using comparison function cmp:

```
template<class T> void heapSort(T s[], int n, int(*cmp)(T,T))
{
   SearchTree<T> t(cmp);
   for (int i = 0; i < n; i++)
      t.insert(s[i]);
   for (i = 0; i < n; i++)
      s[i] = t.removeMin();
}
```

3.6   Braided Binary Search Trees

One problem with binary search trees is that they do not efficiently support these operations:
Given an item in a binary search tree, report the next larger or next smaller item. Although
inorder traversal yields *all* the items in increasing order, it does not help us move efficiently
from an arbitrary item to its successor or predecessor. In this section we cover *braided
binary search trees*, which are binary search trees with a linked list threaded through the
nodes in increasing order. For brevity, we will refer to a braided binary search tree as a
braided search tree, and the linked list that threads through it as a *braid*.

   We will implement braided search trees with the class `BraidedSearchTree`.
This class differs from class `SearchTree` of the previous section in three significant
ways. First, a `BraidedSearchTree` object possesses a linked list—the braid—which
links each node to its successor and predecessor. Second, a `BraidedSearchTree` object
maintains a window which is at all times positioned over some item in the tree. The window
serves the same purpose as it does in class `List`: Many operations refer to the window or
to the item in the window. Third, member `root` of a `BraidedSearchTree` points to a
header node, a "pseudoroot node" whose right child is the actual root of the braided search
tree. Along the braid, the node containing the smallest item in the tree follows the header
node, and the node containing the largest item precedes the header node. Hence the header
node corresponds to a head position which simultaneously occurs before the first position
and after the last position (Figure 3.13).

3.6.1 The `BraidedNode` Class

The nodes of a braided search tree are `BraidedNode` objects. Since nodes behave both
like tree nodes and list nodes, we derive class template `BraidedNode` from the base
classes `TreeNode` and `Node`:

```
template<class T>
class BraidedNode : public Node, public TreeNode<T> {
 public:
    BraidedNode(T);
    BraidedNode<T> *rchild(void);
    BraidedNode<T> *lchild(void);
    BraidedNode<T> *next(void);
    BraidedNode<T> *prev(void);
    friend class BraidedSearchTree<T>;
};
```

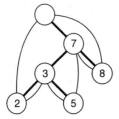

Figure 3.13: A braided search tree with header
node. The braid is represented by the lighter curved
lines.

Class `BraidedNode`'s constructor explicitly initializes base class `TreeNode` in its initialization list; base class `Node` gets initialized implicitly since its constructor takes no arguments:

```
template<classT> BraidedNode<T>::BraidedNode(T val) :
    TreeNode<T>(val)
{
}
```

Member functions `rchild`, `lchild`, `next`, and `prev` yield this node's four links—the first two within the search tree, the last two within the braid:

```
template<class T>
BraidedNode<T> *BraidedNode<T>::rchild(void)
{
    return (BraidedNode<T>*)_rchild;
}
```

```
template<class T>
BraidedNode<T> *BraidedNode<T>::lchild(void)
{
    return (BraidedNode<T>*)_lchild;
}
```

```
template<class T>
BraidedNode<T> *BraidedNode<T>::next(void)
{
    return (BraidedNode<T>*)_next;
}
```

```
template<class T>
BraidedNode<T> *BraidedNode<T>::prev(void)
{
    return (BraidedNode<T>*)_prev;
}
```

3.6.2 The `BraidedSearchTree` Class

Class template `BraidedSearchTree` is defined as follows:

```
template<class T> class BraidedSearchTree {
 private:
    BraidedNode<T> *root;          // header node
    BraidedNode<T> *win;           // current window
    int (*cmp)(T,T);               // comparison function
    void _remove(T, TreeNode<T>* &);
 public:
    BraidedSearchTree(int(*)(T,T));
    ~BraidedSearchTree(void);
```

```
    T next(void);
    T prev(void);
    void inorder(void(*)(T));
    T val(void);
    bool isFirst(void);
    bool isLast(void);
    bool isHead(void);
    bool isEmpty(void);
    T find(T);
    T findMin(void);
    T insert(T);
    void remove(void);
    T removeMin(void);
};
```

3.6.3 Constructors and Destructors

The class constructor `BraidedSearchTree` initializes data member `cmp` to a comparison function and `root` to the empty tree, represented by an isolated header node:

```
template<class T>
BraidedSearchTree<T>::BraidedSearchTree(int(*c)(T,T)) :
    cmp(c)
{
    win = root = new BraidedNode<T>(NULL);
}
```

The class destructor deletes the entire tree by invoking the header node's destructor:

```
template<class T>
BraidedSearchTree<T>::~BraidedSearchTree(void)
{
    delete root;
}
```

3.6.4 Using the Braid

Data member `win` represents the tree's window—`win` points to the node over which the window is positioned. Member functions `next` and `prev` advance the window to the next or previous position. If the window is in the head position, `next` moves it to the first position and `prev` moves it to the last position. Both functions return the item in the window's new position:

```
template<class T> T BraidedSearchTree<T>::next(void)
{
    win = win->next();
    return win->val;
}
```

```
template<class T> T BraidedSearchTree<T>::prev(void)
{
   win = win->prev();
   return win->val;
}
```

Member function `val` returns the item in the window. NULL is returned if the window is in the head position:

```
template<class T> T BraidedSearchTree<T>::val(void)
{
   return win->val;
}
```

Inorder traversal is performed by following the braid from the first position to the last while applying function `visit` to each item along the way:

```
template<class T>
void BraidedSearchTree<T>::inorder(void (*visit)(T))
{
   BraidedNode<T> *n = root->next();
   while (n != root) {
     (*visit)(n->val);
      n = n->next();
   }
}
```

Member functions `isFirst`, `isLast`, and `isHead` return TRUE if the window is in the first position, last position, and head position, respectively:

```
template<class T> bool BraidedSearchTree<T>::isFirst(void)
{
   return (win == root->next()) && (root != root->next());
}
```

```
template<class T> bool BraidedSearchTree<T>::isLast(void)
{
   return (win == root->prev()) && (root != root->next());
}
```

```
template<class T> bool BraidedSearchTree<T>::isHead(void)
{
   return (win == root);
}
```

Function `isEmpty` returns TRUE only if this search tree is empty and consists only of an isolated header node:

```
template<class T> bool BraidedSearchTree<T>::isEmpty()
{
    return (root == root->next());
}
```

3.6.5 Searching

Member function `find` is used to search for an item. The function is similar to function `SearchTree::find` except that it begins its search at `root->rchild()`, the real root. The window is moved over the item found, if any:

```
template<class T> T BraidedSearchTree<T>::find(T val)
{
    BraidedNode<T> *n = root->rchild();
    while (n) {
        int result = (*cmp)(val, n->val);
        if (result < 0)
            n = n->lchild();
        else if (result > 0)
            n = n->rchild();
        else {
            win = n;
            return n->val;
        }
    }
return NULL;
}
```

The smallest item in a braided search tree occurs in the first position along the braid. Member function `findMin` moves the window over the smallest item and returns the item. If the search tree is empty, `NULL` is returned:

```
template<class T> T BraidedSearchTree<T>::findMin(void)
{
    win = root->next();
    return win->val;
}
```

3.6.6 Inserting Items

A new item must be inserted into its proper position within both the search tree and the braid. If the new item becomes a left child, it also becomes its parent's predecessor in the braid; if the item becomes a right child, it also becomes its parent's successor in the braid. Other than inserting the new node into the braid, the following implementation of `insert` parallels that of function `SearchTree::insert`. However, note that `insert` does not need to check for insertion into an empty tree since the header node is always present. The function places the window over the just-inserted item and returns the item if the insertion succeeds:

```
template<class T> T BraidedSearchTree<T>::insert(T val)
{
    int result = 1;
    BraidedNode<T> *p = root;
    BraidedNode<T> *n = root->rchild();
    while (n) {
        p = n;
        result = (*cmp)(val, p->val);
        if (result < 0)
            n = p->lchild();
        else if (result > 0)
            n = p->rchild();
        else
            return NULL;
    }
    win = new BraidedNode<T>(val);
    if (result < 0) {
        p->_lchild = win;
        p->prev()->Node::insert(win);
    }
    else {
        p->_rchild = win;
        p->Node::insert(win);
    }
    return val;
}
```

3.6.7 Removing Items

Member function `remove` removes the item in the window and moves the window to the previous position:

```
template<class T> void BraidedSearchTree<T>::remove(void)
{
    if (win != root)
        _remove(win->val, root->_rchild);
}
```

Private member function `_remove` is passed the item `val` to be removed and a pointer n to the root of the search tree in which the item occurs. The function works much like its counterpart of the same name in class `SearchTree`. However, to remove an item from a *braided* search tree, the item must, of course, be removed from both the search tree and the braid:

```
template<class T>
void BraidedSearchTree<T>::_remove(T val, TreeNode<T>* &n)
{
    int result = (*cmp)(val, n->val);
    if (result < 0)
        _remove(val, n->_lchild);
    else if (result > 0)
        _remove(val, n->_rchild);
    else {    // case 1
        if (n->_lchild == NULL) {
            BraidedNode<T> *old = (BraidedNode<T>*)n;
            if (win == old)
                win = old->prev();
            n = old->rchild();
            old->Node::remove();
            delete old;
        }
        else if (n->_rchild == NULL) {    // case 2
            BraidedNode<T> *old = (BraidedNode<T>*)n;
            if (win == old)
                win = old->prev();
            n = old->lchild();
            old->Node::remove();
            delete old;
        }
        else {    // case 3
            BraidedNode<T> *m = ((BraidedNode<T>*)n)->next();
            n->val = m->val;
            _remove(m->val, n->_rchild);
        }
    }
}
```

Note that _remove uses the braid to find node n's successor in case 3, when the node to be removed has two nonempty children. Note also that the parameter n is a reference to type TreeNode* rather than type BraidedNode*. This is because n references the link stored in the parent of the node to be removed, and this link has type TreeNode*. Had parameter n instead been made type BraidedNode*, it would mistakenly reference an anonomous object; the link field in the parent node would be inaccessible.

Member function removeMin removes the smallest item from the tree and returns it; the function returns NULL if the tree is empty. If the window had contained the smallest item, the window is moved to the head position; otherwise it is not moved:

```
template<class T> T BraidedSearchTree<T>::removeMin(void)
{
    T val = root->next()->val;
    if (root != root->next())
        _remove(val, root->_rchild);
    return val;
}
```

3.7   **Randomized Search Trees**

Searching is fastest when the item being sought is close to the root. Ideally, the binary search tree is *balanced*, shaped such that every item is relatively close to the root. A balanced binary search tree of size n has height $O(\log n)$, implying that the path from the root to each node has length no greater than $O(\log n)$. Yet a very out-of-balance search tree has height $\Omega(n)$; searching in such a tree is little more efficient than searching in a linked list (Figure 3.9c).

The binary search trees produced by the joint use of functions `insert`, `remove`, and `removeMin` have height $\Omega(n)$ in the worst case. However, if we assume that of the three operations only `insert` is used, and if we also assume that the n items to be inserted arrive in random order—that all $n!$ permutations of the items are equally likely—then the binary search tree will have $O(\log n)$ height on average. Although this is an important result, the assumptions it relies on are restrictive, suggesting that binary search trees are not always efficient in practice. First, in many applications, the input order is unlikely to be random (in an extreme case, the items are inserted in increasing or decreasing order, and the binary search tree that results is most out of balance). Second, the order of search operations—interspersed with insert operations—may be biased (searching for recently inserted items is especially expensive since such items tend to occur in the lowest levels of the binary search tree). Third, the expected properties of search trees that result when `remove` operations are also permitted are not well understood.

In this section we discuss *randomized search trees*. The idea is to make the search tree's behavior depend on the values produced by a random number generator, rather than on input order. When an item is inserted into a randomized search tree, the item is assigned a *priority*, a real number from the uniform distribution on the interval $[0, 1]$ (every number in the interval is equally likely to be chosen). The priorities of the items in the randomized search tree determine its shape according to this rule: The priority of each item is no greater than the priority of every one of its descendants. The binary search tree rule also remains in effect: For every item x, the items in x's left subtree are less than x, and those in its right subtree are greater than x. Figure 3.14 gives an example of a randomized search tree.

How do we insert some item x into a randomized search tree? There are two stages. In the first stage, we disregard priorities and insert x by the method with which we are already familiar: We follow the search path for x from the root down to the external node where x belongs, and then replace the external node by a new internal node containing x. In the second stage, we change the shape of the tree in accordance with the priorities of items. We first randomly choose a priority for x. In the simplest case, the priority of x is greater than or equal to the priority of its parent, so we are done. Alternatively, if the priority of x is less than that of its parent y, the priority rule is violated at y. Suppose that x is the left

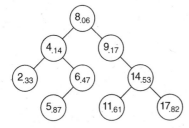

Figure 3.14:   A randomized search tree. The priority of each item is written as a subscript.

child of y. In this case we apply a *right rotation* to y, thereby moving x one level higher in the tree (Figure 3.15). Now the priority rule may be violated at x's new parent. If so, we apply a rotation to the parent—a right rotation if x is a left child, a left rotation if x is a right child—thereby moving x up yet another level higher. We continue to bubble x up until either it is the root or its priority is no less than that of its parent.

Figure 3.16 illustrates item insertion. In this figure, item 6 replaces the proper external node and then is bubbled up according to its priority (.10) and the priorities of its successive parents.

Let us now define the relevant classes. We will consider how to remove items from a randomized search tree a bit later.

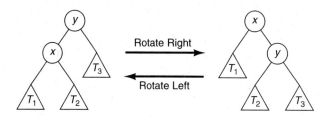

Figure 3.15:   Rotations.

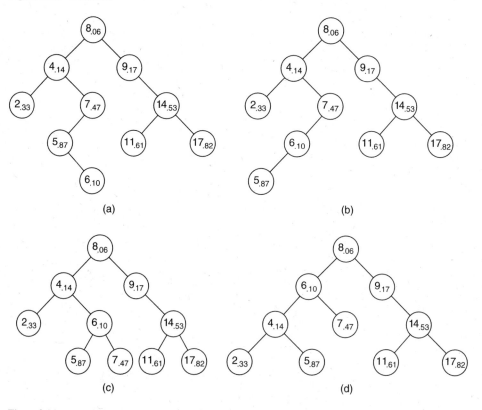

Figure 3.16:   Inserting item 6 into a randomized search tree. (a) and (b) A left rotation at item 5. (b) and (c) A right rotation at item 7. (c) and (d) A left rotation at item 4.

3.7.1 The `RandomizedNode` Class

The nodes of a randomized search tree are objects of class template `RandomizedNode`:

```
template<class T>
class RandomizedNode : public BraidedNode<T> {
 protected:
    RandomizedNode *_parent;
    double _priority;
    void rotateRight(void);
    void rotateLeft(void);
    void bubbleUp(void);
    void bubbleDown(void);
 public:
    RandomizedNode(T v, int seed = -1);
    RandomizedNode *lchild(void);
    RandomizedNode *rchild(void);
    RandomizedNode *next(void);
    RandomizedNode *prev(void);
    RandomizedNode *parent(void);
    double priority(void);
    friend class RandomizedSearchTree<T>;
};
```

Class `RandomizedNode` inherits five data members from its base class: `val`, `_lchild`, `_rchild`, `_prev`, and `_next`. The class introduces two additional data members: `_parent`, which points to this node's parent node, and `_priority`, this node's priority.

The constructor assigns a new `RandomizedNode` a random priority using the standard C++ function `rand`, which generates a random integer between 0 and `RAND_MAX`:

```
template<class T>
RandomizedNode<T>::RandomizedNode(T v, int seed) :
    BraidedNode<T>(v)
{
    if (seed != -1) srand(seed);
    _priority = (rand() % 32767) / 32767.0;
    _parent = NULL;
}
```

It is the *private* member functions of class `RandomizedNode` that are most interesting. The first two perform the two kinds of rotations: right rotations and left rotations. A right rotation is a local operation which changes the shape of a search tree while preserving the ordering of items—both before and after the operation, each node's successor and predecessor are the same. A right rotation on node y pivots the subtree rooted at y around the link from y to its left child x (Figure 3.15). The operation is performed by updating a small number of links: The left-child link of y is set to subtree T_2, the right-child link of x is set to y, and the link to y (in y's parent) is set to x.

Member function `rotateRight` performs a right rotation on this node, which plays the role of *y*.   Node *x* is *y*'s left child.   The function assumes that *y*'s parent exists, a safe assumption because the header node will be assigned a minimum priority—since no node can ascend to the level of the header node, every remaining node must have a parent.

```
template<class T> void RandomizedNode<T>::rotateRight(void)
{
    RandomizedNode<T> *y = this;
    RandomizedNode<T> *x = y->lchild();
    RandomizedNode<T> *p = y->parent();
    y->_lchild = x->rchild();
    if (y->lchild() != NULL)
        y->lchild()->_parent = y;
    if (p->rchild() == y)
        p->_rchild = x;
    else
        p->_lchild = x;
    x->_parent = p;
    x->_rchild = y;
    y->_parent = x;
}
```

Member function `rotateLeft`, also depicted in Figure 3.15, is defined symmetrically:

```
template<class T> void RandomizedNode<T>::rotateLeft(void)
{
    RandomizedNode<T> *x = this;
    RandomizedNode<T> *y = x->rchild();
    RandomizedNode<T> *p = x->parent();
    x->_rchild = y->lchild();
    if (x->rchild() != NULL)
        x->rchild()->_parent = x;
    if (p->lchild() == x)
        p->_lchild = y;
    else
        p->_rchild = y;
    y->_parent = p;
    y->_lchild = x;
    x->_parent = y;
}
```

Member function `bubbleUp` bubbles this node up toward the root through repeated rotations, until this node's priority is greater than or equal to that of its parent. The function is used when an item is lower in the randomized search tree than its priority warrants, which is what holds generally when the second stage of insertion commences. Note that the rotation is applied to this node's parent.

```
template<class T> void RandomizedNode<T>::bubbleUp(void)
{
    RandomizedNode<T> *p = parent();
    if (priority() < p->priority()) {
        if (p->lchild() == this)
            p->rotateRight();
        else
            p->rotateLeft();
        bubbleUp();
    }
}
```

Member function `bubbleDown` moves this node down toward the external nodes of the tree through repeated rotations, until this node's priority is less than or equal to that of both its children. Whenever a rotation is performed, its sense (left or right) depends on which of the two children has smaller priority; if the left child has smaller priority, for instance, a right rotation moves the left child up one level while moving this node down one level. Every external node is assigned priority 2.0, large enough to prevent it from being mistakenly bubbled up. Function `bubbleDown` is used when an item is higher in the tree than its priority warrants. We will use this function later to remove items from the search tree.

```
template<class T> void RandomizedNode<T>::bubbleDown(void)
{
    float lcPriority = lchild() ? lchild()->priority() : 2.0;
    float rcPriority = rchild() ? rchild()->priority() : 2.0;
    float minPriority = (lcPriority<rcPriority) ?
                               lcPriority : rcPriority;
    if (priority() <= minPriority)
        return;
    if (lcPriority < rcPriority)
        rotateRight();
    else
        rotateLeft();
    bubbleDown();
}
```

The public member functions `rchild`, `lchild`, `next`, `prev`, and `parent` yield this node's links to its right child, left child, successor, predecessor, and parent:

```
template<class T>
RandomizedNode<T> *RandomizedNode<T>::rchild(void)
{
    return (RandomizedNode<T>*)_rchild;
}

template<class T>
RandomizedNode<T> *RandomizedNode<T>::lchild(void)
```

```
{
    return (RandomizedNode<T>*)_lchild;
}

template<class T>
RandomizedNode<T> *RandomizedNode<T>::next(void)
{
    return (RandomizedNode<T>*)_next;
}

template<class T>
RandomizedNode<T> *RandomizedNode<T>::prev(void)
{
    return (RandomizedNode<T>*)_prev;
}

template<class T>
RandomizedNode<T> *RandomizedNode<T>::parent(void)
{
    return (RandomizedNode<T>*)_parent;
}
```

Member function `priority` returns this node's priority:

```
template<class T>
double RandomizedNode<T>::priority(void)
{
    return _priority;
}
```

3.7.2 The `RandomizedSearchTree` Class

Randomized search trees are represented by objects of class `RandomizedSearchTree`.
The class template resembles class `BraidedSearchTree` in many respects: Data member `root` points to a header node, `win` represents a window, and `cmp` points to the tree's comparison function.

```
template<class T> class RandomizedSearchTree {
 private:
    RandomizedNode<T> *root;         // header node
    RandomizedNode<T> *win;          // window
    int (*cmp)(T,T);                 // comparison function
    void _remove( RandomizedNode<T>*);
 public:
    RandomizedSearchTree(int(*)(T,T), int  = -1);
    ~RandomizedSearchTree(void);
    T next(void);
    T prev(void);
```

```
    void inorder(void(*)(T));
    T val(void);
    bool isFirst(void);
    bool isLast(void);
    bool isHead(void);
    bool isEmpty(void);
    T find(T);
    T findMin(void);
    T locate(T);
    T insert(T );
    void remove(void);
    T remove(T);
    T removeMin(void);
};
```

3.7.3 Constructors and Destructors

The constructor `RandomizedSearchTree` initializes a new randomized search tree, represented by an isolated header node with minimum priority −1.0:

```
template<class T>
RandomizedSearchTree<T>::RandomizedSearchTree(int (*c)(T,T),
                                              int seed) :
    cmp(c)
{
    win = root = new RandomizedNode<T>(NULL, seed);
    root->_priority = -1.0;
}
```

The destructor deletes the search tree:

```
template<class T>
RandomizedSearchTree<T>::~RandomizedSearchTree(void)
{
    delete root;
}
```

3.7.4 Using the Braid

Member functions `next`, `prev`, `val`, `inorder`, `isFirst`, `isLast`, `isHead`, and `isEmpty` are defined like their counterparts in class `BraidedSearchTree`:

```
template<class T> T RandomizedSearchTree<T>::next(void)
{
    win = win->next();
    return win->val;
}
```

```
template<class T> T RandomizedSearchTree<T>::prev(void)
{
   win = win->prev();
   return win->val;
}


template<class T> T RandomizedSearchTree<T>::val(void)
{
   return win->val;
}


template<class T>
void RandomizedSearchTree<T>::inorder(void (*visit)(T))
{
   RandomizedNode<T> *n = root->next();
   while (n != root) {
      (*visit)(n->val);
      n = n->next();
   }
}


template<class T>
bool RandomizedSearchTree<T>::isFirst(void)
{
   return (win == root->next()) && (root != root->next());
}


template<class T>
bool RandomizedSearchTree<T>::isLast(void)
{
   return (win == root->prev()) && (root != root->next());
}


template<class T>
bool RandomizedSearchTree<T>::isHead(void)
{
   return (win == root);
}


template<class T>
bool RandomizedSearchTree<T>::isEmpty(void)
{
   return (root == root->next());
}
```

3.7.5 Searching

Member functions `find` and `findMin` are also implemented like their counterparts in
class `BraidedSearchTree`:

```
template<class T> T RandomizedSearchTree<T>::find(T val)
{
    RandomizedNode<T> *n = root->rchild();
    while (n) {
        int result = (*cmp)(val, n->val);
        if (result < 0)
            n = n->lchild();
        else if (result > 0)
            n = n->rchild();
        else {
            win = n;
            return n->val;
        }
    }
return NULL;
}

template<class T> T RandomizedSearchTree<T>::findMin(void)
{
    win = root->next();
    return win->val;
}
```

We now introduce *locate*, a new search operation. When applied to argument `val`, function `locate` returns the largest item in the tree that is not greater than `val`. If `val` occurs in the tree, `val` is returned. If `val` does not occur in the tree, the largest item smaller than `val` is returned; if no such item exists in the tree, `NULL` is returned.

To perform the operation, we zigzag down the search path for `val`. As we proceed down the search path, we keep track of the last (lowest) node b at which we branched to the right—node b is the lowest node encountered along the search path whose right child also lies along the search path. If we find `val` in the tree, we simply return it. Alternatively, if we do not find `val` in the tree—the search path terminates at an external node—we return the item stored in node b.

The operation is implemented by member function `locate`, which moves the window over the located item and returns the item:

```
template<class T> T RandomizedSearchTree<T>::locate(T val)
{
    RandomizedNode<T> *b = root;
    RandomizedNode<T> *n = root->rchild();
    while (n) {
        int result = (*cmp)(val, n->val);
        if (result < 0)
            n = n->lchild();
        else if (result > 0) {
            b = n;
            n = n->rchild();
        } else {
```

```
      win = n;
      return win->val;
   }
 }
 win = b;
 return win->val;
}
```

Why does this work? This approach clearly works when `val` occurs in the tree, so let us suppose that `val` does not occur in the tree, that `val`'s search path terminates at an external node. As the pointer n descends the search path, b points to the largest item less than every item in the subtree rooted at node n. It is easy to see that this condition holds initially. Whenever we branch left at n, the condition continues to hold since every item in n's left subtree is less than the item stored in n. Whenever we branch right at n, setting b equal to n restores the condition because (1) every item in n's right subtree is greater than the item stored in n and (2) the item stored in n is greater than the item b had pointed to before being updated. Finally, when n points to an external node, b is the largest item in the tree that is less than any item which might legally replace the external node, of which `val` is one.

3.7.6 Inserting Items

To insert a new item into a randomized search tree, we find the external node where it belongs (stage 1) and then bubble the item up toward the root according to its priority (stage 2). Member function `insert` inserts item `val` into this randomized search tree and then moves the window over the item and returns the item:

```
template<class T> T RandomizedSearchTree<T>::insert(T val)
{
   // stage 1
   int result = 1;
   RandomizedNode<T> *p = root;
   RandomizedNode<T> *n = root->rchild();
   while (n) {
      p = n;
      result = (*cmp)(val, p->val);
      if (result < 0)
         n = p->lchild();
      else if (result > 0)
         n = p->rchild();
      else
         return NULL;
   }
   win = new RandomizedNode<T>(val);
   win->_parent = p;
   if (result < 0) {
      p->_lchild = win;
```

```
        p->prev()->Node::insert(win);
    }
    else {
        p->_rchild = win;
        p->Node::insert(win);
    }
    // stage 2
    win->bubbleUp();
    return val;
}
```

3.7.7 Removing items

Member function `remove` removes the item in the window and then moves the window to the predecessor position. Member function `removeMin` removes the smallest item and returns it; if the window is positioned over this item, the window is moved to the head position:

```
template<class T> void RandomizedSearchTree<T>::remove(void)
{
    if (win != root)
        _remove(win);
}
```

```
template<class T> T RandomizedSearchTree<T>::removeMin(void)
{
    T val = root->next()->val;
    if (root != root->next())
        _remove(root->next());
    return val;
}
```

Both of these functions rely on private member function `_remove`. To remove node n, function `_remove` increases the priority of n to 1.5 and then bubbles it down until it becomes an external node. Priority 1.5 exceeds the priority of every item in the tree but is less than the priority (2.0) of the external nodes. Finally, the function removes n from the randomized search tree. If the window is over the node to be removed, the window is moved to the predecessor position. The algorithm is implemented by function `_remove`, which removes node n from this search tree:

```
template<class T> void
RandomizedSearchTree<T>::_remove(RandomizedNode<T> *n)
{
    n->_priority = 1.5;
    n->bubbleDown();
    RandomizedNode<T> *p = n->parent();
    if (p->lchild() == n)
```

```
        p->_lchild = NULL;
    else
        p->_rchild = NULL;
    if (win == n)
        win = n->prev();
    n->Node::remove();
    delete n;
}
```

Figure 3.16, viewed from (d) to (a), illustrates the removal of item 6 from the rightmost search tree, where the priority of the node containing 6 has been increased to 1.5. The process is reverse that of the insertion of item 6 into tree (a), because right rotation and left rotation are inverse to each other.

For convenience we introduce a second member function `remove`, which, when passed an item, removes the item from the randomized search tree. If the window is over the item to be removed, the window is moved to the previous position; otherwise the window is not moved:

```
template<class T> T RandomizedSearchTree<T>::remove(T val)
{
    T v = find(val);
    if (v) {
        remove();
        return v;
    }
    return NULL;
}
```

3.7.8 Expected Performance

In a randomized search tree of size n, the average depth of a node is $O(\log n)$. This is true regardless of biases in input order and where it is assumed that items may be inserted and removed. Since the operations `insert`, `remove`, and `removeMin`, as well as the search operations `find` and `findMin`, each take time proportional to the depth of the item involved, these operations run in $O(\log n)$ time on average.

Why does the average search path have length $O(\log n)$? To answer this, we consider the expected depth of an item in a randomized search tree T. Let us relabel the items in T by increasing priority as $x_1, x_2, \ldots, x_n$. To determine the expected depth of item x_k, imagine building T from scratch by inserting the items in the order $x_1, x_2, \ldots, x_n$ into an initially empty randomized search tree T'. As each x_i is inserted, we determine the likelihood that it lies along the search path for x_k in T.

Observe three things before continuing. First, the process results in T since a randomized search tree is completely determined by its items and their priorities (if some priority values occur more than once, the items can still be ordered such that T results). Second, because of our insertion order, no rotations will be necessary. Third, our analysis requires that we insert only $x_1, \ldots, x_{k-1}$, since x_k necessarily lies at the end of its own search path, and inserting $x_{k+1}, \ldots, x_n$ cannot increase the depth of x_k since none of these items can be an ancestor of x_k.

We start out with an empty binary tree T', represented by a single external node. To insert x_1 into T', we replace the external node by x_1. As the root of T', x_1 will be an ancestor of x_k, so the probability that x_1 will lie along x_k's search path is one. Next insert x_2 into T'. Item x_2 is equally likely to replace either one of the two external nodes that descend from x_1, yet in only one of the two positions will x_2 lie along x_k's search path. Thus the probability that x_2 will lie along this search path is $\frac{1}{2}$. In general, when we insert x_i into T' for i from 1 to k, x_i is equally likely to replace any one of i external nodes. Since in only one of these positions will x_i lie along x_k's search path, there is probability $\frac{1}{i}$ that x_i will lie along x_k's search path. It follows that the expected depth of item x_k equals $1 + \sum_{i=1}^{k-1} \frac{1}{i}$, which is $O(\log n)$ for $k \le n$.

3.7.9 The Dictionary ADT

The *dictionary* ADT is used to manipulate sets of items drawn from a linear order. It supports dynamic updating of sets (creation, insertion, and deletion) and various forms of searching within a set (e.g., searching for a specific item, for the smallest or largest item, for an item's successor or predecessor). The particular search operations, and the specifics of how they behave, tend to vary slightly from one version to the next. For the purposes of this book, we will let the randomized search tree serve as our dictionary.

Using the preprocessor directive `#define`, we identify `RandomizedSearchTree` as a dictionary:

```
#define Dictionary RandomizedSearchTree
```

Use of the identifier `Dictionary` in our programs is more suggestive of the type's behavior than use of the identifier `RandomizedSearchTree`. Moreover, it allows us to replace one implementation of a dictionary by another by simply changing the `#define` statement accordingly.

3.8   Chapter Notes

Good introductions to data structures are provided by [2, 20, 73, 78, 83, 89, 90]. Robert Tarjan's monograph [83], though somewhat more advanced than the others, captures the interplay between data structures and algorithms in an especially elegant and succinct manner.

Taken together, the aforementioned books present several kinds of balanced search trees guaranteed to have height $\Theta(\log n)$, where n is the size of the tree. Randomized search trees are discussed in [58]. The rotations they rely on are also used by older balanced search tree schemes—most notably by AVL trees, which date to 1962 [1]—and by red-black trees [6, 35].

3.9   Exercises

1. Prove that a binary tree of size n contains $n + 1$ external nodes.

2. Prove that a binary tree of height h has size at most $2^h - 1$. (Hint: Induction on h.)

3. Prove that a binary tree of size n has height at least $\lceil \log(n + 1) \rceil$. (Hint: Use the previous exercise.)

4. Write a member function that computes the height of a `SearchTree` object.

5. Define the copy constructor for class `SearchTree`.

6. Modify the definitions of `RandomizedNode` and `RandomizedSearchTree` so that every `RandomizedSearchTree` object maintains its own random number generator, which gets seeded once when the object is initialized.

7. Show that a set of items with distinct priorities completely determines a randomized search tree.

8. Show that rotation preserves the order of nodes in a binary tree.

9. Given two binary trees T and T' of size n, show that there exists a sequence of left and right rotations that transforms T into T'.

10. Suppose we define a binary search tree whose nodes are connected only by right-child links, left-child links, and parent links. Write the function `next`, which locates the successor to a given node n. (Hint: If n has no right child, its successor is an ancestor.)

11. Show that $\sum_{i=1}^{n} \frac{1}{i} = O(\log n)$.

12. It is claimed that the height of randomized search trees of size n averages about $2.99 \log_2 n + O(\log \log n)$. Experiment with randomized search trees of different sizes to see if you can verify this experimentally. What constant factor is hidden in the term $O(\log_2 \log_2 n)$?

13. In arguing that the expected length of a search path in a randomized search tree of size n is $O(\log n)$, we use the fact that when an item x_i is inserted it is equally likely to replace each of i external nodes of T'. Why is this the case?

4

Geometric Data Structures

In this chapter we define the classes we will need for working with geometric objects in two and three dimensions. In two dimensions, the operations supported by these classes include splitting a polygon along a chord into two smaller polygons, computing the intersection point of two skew lines, and classifying a point relative to a line. In three dimensions they include classifying a point relative to a plane and finding the intersection of a line and a triangle. This chapter also provides what little linear algebra we will need.

4.1 Vectors

A *coordinate system* provides a frame of reference for specifying positions in the plane. Under the *Cartesian coordinate system*, the plane is endowed with two *coordinate axes* with the same origin (their point of intersection) and same unit length; the axes are perpendicular to each other and oriented as in Figure 4.1a. This establishes a one-to-one correspondence between ordered pairs of numbers (x, y) and points in the plane. The point's first coordinate x indicates its displacement along the horizontal axis, and the point's second coordinate y its displacement along the vertical axis.

An ordered pair (x, y) can also be thought of as a *vector*, as shown in Figure 4.1b. Geometrically, vector (x, y) is a directed line segment beginning at the origin $(0, 0)$ and ending at point (x, y). The origin $(0, 0)$—sometimes denoted **0**—is called the *zero vector*.

Vector addition and *scalar multiplication* are two fundamental operations for working with vectors (Figure 4.2). Given two vectors $a = (x_a, y_a)$ and $b = (x_b, y_b)$, vector addition

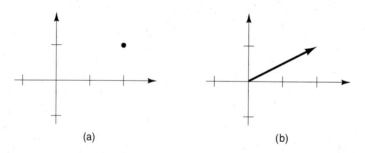

Figure 4.1:   Interpreting the ordered pair (2, 1) as (a) a point and (b) a vector.

is defined by $a + b = (x_a + x_b, y_a + y_b)$. Geometrically, vectors a and b determine the parallelogram with vertices $\mathbf{0}$, a, b, and $a + b$.

Scalar multiplication involves the multiplication of a vector by a real number, the *scalar* (Figure 4.2). Given scalar t and vector $b = (x_b, y_b)$, scalar multiplication is defined by $tb = (tx_b, ty_b)$. The operation scales the length of vector b by factor t. The direction of the vector is unchanged if $t > 0$ and reversed if $t < 0$.

Since a vector begins at the origin, it is fully described by the point at which it terminates. Alternatively, a vector can be characterized by its *length* and *direction*. The length of vector $a = (x_a, y_a)$, denoted $\|a\|$, is defined by $\|a\| = \sqrt{x_a^2 + y_a^2}$. This equals the distance between point a and the origin $\mathbf{0}$. A *unit vector* is a vector with length one. Scaling a nonzero vector a by the reciprocal of its length yields a unit vector $\frac{a}{\|a\|}$ with the same direction, an operation known as *normalization*.

The direction of vector a is described by its *polar angle* θ_a, the angle the vector makes with the positive x-axis. Polar angles are measured in counterclockwise rotation starting at the positive x-axis and lie in the range $0 \le \theta_a < 360$ (we will always measure angles in degrees). Figure 4.3 gives some examples.

Vector subtraction is defined in terms of vector addition and scalar multiplication: Given vectors a and b, we have $b - a = b + (-1)a$. In practice, the operation is carried out with coordinate-wise subtraction: $b - a = (x_b - x_a, y_b - y_a)$. Geometrically, the operation identifies the directed line segment $\overrightarrow{ab}$, beginning at point a and ending at point b, with the vector $b - a$ (Figure 4.4).

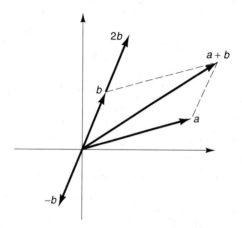

Figure 4.2:   Vector addition and scalar multiplication.

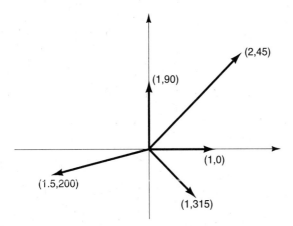

Figure 4.3:   Various vectors, given in polar coordinates $a = (\|a\|, \theta_a)$.

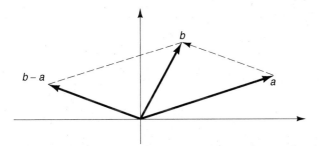

Figure 4.4:   Vector subtraction.

A *directed line segment* $\overrightarrow{ab}$ is a vector fixed in the plane. Endpoint a is called the *origin* of $\overrightarrow{ab}$, and endpoint b the *destination*. Two directed line segments $\overrightarrow{ab}$ and $\overrightarrow{cd}$ that have the same length and direction are translates of each other and can be identified with the same canonical directed line segment, the vector $b - a = d - c$. Vector arithmetic provides the machinery for solving problems involving directed line segments that remain unchanged by translation. We illustrate this fact with the following example.

Given three non-collinear points p_0, p_1, p_2, the triangle $\triangle p_0 p_1 p_2$ they determine is *positively oriented* if p_2 lies to the left of $\overrightarrow{p_0 p_1}$, and *negatively oriented* if p_2 lies to the right of $\overrightarrow{p_0 p_1}$ (Figure 4.5). The problem is to describe a procedure for deciding orientation. It is reasonable to solve this problem using vectors since the orientation of a triangle does not change under translation. Letting $a = p_1 - p_0$ and $b = p_2 - p_0$, the problem reduces to one involving the angle θ_{ab} between the vectors, measured counterclockwise starting at vector a. If $0 < \theta_{ab} < 180$, then $\triangle p_0 p_1 p_2$ has positive orientation; otherwise $(180 < \theta_{ab} < 360)$ the triangle has negative orientation.

Vectors a and b assume one of four possible configurations (Figure 4.6). In cases 1 and 3 we have $0 < \theta_{ab} < 180$, and in cases 2 and 4 we have $180 < \theta_{ab} < 360$; in cases 1 and 2 the positive x-axis pierces the angle θ_{ab}, and in cases 3 and 4 it does not. The four

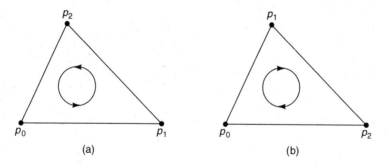

Figure 4.5: Triangle is (a) positively oriented and (b) negatively oriented.

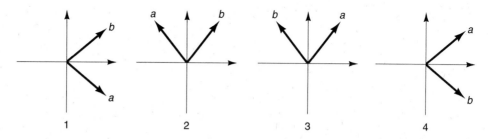

Figure 4.6: The four configurations relevant for deciding a triangle's orientation.

possible configurations correspond to four possible ranges in which the value $Q = \theta_b - \theta_a$ lies:

Case	Range of $Q = \theta_b - \theta_a$	Orientation of $\triangle p_0 p_1 p_2$	$\sin Q$
1	$-360 < Q < -180$	$+$	$+$
2	$-180 < Q < 0$	$-$	$-$
3	$0 < Q < 180$	$+$	$+$
4	$180 < Q < 360$	$-$	$-$

To decide the orientation of the triangle, we could compute $Q = \theta_b - \theta_a$ and then answer based on which of the four ranges Q lies in. A better way makes use of the observation that $\sin(Q)$ has the same sign as the triangle's orientation. Since

$$\sin(\theta_b - \theta_a) = \sin\theta_b \; \cos\theta_a - \cos\theta_b \; \sin\theta_a$$

and

$$\cos\theta_a = \frac{x_a}{\|a\|}, \quad \sin\theta_a = \frac{y_a}{\|a\|}, \quad \cos\theta_b = \frac{x_b}{\|b\|}, \quad \sin\theta_b = \frac{y_b}{\|b\|}$$

we have

$$\sin(\theta_b - \theta_a) = \frac{1}{\|a\| \, \|b\|}(x_a y_b - x_b y_a)$$

Because the lengths $\|a\|$ and $\|b\|$ are positive constants, it follows that

$$\text{sign}(\sin(\theta_b - \theta_a)) = \text{sign}(x_a y_b - x_b y_a)$$

Hence $x_a y_b - x_b y_a$ has the same sign as the triangle's orientation. In the next section we will formulate this as a C++ function which reports the orientation of a triangle. It is noteworthy that the expression $x_a y_b - x_b y_a$ has a simple geometric interpretation: It equals the signed area of the parallelogram with vertices $\mathbf{0}$, a, b, and $a + b$.

4.2 Points

4.2.1 The `Point` Class

The class `Point` contains data members x and y to store a point's coordinates. Its member functions support such operations as classifying this point relative to a given line segment and computing the point's distance from a given line. Additional member functions treat this point as a vector: operator functions for performing vector arithmetic, and functions which return polar angle and length.

```
class Point {
 public:
    double x;
    double y;
    Point(double _x = 0.0, double _y = 0.0);
    Point operator+(Point&);
    Point operator-(Point&);
    friend Point operator*(double, Point&);
    double operator[](int);
    int operator==(Point&);
    int operator!=(Point&);
    int operator<(Point&);
    int operator>(Point&);
    int classify(Point&, Point&);
    int classify(Edge&);
    double polarAngle(void);
    double length(void);
    double distance(Edge&);
};
```

4.2.2 Constructors

The constructor initializes a new point with x and y coordinates:

```
Point::Point(double _x, double _y) :
    x(_x), y(_y)
{
}
```

If arguments are not provided, default arguments initialize the point to $(0, 0)$.

A point can also be initialized with a second point. For example, the declaration `Point p(q)` initializes a new point p with the same coordinates as point q. In this case, initialization is performed by the default copy constructor (supplied by the C++ compiler), which performs a member-wise copy.

4.2.3 Vector Arithmetic

Vector addition and vector subtraction are invoked by the operators + and −:

```
Point Point::operator+(Point &p)
{
   return Point(x + p.x, y + p.y);
}


Point Point::operator-(Point &p)
{
   return Point(x - p.x, y - p.y);
}
```

The scalar multiplication operator is made a friend of class `Point`, rather than a member of the class, because its first operand is not of type `Point`. The operator is defined as follows:

```
Point operator*(double s, Point &p)
{
   return Point(s * p.x, s * p.y);
}
```

The `operator[]` member returns this point's x-coordinate if called with *coordinate index* 0, or its y-coordinate if called with 1:

```
double Point::operator[](int i)
{
   return (i == 0) ? x : y;
}
```

4.2.4 Relational Operators

The relational operators == and ! = are used to determine whether two points are equivalent:

```
int Point::operator==(Point &p)
{
   return (x == p.x) && (y == p.y);
}


int Point::operator!=(Point &p)
{
   return !(*this == p);
}
```

Operators < and > implement the *lexicographic* order relation in which point *a* is less than point *b* if either (1) $a.x < b.x$ or (2) $a.x = b.x$ and $a.y < b.y$. Given two points, we first compare their *x*-coordinates; if their *x*-coordinates are equal, we then compare their *y*-coordinates. This is sometimes called the *dictionary order relation* because the same rule orders two-letter words in a dictionary.

```
int Point::operator<(Point &p)
{
   return ((x < p.x) || ((x == p.x) && (y < p.y)));
}

int Point::operator>(Point &p)
{
   return ((x > p.x) || ((x == p.x) && (y > p.y)));
}
```

Infinitely many other orderings of the points in the plane are possible. Nonetheless, it is convenient to use operators < and > to establish a canonical ordering since we will often be storing points in dictionaries, and these operators can be used to help define the necessary comparison functions.

Before turning to the remaining member functions of class Point, let us consider the following simple example, which illustrates the use of Point objects. The function orientation returns 1 if the three points it is handed are positively oriented, -1 if they are negatively oriented, or 0 if they are collinear. The function implements the method explained at the end of the previous section.

```
int orientation(Point &p0, Point &p1, Point &p2)
{
   Point a = p1 - p0;
   Point b = p2 - p0;
   double sa = a.x * b.y - b.x * a.y;
   if (sa > 0.0)
      return 1;
   if (sa < 0.0)
      return -1;
   return 0;
}
```

4.2.5 Point-Line Classification

One important operation is that of classifying a point relative to a directed line segment. The operation reports whether the point lies to the left or right of the directed line segment; and if neither, whether the point lies beyond the directed line segment's destination or behind its origin; and if neither of these, whether it coincides with the origin, coincides with the destination, or lies between them. The directed line segment effectively partitions the plane into seven non-overlapping regions, and the operation reports in which region the point lies (Figure 4.7).

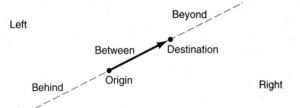

Figure 4.7: Partition of the plane into seven regions by a directed line segment.

Member function `classify` is used to classify this point relative to the directed line segment $\overrightarrow{p_0 p_1}$ from p0 to p1. It returns an enumeration value indicating the point's classification:

```
enum { LEFT, RIGHT, BEYOND, BEHIND, BETWEEN, ORIGIN, DESTINATION };

int Point::classify(Point &p0, Point &p1)
{
    Point p2 = *this;
    Point a = p1 - p0;
    Point b = p2 - p0;
    double sa = a.x * b.y - b.x * a.y;
    if (sa > 0.0)
        return LEFT;
    if (sa < 0.0)
        return RIGHT;
    if ((a.x * b.x < 0.0) || (a.y * b.y < 0.0))
        return BEHIND;
    if (a.length() < b.length())
        return BEYOND;
    if (p0 == p2)
        return ORIGIN;
    if (p1 == p2)
        return DESTINATION ;
    return BETWEEN;
}
```

The orientation of points p0, p1, and p2 is first used to decide whether point p2 lies to the left of, to the right of, or collinear with $\overrightarrow{p_0 p_1}$. In the last case, additional calculations are needed. If vectors a=p1-p0 and b=p2-p0 point in opposite directions, then point p2 lies behind directed segment $\overrightarrow{p_0 p_1}$. If vector a is shorter than vector b, then p2 lies beyond $\overrightarrow{p_0 p_1}$. Otherwise p2 is compared to p0 and p1 to decide whether it coincides with one of these two endpoints or lies between them.

A second version of member function `classify`, which is passed an edge rather than a pair of points, is provided for convenience:

```
int Point::classify(Edge &e)
{
    return classify(e.org, e.dest);
}
```

Point-line classification will be used frequently throughout this book. In some applications a more coarse classification suffices (such as deciding whether a point lies to the left of a given directed line segment). Other applications will make full use of this classification scheme.

4.2.6 Polar Coordinates

The *polar coordinate system* provides a second frame of reference for fixing positions in the plane. Originating from the origin **0** is a *polar axis*, a rightward-pointing horizontal ray as in Figure 4.8. A point *a* is represented by the pair (r_a, θ_a). Regarding point *a* as a vector originating at the origin, r_a is its length and θ_a its polar angle (the angle that *a* makes with the polar axis, measured in counterclockwise rotation).

The correspondence between pairs (r_a, θ_a) and points is not one to one; many pairs can represent the same point. The pair $(0, \theta)$ corresponds to the origin for *every* value of θ. Moreover, $(r, \theta + 360k)$ corresponds to the same point as k ranges over the integers.

Points can be represented in Cartesian coordinates or in polar coordinates, and it is sometimes necessary to switch from one coordinate system to the other. As evident in Figure 4.8, the two equations

$$x = r \cos \theta, \qquad y = r \sin \theta$$

transform a point from polar coordinates (r, θ) into Cartesian coordinates (x, y).

To transform back, the distance coordinate r is given by

$$r = \sqrt{x^2 + y^2}$$

To express polar angle θ as a function of x and y, observe that the relation $\tan \theta = \frac{y}{x}$ holds, from which it follows that

$$\theta = \tan^{-1} \frac{y}{x}, \quad x \neq 0 \qquad\qquad [4.1]$$

To use Equation 4.1 in function `polarAngle`, it is necessary to distinguish between the quadrants of the plane and to handle the case in which x equals zero:

```
double Point::polarAngle(void)
{
    if ((x == 0.0) && (y == 0.0))
        return -1.0;
    if (x == 0.0)
        return ((y > 0.0) ? 90 : 270);
```

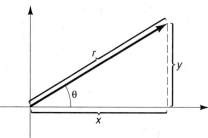

Figure 4.8:   Point *p* is described by polar coordinates (r, θ) and Cartesian coordinates (x, y).

```
    double theta = atan(y / x);        // in radians
    theta *= 360 / (2 * 3.1415926);    // convert to degrees
    if (x > 0.0)    // quadrants 1 and 4
       return ((y >= 0.0) ? theta : 360 + theta);
    else    // quadrants 2 and 3
       return (180 + theta);
}
```

Note that function `polarAngle` returns -1.0 if this vector is the zero vector (it returns a nonnegative value otherwise). This will be used later to simplify the definition of comparison functions based on polar angle.

Member function `length` returns the length of this vector:

```
double Point::length(void)
{
    return sqrt(x*x + y*y);
}
```

Member function `distance` returns the signed distance from this point to an edge. We will define the function in subsection 4.5.3.

4.3 Polygons

Polygons are fascinating—surprisingly so, given how simple they are in concept. In this section we present basic definitions and concepts for talking about polygons and tools for handling them.

4.3.1 What Are Polygons?

A polygon is a closed curve in the plane composed of straight line segments. The segments are called the *edges* or *sides* of the polygon, and the endpoints where two segments meet are called its *vertices*. The number of vertices (or, equivalently, sides) that a polygon possesses is its *size*. For brevity, we will often use *n-gon* to mean a polygon of size n, and $|P|$ to denote the size of some polygon P.

A polygon is *simple* if it does not cross itself. A simple polygon encloses a connected region of the plane, referred to as its *interior*. The unbounded region surrounding a simple polygon forms its *exterior*, and the set of points lying on the polygon itself forms its *boundary*. In this book we will take *polygon* to mean *simple filled polygon*: the union of the boundary and interior of a simple polygon. To say, for instance, that a point lies in a polygon means that the point belongs either to the (simple) polygon's boundary or interior.

Vertices are ordered cyclically around a polygon boundary. Two vertices that are the endpoints of a common edge are *neighbors* and are said to be *adjacent* to one another. A vertex's clockwise neighbor is called its *successor*, and its counterclockwise neighbor its *predecessor*. A *vertex chain*, or simply *chain*, is a section of a polygon boundary. Polygon *traversal* involves moving along a chain from vertex to adjacent vertex, in either clockwise or counterclockwise rotation. Traversal often proceeds full circle around the entire polygon boundary, such as when it is necessary to visit every vertex.

The vertices of a polygon are classified as convex or reflex. A vertex is *convex* if the interior angle at the vertex—through the polygon interior—measures less than or equal to 180 degrees. A vertex is *reflex* otherwise (its interior angle measures greater than 180 degrees).

A line segment between any two nonadjacent vertices is called a *diagonal*. A diagonal is called a *chord* or *internal diagonal* if it lies in the polygon, not crossing the polygon's exterior. Adding a chord to a polygon splits it into smaller subpolygons. Figure 4.9 illustrates some of the notions we have covered relating to polygons.

It is sometimes convenient to regard a point or a line segment as a *degenerate polygon*. A 1-gon consists of a single vertex and a single zero-length edge that connects the vertex to itself. A 2-gon consists of two vertices and two coincident edges that connect the two vertices. Among other benefits, the use of degenerate polygons often simplifies polygon construction: Starting with a 1-gon, we insert a second vertex to form a 2-gon, followed by additional vertices to form conventional polygons of size 3 or greater. By regarding points and line segments as polygons, the initial stages of the process are no different in kind from later stages: Every stage involves the manipulation of polygons.

4.3.2 Convex Polygons

A region in the plane is *convex* if for any two points in the region, the line segment between the two points lies in the region. In Figure 4.9, polygon (a) is convex whereas polygon (b) is not (since the line segment $\overline{pq}$ leaves the polygon). Note that the *boundary* of a convex polygon is *not* convex, but the interior of a convex polygon is.

Convexity has a number of properties that make convex polygons easier to work with than arbitrary polygons. For example, every diagonal of a convex polygon is a chord. In addition, every vertex of a convex polygon is convex. (In a nonconvex polygon, at least one vertex is reflex.) From this it follows that a clockwise traversal of a convex polygon either continues straight or turns right at every vertex.

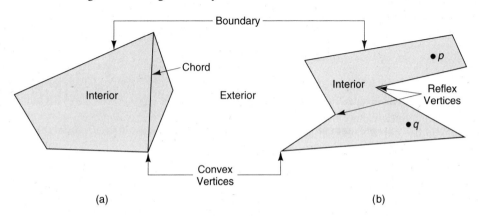

Figure 4.9:   Basic concepts involving polygons.

Another property is that the intersection $A \cap B$ of any two convex regions A and B is convex. (To see why, suppose that p and q are any two points in $A \cap B$. Since both p and q lie in A and A is convex, line segment $\overline{pq}$ lies in A. Similarly, $\overline{pq}$ lies in B. Hence $\overline{pq}$ lies in $A \cap B$, so $A \cap B$ must be convex.) It follows that the intersection of two convex polygons is convex—in fact, a (possibly degenerate) convex polygon. Moreover, since a line is convex, the intersection of a line and a convex polygon must be convex: a line segment, or a single point if the line merely grazes the polygon at some vertex. For these and other properties, we will often work with convex polygons in this book.

4.3.3 The `Vertex` Class

We will represent a polygon by its cycle of vertices, stored in a circular doubly linked list. Each node corresponds to a vertex and links to its two neighbors. By following links we can traverse the polygon boundary in either sense of rotation, and by inserting and removing nodes—and updating links generally—we can create and dynamically modify the polygon.

The classes `Vertex` and `Polygon` support this scheme. The polygon is stored in a circular doubly linked list of `Vertex` objects. Since a vertex of a polygon behaves both like a point in the plane and like a node in a linked list, class `Vertex` is derived from both class `Point` and class `Node`. The `Polygon` class contains a data member which points to some vertex of the linked list representing the polygon. Class `Polygon` serves as the public interface for polygons.

Class `Vertex` inherits data members _next and _prev from base class `Node`, and x and y from base class `Point`. By convention, _next points to this vertex's successor (its clockwise neighbor), and _prev to this vertex's predecessor (its counterclockwise neighbor).

```
class Vertex : public Node, public Point {
 public:
    Vertex(double x, double y);
    Vertex(Point&);
    Vertex *cw(void);
    Vertex *ccw(void);
    Vertex *neighbor(int rotation);
    Point point(void);
    Vertex *insert(Vertex*);
    Vertex *remove(void);
    void splice(Vertex*);
    Vertex *split(Vertex*);
    friend class Polygon;
};
```

A `Vertex` object can be initialized from a point or from x- and y-coordinates:

```
Vertex::Vertex(double x, double y) :
    Point(x,y)
{
}
```

```
Vertex::Vertex(Point &p) :
    Point(p)
{
}
```

Member functions cw and ccw yield this vertex's successor and predecessor, respectively:

```
Vertex *Vertex::cw(void)
{
    return (Vertex*)_next;
}
```

```
Vertex *Vertex::ccw(void)
{
    return (Vertex*)_prev;
}
```

Member function neighbor returns whichever neighbor is specified by parameter rotation, one of the enumeration values CLOCKWISE or COUNTER_CLOCKWISE:

```
Vertex *Vertex::neighbor(int rotation)
{
    return ((rotation == CLOCKWISE) ? cw() : ccw());
}
```

Member function point returns the point in the plane where this vertex lies:

```
Point Vertex::point(void)
{
    return *((Point*)this);
}
```

Member functions insert, remove, and splice correspond to their counterparts defined in base class Node:

```
Vertex *Vertex::insert(Vertex *v)
{
    return (Vertex *)(Node::insert(v));
}
```

```
Vertex *Vertex::remove(void)
{
    return (Vertex *)(Node::remove());
}
```

```
void Vertex::splice(Vertex *b)
{
    Node::splice(b);
}
```

Note that `remove` and `insert` cast their return values to type pointer-to-`Vertex` before returning. Explicit type coersion is needed here because C++ will not automatically convert a pointer to the base class to point to a derived class object. The reason is that the C++ compiler cannot be sure that there is a derived class object present to be pointed to, since the base class object need not be part of a derived class object. (C++ *will*, on the other hand, automatically convert a pointer to the derived class to point to a base class object since every derived class object includes within itself a base class object.)

The last member function, `Vertex::split`, will be defined shortly.

4.3.4 The `Polygon` Class

A polygon is represented by a `Polygon` object. The class contains two data members. The first, `_v`, points to some vertex of the polygon, the current position of the polygon's window. Most operations on polygons refer either to this window or to the vertex in the window. We will sometimes refer to the vertex in the window as the *current vertex*. The second data member, `_size`, holds the size of the polygon:

```
class Polygon {
 private:
   Vertex *_v;
   int _size;
   void resize(void);
 public:
   Polygon(void);
   Polygon(Polygon&);
   Polygon(Vertex*);
   ~Polygon(void);
   Vertex *v(void);
   int size(void);
   Point point(void);
   Edge edge(void);
   Vertex *cw(void);
   Vertex *ccw(void);
   Vertex *neighbor(int rotation);
   Vertex *advance(int rotation);
   Vertex *setV(Vertex*);
   Vertex *insert(Point&);
   void remove(void);
   Polygon *split(Vertex*);
};
```

CONSTRUCTORS AND DESTRUCTORS

There are several constructors for class `Polygon`. The constructor that takes no arguments initializes an empty polygon:

```
Polygon::Polygon(void) :
   _v(NULL), _size(0)
{
}
```

   The copy constructor takes some polygon p and initializes a new polygon with p. It
performs a deep copy, duplicating the linked list in which p is stored. The new polygon's
window is placed over the vertex corresponding to p's current vertex:

```
Polygon::Polygon(Polygon &p)
{
   _size = p._size;
   if (_size == 0)
      _v = NULL;
   else {
      _v = new Vertex(p.point());
      for (int i = 1; i < _size; i++) {
         p.advance(CLOCKWISE);
         _v = _v->insert(new Vertex(p.point()));
      }
      p.advance(CLOCKWISE);
      _v = _v->cw();
   }
}
```

   The third constructor initializes a polygon with a circular doubly linked list of vertices:

```
Polygon::Polygon(Vertex *v) :
   _v(v)
{
   resize();
}
```

   The constuctor calls private member function `resize` to update member `_size`.
In general, `resize` must be called whenever a vertex chain of unknown length is added to
or removed from a polygon. Function `resize` is defined as follows:

```
void Polygon::resize(void)
{
   if (_v == NULL)
      _size = 0;
   else {
      Vertex *v = _v->cw();
      for (_size = 1; v != _v; ++_size, v = v->cw())
         ;
   }
}
```

   The destructor `~Polygon` deallocates this polygon's vertices before deleting the
`Polygon` object itself:

```
Polygon::~Polygon(void)
{
   if (_v) {
      Vertex *w = _v->cw();
```

```
     while (_v != w) {
        delete w->remove();
        w = _v->cw();
     }
   delete _v;
   }
}
```

ACCESS FUNCTIONS

The next several member functions access data about this polygon. Function v returns this polygon's current vertex, and function size this polygon's size:

```
Vertex *Polygon::v(void)
{
   return _v;
}
```

```
int Polygon::size(void)
{
   return _size;
}
```

The pointer returned by member function v can be used as an additional window into the polygon, to supplement the polygon's implicit window. Some applications will require the simultaneous use of several windows into the same polygon—the sole window maintained implicitly by the class does not always suffice.

Member function point returns the point in the plane where the current vertex lies. Member function edge returns the *current edge*. The current edge originates at the current vertex and terminates at the current vertex's successor:

```
Point Polygon::point(void)
{
   return _v->point();
}
```

```
Edge Polygon::edge(void)
{
   return Edge(point(), _v->cw()->point());
}
```

We will define the Edge class in the next section.

Member functions cw and ccw return the current vertex's successor and predecessor without moving the window, and neighbor returns the current vertex's successor or predecessor, depending on the argument it is called with (CLOCKWISE or COUNTER_CLOCKWISE):

```
Vertex *Polygon::cw(void)
{
   return _v->cw();
}
```

```
Vertex *Polygon::ccw(void)
{
    return _v->ccw();
}


Vertex *Polygon::neighbor(int rotation)
{
    return _v->neighbor(rotation);
}
```

UPDATE FUNCTIONS

Member functions `advance` and `setV` move the window over a different vertex; `advance` moves it to the current vertex's successor or predecessor, as specified by the argument:

```
Vertex *Polygon::advance(int rotation)
{
    return _v = _v->neighbor(rotation);
}
```

Member function `setV` moves the window over the vertex v supplied as an argument:

```
Vertex *Polygon::setV(Vertex *v)
{
    return _v = v;
}
```

It is the application's responsibility to ensure that v is a vertex of *this* polygon.

Member function `insert` inserts a new vertex after the current vertex and then moves the window over the new vertex:

```
Vertex *Polygon::insert(Point &p)
{
    if (_size++ == 0)
        _v = new Vertex(p);
    else
        _v = _v->insert(new Vertex(p));
    return _v;
}
```

Member function `remove` removes the current vertex. The window is moved over the predecessor, or is undefined if the polygon is now empty:

```
void Polygon::remove(void)
{
    Vertex *v = _v;
    _v = (--_size == 0) ? NULL : _v->ccw();
    delete v->remove();
}
```

SPLITTING POLYGONS

Polygon splitting involves subdividing a polygon into two smaller subpolygons. The cut is made along some chord. To split along chord $\vec{ab}$, we first insert a duplicate of vertex *a* after *a* and a duplicate of vertex *b* before *b* (call the duplicates *ap* and *bp*). Then we splice *a* and *bp*. The process is illustrated in Figure 4.10.

Member function `Polygon::split` is defined in terms of `Vertex::split`. The latter function partitions a polygon along the chord connecting this vertex (which plays the role of *a*) to vertex b. It returns a pointer to vertex bp, the duplicate of b:

```
Vertex *Vertex::split(Vertex *b)
{                                     // insert bp before vertex b
   Vertex *bp = b->ccw()->insert(new Vertex(b->point()));
   insert(new Vertex(point()));    // insert ap after this vertex
   splice(bp);
   return bp;
}
```

Function `Polygon::split` splits this polygon along the chord connecting its current vertex to vertex b. It returns a pointer to the new polygon, whose window is placed over bp, the duplicate of b. This polygon's window is not moved:

```
Polygon *Polygon::split(Vertex *b)
{
   Vertex *bp = _v->split(b);
   resize();
   return new Polygon(bp);
}
```

Function `Polygon::split` must be used with some care. If vertex b is the successor to the current vertex _v, the operation leaves this polygon unchanged. If the cut occurs along a diagonal that is not a chord, one or both of the resulting "polygons" may self-cross. If vertices b and _v belong to different polygons, the split operation joins the two polygons by two coincident edges that connect the two vertices.

4.3.5 Point Enclosure in a Convex Polygon

In this and the following subsection, we present two simple programs involving polygons. Program `pointInConvexPolygon` is handed a point s and convex polygon p, and

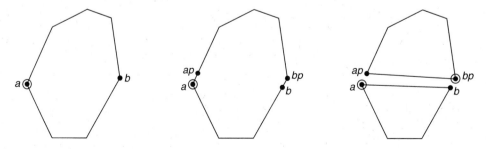

Figure 4.10:   Splitting a polygon along chord $\overline{ab}$. The current vertices (in each polygon's window) are circled.

returns TRUE just if the point lies in (the interior or boundary of) polygon p:

```
bool pointInConvexPolygon(Point &s, Polygon &p)
{
   if (p.size() == 1)
      return (s == p.point());
   if (p.size() == 2) {
      int c = s.classify(p.edge());
      return ((c==BETWEEN) || (c==ORIGIN) || (c==DESTINATION));
   }
   Vertex *org = p.v();
   for (int i = 0; i < p.size(); i++, p.advance(CLOCKWISE))
      if (s.classify(p.edge()) == LEFT) {
         p.setV(org);
         return FALSE;
      }
   return TRUE;
}
```

The preceding function first handles the special cases in which polygon p is a 1-gon or a 2-gon. In the general case, the algorithm traverses the polygon boundary—moves the window from vertex to adjacent vertex—while comparing point s to each edge in turn. Since p is assumed to be convex, point s lies outside the polygon only if s lies to the left of some edge. Note that the program restores the initial position of p's window upon returning.

4.3.6 Finding the Least Vertex in a Polygon

The following function is passed a polygon p and a comparison function cmp, and then finds the least vertex in p. Here *least vertex* means whichever vertex is less than the others under the linear ordering of points given by cmp. Function leastVertex moves p's window over the least vertex and returns the vertex:

```
Vertex *leastVertex(Polygon &p, int (*cmp)(Point*,Point*))
{
   Vertex *bestV = p.v();
   p.advance(CLOCKWISE);
   for (int i = 1; i < p.size(); p.advance(CLOCKWISE), i++)
      if ((*cmp)(p.v(), bestV) < 0)
         bestV = p.v();
   p.setV(bestV);
   return bestV;
}
```

For instance, to find the leftmost vertex in a polygon, we call leastVertex with the following comparison function:

```
int leftToRightCmp(Point *a, Point *b)
{
   if (*a < *b) return -1;
   if (*a > *b) return 1;
   return 0;
}
```

We use the following comparison function to find the rightmost vertex:

```
int rightToLeftCmp(Point *a, Point *b)
{
    return leftToRightCmp(b, a);
}
```

We will use functions `pointInConvexPolygon` and `leastVertex` often in this book. We will also use the two comparison functions defined here, as well as others to be defined later as the need arises.

4.4   Edges

Most every algorithm we will cover involves lines in one form or another. The *line segment* $\overline{p_0 p_1}$ consists of the *endpoints* p_0 and p_1 together with the points that lie between them. When the order of p_0 and p_1 is important, we speak of the *directed line segment* $\overrightarrow{p_0 p_1}$. Endpoint p_0 is the *origin* of the directed line segment, and p_1 the *destination*. We will usually refer to a directed line segment as an *edge* when it is the side of some polygon; the edge is directed so that the polygon's interior lies to its right. An *infinite (directed) line* is determined by two points and is directed from the first point to the second. A *ray* is a semi-infinite line starting at the origin and passing through the destination.

4.4.1 The `Edge` **Class**

The `Edge` class will be used to represent all forms of lines. The class is defined as follows:

```
class Edge {
 public:
    Point org;
    Point dest;
    Edge(Point &_org, Point &_dest);
    Edge(void);
    Edge &rot(void);
    Edge &flip(void);
    Point point(double);
    int intersect(Edge&, double&);
    int cross(Edge&, double&);
    bool isVertical(void);
    double slope(void);
    double y(double);
};
```

An edge's origin and destination endpoints are stored in data members `org` and `dest`, respectively. The `Edge` constructor initializes these data members:

```
Edge::Edge(Point &_org, Point &_dest) :
    org(_org), dest(_dest)
{
}
```

It is also useful to have a constructor for class `Edge` which takes no arguments:

```
Edge::Edge(void) :
   org(Point(0,0)), org(Point(1,0))
{
}
```

4.4.2 Edge Rotations

An *edge rotation* pivots an edge 90 degrees clockwise around its midpoint. Two successive edge rotations are called an *edge flip* since they reverse the direction of an edge. Three successive rotations effectively pivot an edge 90 degrees counterclockwise around its midpoint. Four successive edge rotations leave an edge unchanged. This is illustrated in Figure 4.11.

Figure 4.12 shows how we rotate edge $\overrightarrow{ab}$ into edge $\overrightarrow{cd}$. Where vector $b - a = (x, y)$, the vector n, perpendicular to vector $b - a$, is given by $n = (y, -x)$. The midpoint m between endpoints a and b is given by $m = \frac{1}{2}(a + b)$. Points c and d are then given by $c = m - \frac{1}{2}n$ and $d = m + \frac{1}{2}n$. Rotation is implemented by member function `rot` as follows:

```
Edge &Edge::rot(void)
{
    Point m = 0.5 * (org + dest);
    Point v = dest - org;
    Point n(v.y, -v.x);
    org = m - 0.5 * n;
    dest = m + 0.5 * n;
    return *this;
}
```

Observe that function `rot` is *destructive*: It changes the current edge instead of creating a new edge. The function returns a reference to this edge so calls to `rot` can be readily employed in more complex expressions. This permits, for example, the following concise definition of member function `flip`, for flipping the direction of this edge:

```
Edge &Edge::flip(void)
{
    return rot().rot();
}
```

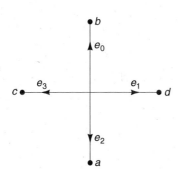

Figure 4.11: Edge e_i is the result of applying i successive edge rotations to edge e_0.

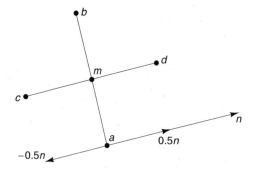

Figure 4.12:   Vectors involved in rotating edge $\overline{ab}$. The rotated edge $\overline{cd}$ has endpoints $c = m - \frac{1}{2}n$ and $d = m + \frac{1}{2}n$.

Within the definition of member function `flip`, the first call to `rot` (to the left of the member-access operator) rotates this edge; the second call to `rot` then rotates this edge once again.

4.4.3 Finding the Intersection of Two Lines

The infinite line $\overleftrightarrow{ab}$ through points a and b can be written in parametric form as

$$P(t) = a + t(b - a) \qquad\qquad [4.2]$$

where the value of parameter t ranges over the real numbers. (If the value of t is restricted to the range $0 \leq t \leq 1$, Equation 4.2 represents the line segment $\overline{ab}$.) The parametric form of a line establishes a correspondence between the real numbers and the points on the line. Figure 4.13 shows the points on an infinite line corresponding to various values of parameter t.

Member functions `Edge::intersect` and `Edge::point` are designed to work together to find the intersection point of two infinite lines e and f. Where e and f are `Edge` objects, the code fragment

```
double t;
Point p;
if (e.intersect(f, t) == SKEW)
    p = e.point(t);
```

assigns t the parametric value (along line e) of the point at which lines e and f intersect, and then sets p to this point. Function `intersect` returns the enumeration value SKEW if the infinite lines cross at a point, COLLINEAR if the lines are collinear, or PARALLEL if they are parallel. Function `point` is handed a parametric value t and returns the corresponding point. The task is performed by two coordinated functions, rather than by a single function,

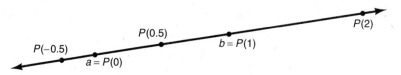

Figure 4.13:   Various points on the line through points a and b.

because we are sometimes interested only in the paramet
rather than in the intersection point itself.

The implementation of member function `point` is simple
is substituted into the parametric equation for this line:

```
Point Edge::point(double t)
{
    return Point(org + t * (dest - org));
}
```

The implementation of member function `intersect` relies on the notion of the *dot product* $a \cdot b$ of two vectors $a = (x_a, y_a)$ and $b = (x_b, y_b)$, which is defined by $a \cdot b = x_a x_b + y_a y_b$. The dot product has a number of important properties, including the following basic ones:

1. Where a, b, and c are vectors, we have $a \cdot b = b \cdot a$ and

2. $a \cdot (b + c) = a \cdot b + a \cdot c = (b + c) \cdot a$.

3. Where s is a scalar, $(sa) \cdot b = s(a \cdot b)$ and $a \cdot (sb) = s(a \cdot b)$.

4. If a is the zero vector, then $a \cdot a = 0$; otherwise $a \cdot a > 0$.

5. $\|a\|^2 = a \cdot a$.

Using these basic properties, we can show the following property on which our line-intersection technique depends: Two vectors a and b are perpendicular if and only if $a \cdot b = 0$. To see why this is true, observe that a and b are perpendicular if and only if

$$\|a - b\| = \|a + b\|$$

This is illustrated in Figure 4.14a. Squaring both sides yields

$$(a - b) \cdot (a - b) = (a + b) \cdot (a + b)$$

Using the aforementioned properties 1 through 3, this expands to

$$a \cdot a - 2a \cdot b + b \cdot b = a \cdot a + 2a \cdot b + b \cdot b$$

Making cancellations yields

$$4a \cdot b = 0$$

or

$$a \cdot b = 0$$

Hence $a \cdot b = 0$ if and only if vectors a and b are perpendicular.

We can say even more. If the angle between vectors a and b measures less than 90 degrees, then $\|a - b\| < \|a + b\|$ (Figure 4.14b). The same sort of argument can be used to show that this is equivalent to the condition $a \cdot b > 0$. It can be shown similarly that the angle between a and b measures greater than 90 degrees if and only if $a \cdot b < 0$ (Figure 4.14c). These results are summarized by the following theorem:

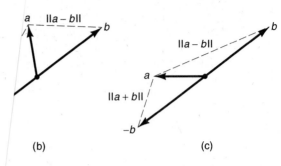

(b)   (c)

...nd b measures (a) 90 degrees if $\|a - b\| = \|a + b\|$, (b)
...eater than 90 if $\|a - b\| > \|a + b\|$.

) *Let a and b be vectors, and let θ be the angle between*

$$a \cdot v \begin{Bmatrix} \\ < \end{Bmatrix} \quad \text{if and only if } \theta \begin{Bmatrix} < \\ = \\ > \end{Bmatrix} 90 \text{ degrees.}$$

The dot product theorem can be used to find the intersection point of two lines $\overleftrightarrow{ab}$
and $\overleftrightarrow{cd}$. Where $\overleftrightarrow{ab}$ is described by $P(t) = a + t(b - a)$, we seek the value of t such
that lines $\overleftrightarrow{ab}$ and $\overleftrightarrow{cd}$ cross at point $P(t)$. Since vector $P(t) - c$ is to coincide with
line $\overleftrightarrow{cd}$, both $P(t) - c$ and $\overleftrightarrow{cd}$ must be perpendicular to the same vector n. Therefore,
using the dot product theorem, we wish to solve for t in the equation

$$n \cdot (P(t) - c) = 0 \qquad\qquad [4.3]$$

Since $P(t) = a + t(b - a)$, we can rewrite Equation 4.3 as

$$n \cdot ((a + t(b - a)) - c) = 0$$

Using the basic properties of dot product yields

$$n \cdot (a - c) + n \cdot (t(b - a)) = 0$$

Then distributing out t gives us

$$n \cdot (a - c) + t[n \cdot (b - a)] = 0$$

From this it follows that

$$t = -\frac{n \cdot (a - c)}{n \cdot (b - a)}, \quad n \cdot (b - a) \neq 0 \qquad\qquad [4.4]$$

Equation 4.4 holds if and only if infinite lines $\overleftrightarrow{ab}$ and $\overleftrightarrow{cd}$ are skew, implying
that they intersect in a single point. If the two lines are parallel or coincident, the fact is
indicated by the condition that $n \cdot (b - a) = 0$, since vectors $b - a$ and $d - c$ are then both
perpendicular to the same vector n. The following implementation of member function
`intersect` results:

```
enum { COLLINEAR, PARALLEL, SKEW, SKEW_CROSS, SKEW_NO_CROSS };

int Edge::intersect(Edge &e, double &t)
{
    Point a = org;
    Point b = dest;
    Point c = e.org;
    Point d = e.dest;
    Point n = Point((d-c).y, (c-d).x);
    double denom = dotProduct(n, b-a);
    if (denom == 0.0) {
        int aclass = org.classify(e);
        if ((aclass==LEFT) || (aclass==RIGHT))
            return PARALLEL;
        else
            return COLLINEAR;
    }
    double num = dotProduct(n, a-c);
    t = -num / denom;
    return SKEW;
}
```

The implementation of function dotProduct is straightforward:

```
double dotProduct(Point &p, Point &q)
{
    return (p.x * q.x + p.y * q.y);
}
```

Member function Edge::cross returns SKEW_CROSS if and only if this line segment intersects line segment e. If the line segments do intersect, the parametric value along this line segment corresponding to the point of intersection is returned through reference parameter t. Otherwise the function returns COLLINEAR, PARALLEL, or SKEW_NO_CROSS, as appropriate:

```
int Edge::cross(Edge &e, double &t)
{
    double s;
    int crossType = e.intersect(*this, s);
    if ((crossType==COLLINEAR) || (crossType==PARALLEL))
        return crossType;
    if ((s < 0.0) || (s > 1.0))
        return SKEW_NO_CROSS;
    intersect(e, t);
    if ((0.0 <= t) && (t <= 1.0))
        return SKEW_CROSS;
    else
        return SKEW_NO_CROSS;
}
```

4.4.4 Distance from a Point to a Line

The definition of function `Point::distance` illustrates some of the ideas we have just
covered. This member function of class `Point` is passed an edge e, and it returns the
signed distance from this point to edge e. Here the *distance* from point p to edge e equals
the minimum distance from p to any point along the infinite line determined by e. The
signed distance is positive if p lies to the right of e, negative if p lies to the left of e, and
zero if p is collinear with e.

   Member function `distance` is defined as follows:

```
double Point::distance(Edge &e)
{
   Edge ab = e;
   ab.flip().rot();   // rotate ab 90 degrees counter-clockwise
   Point n(ab.dest - ab.org);  // n = vector perpendicular to e
   n = (1.0 / n.length()) * n; // normalize n
   Edge f(*this, *this + n);   // f = n, positioned at this point
   double t;
   f.intersect(e, t);          // t = signed distance along f
                               // at which f crosses edge e
   return t;
}
```

   The function first obtains the unit-length vector n, such that n is perpendicular to
edge e and n points to the left of e. It then translates n such that n's origin coincides with
this point, yielding edge f. Finally, the function computes the parametric value of edge f's
intersection with edge e. Since f is perpendicular to e, is of unit length, and originates at
this point, parametric value t equals the signed distance from this point to edge e.

4.4.5 Additional Utilities

The last three member functions of class `Edge` are provided for convenience. Member
function `isVertical` returns `TRUE` only if this edge is vertical:

```
bool Edge::isVertical(void)
{
   return (org.x == dest.x);
}
```

   Member function `slope` returns the slope of this edge, or DBL_MAX if this edge is
vertical:

```
double Edge::slope(void)
{
   if (org.x != dest.x)
      return (dest.y - org.y) / (dest.x - org.x);
   return DBL_MAX;
}
```

Member function y is passed a value x and returns the value y such that (x, y) is a point on this infinite line. The function is defined only if this edge is not vertical:

```
double Edge::y(double x)
{
   return slope() * (x - org.x) + org.y;
}
```

4.5   Geometric Objects in Space

Although we will work mainly in the plane, a few sections of this book will involve geometric objects in three-dimensional space. In this section we will present the classes Point3D, Triangle3D, and Edge3D for manipulating points, triangles, and edges lying in space. The class definitions will be bare bones, providing little more than the functionality we will need. Moreover, for the sake of conciseness, many of the member functions will be defined within the definition of their classes and will be described tersely. This should not hinder clarity since most of the relevant concepts have already been explained in the setting of the two-dimensional plane; new concepts will be discussed in more detail.

4.5.1   Points

Under the Cartesian coordinate system, a point in space is represented by an ordered triple (x, y, z) of real numbers. The Point3D class contains data members x, y, and z to hold a point's coordinates, a constructor, operator functions for the basic vector operations, the operator function [] for coordinate access, a member function for computing dot product, and one for classifying a point relative to a plane:

```
class Point3D {
 public:
   double x;
   double y;
   double z;
   Point3D(double _x, double _y, double _z) :
      x(_x), y(_y), z(_z) {}
   Point3D(void)
      {}
   Point3D operator+(Point3D &p)
      { return Point3D(x + p.x, y + p.y, z + p.z); }
   Point3D operator-(Point3D &p)
      { return Point3D(x - p.x, y - p.y, z - p.z); }
   friend Point3D operator*(double, Point3D &);
   int operator==(Point3D &p)
      { return ((x == p.x) && (y == p.y) && (z == p.z)); }
   int operator!=(Point3D &p)
      { return !(*this == p); }
   double operator[](int i)
      { return ((i == 0) ? x : ((i == 1) ? y : z)); }
```

```
    double dotProduct(Point3D &p)
        { return (x*p.x + y*p.y + z*p.z); }
    int classify(Triangle3D &t);
};
```

Scalar multiplication is implemented like this:

```
Point3D operator*(double s, Point3D &p)
{
    return Point3D(s * p.x, s * p.y, s * p.z);
}
```

Member function `classify` reports which side of the plane determined by triangle t this point lies in. Its definition will be given in the following subsection.

4.5.2 Triangles

A triangle is determined by its three vertices. For working with triangles in space, it is useful to keep track of each triangle's bounding box and normal vector, as well as its vertices. The *bounding box* of a geometric object is the smallest box that contains the object, where the edges of the box are parallel to the major axes. Figure 4.15 gives some examples.

A vector perpendicular to a given plane P is called a *normal* to P. Given any three non-collinear points p_0, p_1, and p_2 lying in plane P, a normal to P is given by the *cross product* vector $a \times b$, where vectors $a = p_1 - p_0$ and $b = p_2 - p_0$. Letting $a = (x_a, y_a, z_a)$ and $b = (x_b, y_b, z_b)$, the cross product vector is defined by

$$a \times b = (y_a z_b - z_a y_b, z_a x_b - x_a z_b, x_a y_b - y_a x_b) \qquad [4.5]$$

The cross product of vectors a and b is returned by the following function:

```
Point3D crossProduct(Point3D &a, Point3D &b)
{
    return Point3D(a.y * b.z - a.z * b.y,
                   a.z * b.x - a.x * b.z,
                   a.x * b.y - a.y * b.x);
}
```

(a)

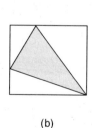

(b)

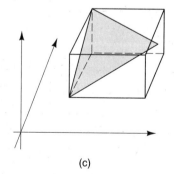

(c)

Figure 4.15:   Bounding box of (a) a blob in the plane, (b) a triangle in the plane, and (c) a triangle in space.

To show that the cross product vector $a \times b$ is perpendicular to the plane spanned by vectors a and b, we need only show that $a \cdot (a \times b) = 0$ and $b \cdot (a \times b) = 0$. We have

$$a \cdot (a \times b) = (x_a, y_a, z_a) \cdot (y_a z_b - z_a y_b, z_a x_b - x_a z_b, x_a y_b - y_a x_b)$$

$$= 0$$

since all terms cancel. That $b \cdot (a \times b) = 0$ is shown similarly.

The direction of the cross product vector is shown in Figure 4.16. When viewed from point $a \times b$ in space, triangle $\triangle 0ab$ is positively oriented. The normal vector having the same length but opposite direction is given by $-a \times b = b \times a$.

Observe that if vectors a and b lie in the xy-plane, then the length of their cross product is $\|a \times b\| = |x_a y_b - y_a x_b|$, the area of the parallelogram with vertices 0, a, b, and $a + b$.

Having discussed bounding boxes and normal vectors, we can define the `Triangle3D` class:

```
class Triangle3D {
 private:
    Point3D _v[3];
    Edge3D _boundingBox;
    Point3D _n;
 public:
    int id;
    int mark;
    Triangle3D(Point3D &v0, Point3D &v1, Point3D &v2, int id);
    Triangle3D(void)
       {}
    Point3D operator[](int i)
       { return _v[i]; }
    Edge3D boundingBox()
       { return _boundingBox; }
    Point3D n(void)
       { return _n; }
    double length(void)
       { return sqrt(x*x + y*y + z*z);
};
```

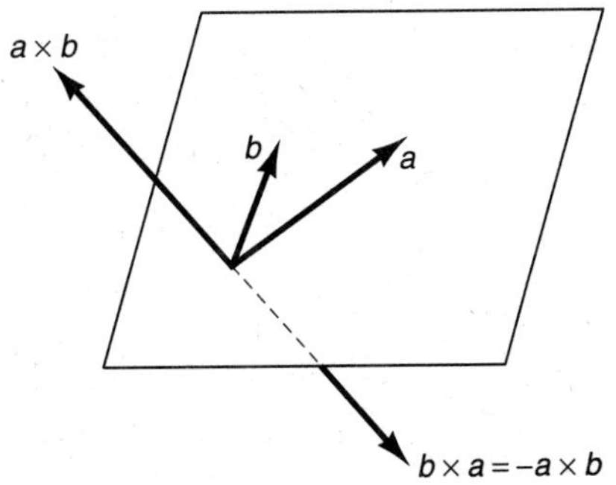

Figure 4.16:   The cross product $a \times b$ of vectors a and b.

This triangle's vertices are stored in array _v. Its bounding box is represented by the edge
_boundingBox extending from the bounding box's minimum-coordinate corner to its
maximum-coordinate corner. The unit normal to the triangle, stored in data member _n,
equals the cross product vector (_v[1]-_v[0]) × (_v[2]-_v[0]), divided by its
length. Data member id is an identifier for this triangle.

The first constructor Triangle3 makes use of the macro functions max3 and min3
for finding the largest and smallest of three numbers:

```
#define min3(A,B,C)    \\
   ((A)<(B)  ?  ((A)<(C)?(A):(C))  :  ((B)<(C)?(B):(C)))
#define max3(A,B,C)    \\
   ((A)>(B)  ?  ((A)>(C)?(A):(C))  :  ((B)>(C)?(B):(C)))


Triangle3D::Triangle3D(Point3D &v0, Point3D &v1, Point3D &v2,
                       int _id)
{
    id = _id;
    mark = 0;
    _v[0] = v0;
    _v[1] = v1;
    _v[2] = v2;
    _boundingBox.org.x = min3(v0.x, v1.x, v2.x);
    _boundingBox.org.y = min3(v0.y, v1.y, v2.y);
    _boundingBox.org.z = min3(v0.z, v1.z, v2.z);
    _boundingBox.dest.x = max3(v0.x, v1.x, v2.x);
    _boundingBox.dest.y = max3(v0.y, v1.y, v2.y);
    _boundingBox.dest.z = max3(v0.z, v1.z, v2.z);
    _n = crossProduct(v1 - v0, v2 - v0);
    _n = (1.0 / _n.length()) * _n;
}
```

The vertices of a Triangle3D object are accessed through operator [], which
is passed the index of the vertex (0, 1, or 2). For instance, where t is a Triangle3D
object, t[0] yields t's first vertex. The bounding box and the unit normal vector are
accessed through member functions boundingBox and n, respectively. The geometric
data members are declared private so the class can ensure self-consistency.

The plane determined by a triangle subdivides space into two half-spaces. The
half-space into which the triangle's normal vector points is called the triangle's *positive
half-space* since the triangle appears to be positively oriented when viewed from this half-
space. The other half-space is called the triangle's *negative half-space*.

With the definition of class Triangle3D in hand, we are in a position to define member function Point3D::classify. Recall that the function reports the half-space—
relative to a given triangle p—in which this point lies. The function returns POSITIVE
or NEGATIVE if this point lies in p's positive or negative half-space; it returns ON if this
point lies on the plane determined by p:

```
#define EPSILON1    1E-12
enum { POSITIVE, NEGATIVE, ON };
```

```
int Point3::classify(Triangle3 &p)
{
   Point3 v = *this - p[0];
   double len = v.length();
   if (len == 0.0)
      return ON;
   v = (1.0 / len) * v;
   double d = v.dotProduct(p.n());
   if (d > EPSILON1)
      return POSITIVE;
   else if (d < -EPSILON1)
      return NEGATIVE;
   else
      return ON;
}
```

Vector v represents a directed line segment which originates at some point on the plane (p[0]) and terminates at the point to be classified (*this). The dot product theorem is used to decide whether the angle between v and the plane's normal vector n is less than, equal to, or greater than 90 degrees.

The function centers the plane of triangle tri within a slab of width 2*EPSILON1. A point which lies within this slab is considered to lie on the plane. This is intended to avoid faulty decisions attributable to round-off, such as when a point on the plane appears to lie off the plane due to limitations of representation.

4.5.3 Edges

The Edge3D class is defined as follows:

```
class Edge3D {
 public:
   Point3D org;
   Point3D dest;
   Edge3D(Point3D &_org, Point3D &_dest) :
      org(_org), dest(_dest) {}
   Edge3D(void)
      {}
   int intersect(Triangle3D &p, double &t);
   Point3D point(double t);
};
```

The first constructor initializes an edge with origin and destination endpoints, which are stored in data members org and dest. Member functions intersect and point play the same role as their counterparts in class Edge. Function intersect finds the parametric value of the infinite line determined by this edge, at the point where the line crosses the plane of triangle p. If the line and plane intersect at a point, the function passes back the parametric value via reference parameter t and returns the enumeration value SKEW; otherwise it returns either PARALLEL or COLLINEAR. Like its counterpart Edge::intersect, member function intersect is implemented using Equation 4.4:

```
int Edge3D::intersect(Triangle3D &p, double &t)
{
   Point3D a = org;
   Point3D b = dest;
   Point3D c = p[0];    // some point on the plane
   Point3 n = p.n();
   double denom = n.dotProduct(b - a);
   if (denom == 0.0) {
      int aclass = org.classify(p);
      if (aclass!=ON)
         return PARALLEL;
      else
         return COLLINEAR;
   }
   double num = n.dotProduct(a - c);
   t = -num / denom;
   return SKEW;
}
```

Member function point returns the point along this line corresponding to parametric value t:

```
Point3D Edge3D::point(double t)
{
   return org + t * (dest - org);
}
```

4.6   Finding the Intersection of a Line and a Triangle

In this section we solve a problem using some of the tools presented in this chapter. Our solution to the problem—that of deciding whether a line pierces a triangle in space—will prove useful later in this book.

A *projection* is a mapping from a higher-dimensional space into a lower-dimensional space. One of its uses is to transform a problem from a higher-dimensional setting to an equivalent problem in a lower-dimensional setting, where there are techniques to solve it. Consider the problem of deciding whether a given infinite line intersects a given triangle p in space. Figure 4.17a depicts one approach to this problem. First compute the point q where the infinite line pierces the plane of triangle p. Then perpendicularly project both p and q into the xy-plane, yielding triangle p' and point q'. The resulting problem in two dimensions—that of deciding whether p' contains q'—is equivalent to the original problem: The answer to the two-dimensional problem is yes if and only if the answer to the original three-dimensional problem is yes. The advantage in applying this transformation is that the two-dimensional problem is easier to solve than the original three-dimensional problem.

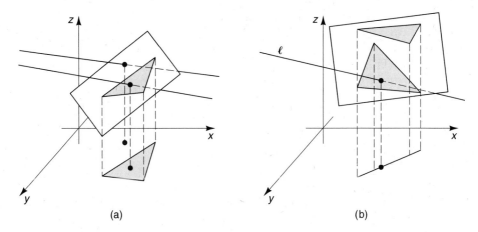

Figure 4.17:   (a) Deciding whether a line pierces triangle p. (b) Both triangles project degenerately to the same line segment.

Projection is a many-to-one mapping, and difficulties can arise when too much information is lost. In Figure 4.17b, both triangles project (degenerately) to the same line segment in the xy-plane. It is not hard to see why this two-dimensional problem is not equivalent to the original problem. Given two triangles p_1 and p_2 that project to the same line segment and an infinite line ℓ in space, the two three-dimensional problems that result—one involving ℓ and p_1, the other involving ℓ and p_2—transform to the same two-dimensional problem in the xy-plane. Yet if ℓ pierces (say) triangle p_1 but not triangle p_2, the two-dimensional problem must report a wrong answer in one of the two cases.

To save the algorithm, we test for degeneracy before projecting. A triangle p projects to a line segment in the xy-plane if the triangle's normal vector n is perpendicular to the z-axis. Before projecting, we perform this test; if n is perpendicular to the z-axis, we consider projecting into the yz-plane instead; and if this too would be degenerate, we finally project into the zx-plane. Since vector n cannot be perpendicular to all three axes, at least one of the three projections proves non-degenerate.

The algorithm is implemented by the following function, whose return value—PARALLEL, COLLINEAR, SKEW_CROSS, or SKEW_NO_CROSS—indicates the relationship between infinite line e and triangle p. If the function returns either SKEW_CROSS, indicating that the line pierces the triangle, or SKEW_NO_CROSS, indicating that the line crosses the plane of the triangle without piercing the triangle itself, then the parametric value of the intersection point along e is passed back through reference parameter t:

```
int lineTriangleIntersect(Edge3D &e, Triangle3D &p, double &t)
{
    Point3D q;
    int aclass = e.intersect(p, t);
    if ((aclass==PARALLEL) || (aclass==COLLINEAR))
        return aclass;
    q = e.point(t);
    int h, v;
```

```
    if (p.n().dotProduct(Point3D(0,0,1)) != 0.0) {
        h = 0;
        v = 1;
    } else if (p.n().dotProduct(Point3D(1,0,0)) != 0.0) {
        h = 1;
        v = 2;
    } else {
        h = 2;
        v = 0;
    }
    Polygon *pp = project(p, h, v);
    Point qp = Point(q[h], q[v]);
    int answer = pointInConvexPolygon(qp, *pp);
    delete pp;
    return (answer ? SKEW_CROSS : SKEW_NO_CROSS);
}
```

The function call `project(p,h,v)` returns a polygon representing the projection of triangle p into the hv-plane. Arguments h and v are axis indices; for instance, `project(p,0,1)` projects p into the xy-plane. Function `project` assumes that the projection of triangle p is non-degenerate, so its projection is a triangle. The function is defined as follows:

```
Polygon *project(Triangle3D &p, int h, int v)
{
    // project vertices of triangle p
    Point3D a;
    Point pts[3];
    for (int i = 0; i < 3; i++) {
        a = p.v(i);
        pts[i] = Point(a[h], a[v]);
    }
    // insert first two projected vertices into polygon
    Polygon *pp = new Polygon;
    for (i = 0; i < 2; i++)
        pp->insert(pts[i]);
    // insert third projected vertex into polygon
    if (pts[2].classify(pts[0], pts[1]) == LEFT)
        pp->advance(CLOCKWISE);
    pp->insert(pts[2]);
    return pp;
}
```

The only tricky part of function `project` involves insertion of the last of the three projected vertices (`pts[2]`) into the polygon under construction. If the three projected vertices are negatively oriented, then `pts[2]` belongs after `pts[1]`; if positively oriented, `pts[2]` belongs after `pts[0]`. This ensures that the interior of the resulting polygon pp lies to the *right* of each of its edges—that successive calls to pp->advance(CLOCKWISE) corresponds to clockwise traversal. Advancing pp's window if the projected vertices are positively oriented does the trick.

4.7 Chapter Notes

Most of the mathematics in this chapter comes from vector algebra, also known as linear algebra. Vectors are the elements of an algebraic structure known as a vector space. Although most aspects of linear algebra admit a geometric interpretation (and our presentation has concentrated on such an interpretation), all the results of linear algebra can be derived using algebra, without appealing to geometry. Introductions to linear algebra are provided by [41, 44].

A number of other books present geometric tools at the level of working code and put them to work in geometric algorithms [3, 20, 61, 66, 73]. Some of the ideas of this chapter can be found in these sources.

4.8 Exercises

1. Show that $x_a y_b - x_b y_a$ equals the signed area of the parallelogram determined by vectors $a = (x_a, y_a)$ and $b = (x_b, y_b)$.

2. Given nonzero vectors a and b, show that $a \cdot b = \|a\| \, \|b\| \, \cos\theta$, where θ is the angle between a and b.

3. Show that $\sin(\alpha - \beta) = \sin\alpha \, \cos\beta - \cos\alpha \, \sin\beta$.

4. Show that the convex polygon with vertices $v_1, \ldots, v_k$ consists of the set of points of the form $p = \alpha_1 v_1 + \cdots + \alpha_k v_k$, where $\alpha_1 + \cdots + \alpha_k = 1$ and each $\alpha_i \geq 0$. (This expression is known as the *convex combination* of points $v_1, \ldots, v_k$.)

5. Show that the dot product theorem remains valid for vectors in three-dimensional space.

6. Why does the copy constructor `Polygon::Polygon(Polygon&)` perform a deep copy? (Hint: If two polygon objects referred to the same linked list of vertices, what could go wrong?)

7. What are the advantages and disadvantages of representing the various kinds of lines (infinite lines, line segments, rays, etc.) using a single `Edge` class?

8. Write a version of `Polygon::split` that performs error checking.

9. Using the splice operation for circular doubly linked lists, write a (destructive) function `join(Polygon &p, Polygon &q)` which merges polygons p and q into a single polygon and returns a pointer to the new polygon.

10. Write a function that decides whether a polygon is convex.

11. Devise a data structure for representing a convex n-gon that permits us to decide in $O(\log n)$ time whether a given point belongs to the polygon.

12. Write a function to determine whether a given diagonal of a given polygon is a chord.

13. Write a function to determine whether a given `Polygon` object represents an illegal
    n-gon, one that crosses itself. [The obvious approach, that of comparing all pairs of
    edges, takes $O(n^2)$ time. Can you think of an algorithm that takes $O(n \log n)$ time?]

14. Devise an algorithm to decide whether a point belongs to an arbitrary (i.e., convex or
    nonconvex) n-gon that runs in $O(n)$ time.

15. Devise an $O(n \log n)$ time algorithm to decide whether two polygons intersect, where
    n equals the sum of their sizes.

16. Devise an $O(n)$ time algorithm to decide whether two *convex* polygons intersect,
    where n equals the sum of their sizes.

17. Write a function to find the intersection point of a line and a triangle in space which
    does not rely on projection into a plane.

18. Write a function to determine whether two triangles in space intersect.

II

Applications

5

Incremental Insertion

The algorithmic design approach of *incremental insertion* examines the input to a problem one item at a time while maintaining a current solution for those items seen so far. At each increment, the next input item is examined and processed, and the current solution is updated to accommodate the new item. When all the input has been processed, the problem as a whole has been solved.

One reads a mystery novel in much the same manner. The reader maintains a working hypothesis concerning who committed the murder and how and why it took place. Each new clue either confirms the hypothesis or requires that it be revised, or even abandoned and formulated anew. By the book's end when all the clues are in, the reader will have solved the crime, assuming he or she is clever enough and the writer has been fair.

In some cases, the algorithm is capable of maintaining only a current *state* as opposed to a current *solution*, since the portion of the input seen so far is too incomplete to represent a coherent situation. This often happens, for instance, when solving problems involving polygons: If the polygon boundary is processed a vertex at a time, we may not even have our hands on a simple polygon until all the input has been processed. Returning to our mystery novel analogy, we see this is similar to the way the reader's outlook develops even before any murder has taken place—although there is not yet a problem to solve, early clues and insights are organized and readied for use at the first sign of trouble.

The most obvious approach to finding the smallest integer in an array—stepping down the array while keeping track of the smallest integer seen so far—is a computational example of incremental insertion. Insertion involves a conditional assignment to the variable holding the current minimum. At each stage, this variable holds the answer to the problem involving those integers processed so far. Incremental insertion is not usually so simple.

In this chapter we will study a number of (more interesting) algorithms that employ this strategy. The first, insertion sort, is a well-known sorting method most useful for sorting a relatively short list of items. The remaining algorithms solve geometric problems: finding a star-shaped polygon in a finite set of points, finding the convex hull of a set of points, deciding whether a given point lies in a polygon, clipping geometric objects (lines and polygons) to a convex polygon, and triangulating a monotone polygon.

5.1 Insertion Sort

Insertion sort works the way a card player keeps a hand of cards. With the deck face down on the table, the card player draws a number of cards; as the player draws each card, he or she inserts it into the proper position in the hand. When each new card is about to be drawn, the hand is sorted over all the cards that have been drawn so far.

Let us consider how to use insertion sort to arrange array items `a[0]`,...,`a[n-1]` in increasing order. (For brevity, we will refer to this range of items as `a[0..n-1]`.) For each `i` from 1 through $n-1$, at the start of iteration `i` the subarray `a[0..i-1]` is sorted. Our task in iteration i is to sort `a[0..i]` by putting item `a[i]` in its proper position. To do this, we save `a[i]` in some variable `v` and then move items `a[i-1]`, `a[i-2]`,... in turn one position to the right until reaching the first item `a[j-1]` not greater than `v`. Finally, we copy `v` into the "hole" that has been created in position `j`. Figure 5.1 shows how the algorithm sorts a short array of integers.

The algorithm is implemented by function template `insertionSort`, which sorts the array `a[0..n-1]`. Argument `cmp` is a comparison function that returns $-1, 0$, or 1 if its first argument is less than, equal to, or greater than its second argument:

```
template<class T>
void insertionSort(T a[], int n, int (*cmp)(T,T))
{
    for (int i = 1; i < n; i++) {
        T v = a[i];
        int j = i;
        while ((j > 0) && ((*cmp)(v, a[j-1]) < 0)) {
            a[j] = a[j-1];
            j--;
        }
        a[j] = v;
    }
}
```

In each iteration i from 1 to $n-1$, the `while` loop inserts item `a[i]` into the sorted subarray `a[0..i-1]`. The test `j > 0` of the `while` loop ensures that the program does not fall off the left end of array `a` during insertion.

For the sorting programs presented in this book, we will assume that the template type parameter `T` represents a pointer type. Nonetheless, function template `insertionSort` can be used to sort objects of any type that defines both the assignment operator = and a copy

3	(6)	2	5	9	4
3	6	(2)	5	9	4
2	3	6	(5)	9	4
2	3	5	6	(9)	4
2	3	5	6	9	(4)
2	3	4	5	6	9

Figure 5.1:   Insertion sorting an array of six integers. The next number to be inserted at each step is circled.

constructor. For example, the following code fragment reads 100 strings into array s and then sorts them using the standard C++ library function strcmp to compare two strings by dictionary order:

```
char buffer[80];
char *s[100];
for (int i = 0; i < 100 ; i++) {
   cin >> buffer;
   s[i] = new char[strlen(buffer)+1];
   strcpy(s[i], buffer);
}
insertionSort(s, 100, strcmp);
```

Note that this code fragment sorts an array of pointer-to-strings (array s), rather than the strings themselves. It is often more efficient to sort pointers instead of the objects pointed to. Unless the objects are small (4 bytes or less), a sorting program can move pointers around faster than the objects to which they point.

5.1.1 Analysis

To analyze insertion sort, it suffices to count the number of times the comparison function is called (assuming a comparison takes constant time). The running time of insertionSort is $T(n) = \sum_{i=1}^{n} I(i)$, where $I(i)$ time is needed to insert the ith item. Since $I(i)$ costs at most i comparisons, insertion sort requires $T(n) = \sum_{i=1}^{n} i = \frac{n(n+1)}{2}$ comparisons, or about $n^2/2$ comparisons in the worst case. This worst-case behavior in fact occurs whenever the input array is initially sorted in reverse (decreasing) order.

On average, the ith item is compared to about $i/2$ items before its insertion position is found. Thus insertion sort performs about $n^2/4$ comparisons on average, twice as good as the worst case. If the input array is initially almost sorted, the program's expected running time is linear since the ith item is compared to only a constant number of items before reaching its position, on average. Hence insertion sort is a good way to sort an input array known to be almost sorted.

5.2   Finding Star-Shaped Polygons

A finite set of points in the plane can be connected by edges to form a polygon in different ways. Each such polygon is called a *polygonization* of the point set. In this section we devise a method for constructing *star-shaped* polygonizations. More simply, our method "connects the dots" (or points) to form star-shaped polygons.

5.2.1 What Are Star-Shaped Polygons?

Suppose points p and q lie in some polygon. We say that p *sees* q if the line segment $\overline{pq}$ lies in the polygon. Here we are imagining the boundary of polygon P to be composed of opaque walls, and its interior some transparent medium such as air. One point can see another only if no wall stands between them. Seeing is symmetric (if p sees q, then q sees p) but not transitive (if p sees q and q sees point r, it does not follow that p sees r) (Figure 5.2).

 The set of those points in a polygon that see every point is called the *kernel* of the polygon. A polygon is said to be *star shaped* (Figure 5.3) if its kernel is nonempty. A polygon is *fan shaped* if its nonempty kernel contains one or more vertices (each such vertex is called an *apex* of the polygon). Every convex polygon is fan shaped since the kernel contains some vertex (in fact, every vertex). Every fan-shaped polygon is star shaped since its kernel is nonempty.

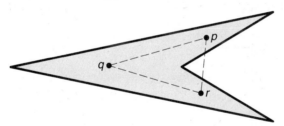

Figure 5.2:   Points p and q see one another as do points q and r, yet points p and r do not see each other.

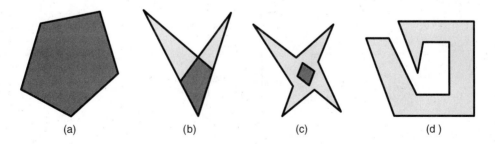

(a)   (b)   (c)   (d)

Figure 5.3:   Polygons with darkened kernels: (a) a convex polygon; (b) a fan-shaped polygon that is not convex; (c) a star-shaped polygon that is not fan shaped; and (d) a polygon that is not star shaped.

5.2.2 Finding Star-Shaped Polygonizations

Given a set S of points $s_0, s_1, \ldots, s_{n-1}$ in the plane, the problem is to construct a star-shaped polygonization of set S. It is not difficult to see that there may exist more than one such polygon. We will specifically seek one whose kernel contains the first point s_0.

The algorithm works by iteratively constructing a *current polygon* over the points of S. Initially, the current polygon is the 1-gon s_0. In each iteration i from 1 to $n-1$, the next point s_i is inserted into the current polygon. At completion, the current polygon is the star-shaped polygon we seek.

To insert each new point s_i into the current polygon, we perform a clockwise traversal of the current polygon starting from vertex s_0. The traversal proceeds clockwise around the polygon boundary until arriving at the vertex which is to become s_i's successor; s_i is then inserted before this vertex. If the traversal proceeds full circle, returning to s_0, then s_i is inserted before s_0. Here s_0 serves as a *sentinel* which ensures that the traversal does not proceed too far. Figure 5.4 shows snapshots of the algorithm running on a small problem.

Function `starPolygon` is handed an array `s` of `n` points and returns a star-shaped polygon whose kernel contains point `s[0]`:

```
Point originPt;   // global: originPt = s[0]

Polygon *starPolygon(Point s[], int n)
{
    Polygon *p = new Polygon;
    p->insert(s[0]);
```

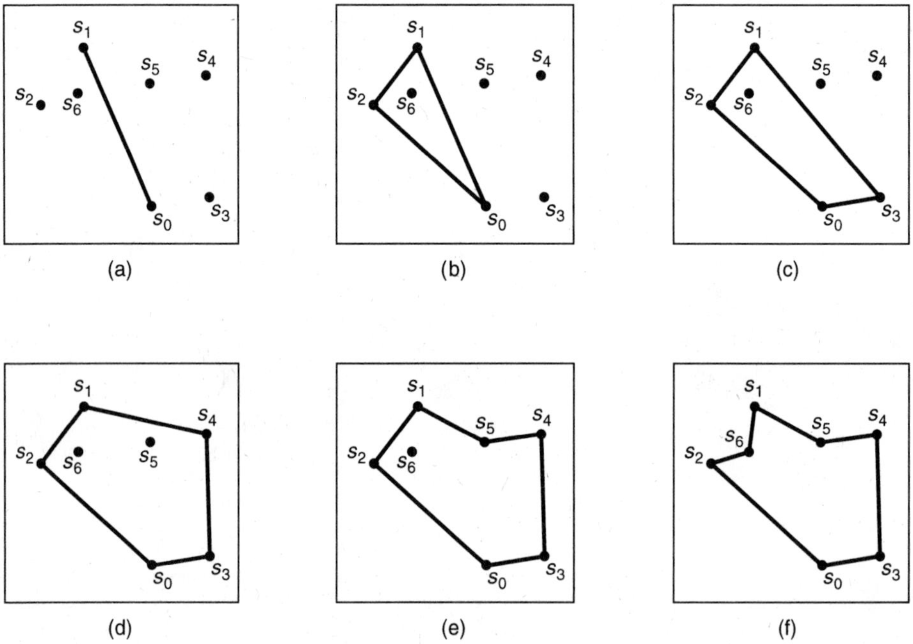

Figure 5.4:   Finding a star-shaped polygon in a point set.

```
    Vertex *origin = p->v();
    originPt = origin->point();
    for (int i = 1; i < n; i++) {
        p->setV(origin);
        p->advance(CLOCKWISE);
        while (polarCmp(&s[i], p->v()) < 0)
            p->advance(CLOCKWISE);
        p->advance(COUNTER_CLOCKWISE);
        p->insert(s[i]);
    }
    return p;
}
```

In each iteration i, how do we determine where to insert point s_i along the boundary of the current polygon? We use the fact that the vertices of a star-shaped polygon are ordered radially around each point in its kernel. Since point s_0 is to lie in the kernel, we define a comparison function `polarCmp` based on the polar coordinates of points relative to point s_0 (i.e., where s_0 is regarded as the origin). Under this relation, point $p = (r_p, \theta_p)$ is considered less than point $q = (r_q, \theta_q)$ if (1) $\theta_p < \theta_q$ or (2) $\theta_p = \theta_q$ and $r_p < r_q$. With respect to this ordering, clockwise traversal of the current polygon proceeds from greater points to lesser points.

Comparison function `polarCmp` is passed two points p and q and compares them with respect to their radial ordering about point `originPt`, a global variable. It returns $-1, 0$, or 1 depending on whether its first argument p is less than, equal to, or greater than its second argument q:

```
int polarCmp(Point *p, Point *q)
{
    Point vp = *p - originPt;
    Point vq = *q - originPt;
    double pPolar = vp.polarAngle();
    double qPolar = vq.polarAngle();
    if (pPolar < qPolar) return -1;
    if (pPolar > qPolar) return 1;
    if (vp.length() < vq.length()) return -1;
    if (vp.length() > vq.length()) return 1;
    return 0;
}
```

Under function `polarCmp`, `originPt` is less than every other point in the plane. This is because function `Point::polarAngle` returns -1.0 if this point equals `originPt`, and returns a value in the range $[0, 360)$ otherwise. This fact allows point s[0] (=originPt) to serve as a sentinel. Function `starPolygon` runs in $O(n^2)$ time. Iteration i requires as many as i comparisons, and there are $n - 1$ iterations (the analysis parallels that of insertion sort).

The algorithm for finding star-shaped polygons closely parallels insertion sort. Both algorithms incrementally grow a current solution, represented by an ordering of items, into a complete solution. To insert each new item into the current ordering, both algorithms sequentially traverse the ordering from greatest to least until the item's proper position is reached. Furthermore, both algorithms run in quadratic time in the worst case.

5.3   Finding Convex Hulls: Insertion Hull

The algorithm we consider in this section—for finding the convex hull of a set of points—is more complicated than both insertion sort and our star-shaped polygonization algorithm. First, finding the proper position of each new item is more involved. Second, it is sometimes necessary to *remove* items from the current solution, so the current solution grows and shrinks as the algorithm proceeds.

5.3.1 What Are Convex Hulls?

Let S be a finite set of points in the plane. The convex hull of set S, denoted $\mathcal{CH}(S)$, equals the intersection of all convex polygons which contain S. Equivalently, $\mathcal{CH}(S)$ is the convex polygon of minimum area which contains all the points of S. Yet another equivalent definition states that $\mathcal{CH}(S)$ equals the union of all triangles determined by points of S.

Imagine the plane to be a sheet of wood with a nail protruding from every point in S. Now stretch a rubber band around all the nails and then release it, allowing it to snap taut against the nails. The taut rubber band conforms to the convex hull boundary. Figure 5.5 gives some examples.

Because they provide a way to approximate a point set or other nonconvex set by a convex region, convex hulls prove useful in a wide range of geometric applications. In pattern recognition, an unknown shape may be represented by its convex hull or by a hierarchy of convex hulls, which is then matched to a database of known shapes. As another example, motion planning, required when a moving robot must negotiate a landscape of obstacles, becomes much easier if the robot is approximated by its convex hull.

A useful scheme for classifying the points of a point set S refers to the convex hull $\mathcal{CH}(S)$. A point is a *boundary point* if it lies in the convex hull boundary, and an *interior point* if it lies in the convex hull interior. Those boundary points which form the

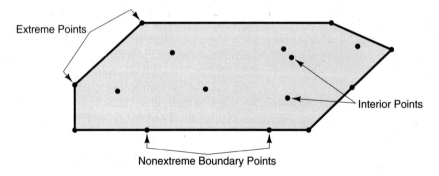

Figure 5.5:   A finite set of points and its convex hull.

"corner" vertices of the convex hull are known as *extreme points*. Equivalently, a boundary point is extreme if it does not lie between any two other points of S. Figure 5.5 illustrates these notions. Note that this scheme for classifying points applies even if we are not interested in finding their convex hull per se.

5.3.2 Insertion Hull

Insertion hull, an incremental insertion approach to finding the convex hull of a finite set S of points, inserts a point at a time while maintaining the convex hull of those points inserted so far. We will refer to the convex hull built along the way as the *current hull*. Initially, the current hull consists of a single point of S; at completion, when all points have been inserted, the current hull equals $CH(S)$ and we are done.

When a new point s is inserted into the current hull, one of two cases occurs. In the first case, s may lie in (the boundary or interior of) the current hull, in which case the current hull does not need to be updated.

In the second case, s lies outside the current hull, requiring that the current hull be modified as in Figure 5.6. Through point s can be drawn two *supporting lines*, each tangent to the current hull. (A line is a *supporting line* of a convex polygon P if the line passes through a vertex of P and the interior of P lies entirely to one side of the line.) The left (right) supporting line $\overrightarrow{sr}$ passes through some vertex ℓ (r) of the current hull and lies to the left (right) of the current hull. If you were positioned at point s facing the convex hull, the left supporting line would appear to your left and the right supporting line to your right.

The two supporting vertices ℓ and r split the current hull boundary into two vertex chains: a *near chain* that is nearer point s and a *far chain* that is farther from s. (The near chain lies on the same side of line $\overline{\ell r}$ as s, and the far chain lies on the other side of $\overline{\ell r}$.) To update the current hull, we first find the two vertices ℓ and r which terminate the near and far chains. Then we remove the vertices of the near chain (except for vertices ℓ and r) and insert point s in their place.

The following program `insertionHull` returns the convex hull of the n points of array `s`:

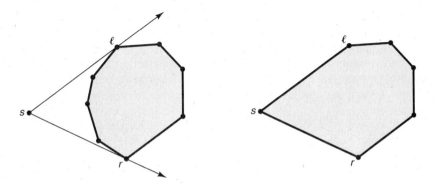

Figure 5.6:   Inserting point s into the current hull.

```
Point somePoint;   // global

Polygon *insertionHull(Point s[], int n)
{
   Polygon *p = new Polygon;
   p->insert(s[0]);
   for (int i = 1; i < n; i++) {
      if (pointInConvexPolygon(s[i], *p))
         continue;
      somePoint = s[i];
      leastVertex(*p, closestToPolygonCmp);
      supportingLine(s[i], p, LEFT);
      Vertex *l = p->v();
      supportingLine(s[i], p, RIGHT);
      delete p->split(l);
      p->insert(s[i]);
   }
   return p;
}
```

In iteration i, point s[i] is inserted into the current hull p. The call to function leastVertex moves p's window over the vertex that is closest to point s[i]. This prepares for the subsequent call to supportingLine(s[i],p,LEFT), which moves the window over the vertex ℓ through which the left supporting line passes. The second call to supportingLine then moves the window over vertex r. The split operation is used to subdivide polygon p along the diagonal $\overline{\ell r}$, thereby separating the near chain from the far chain. The subpolygon consisting of the near chain is returned by split and deleted. Finally, point s[i] is inserted into polygon p, which, after split is performed, consists of the far chain.

Let us consider function supportingLine. To find the vertex ℓ through which the left supporting line passes, we start at some vertex of the near chain and then traverse clockwise around the current hull until arriving at the first vertex v whose successor is neither to the left of nor beyond directed line segment $\overrightarrow{sv}$. Vertex v is ℓ, the vertex we seek. Note why the process continues if the successor to v (i.e., vertex w) is *beyond* $\overrightarrow{sv}$: v cannot be an extreme point if it lies between s and w, so we must search further.

Function supportingLine is called with a polygon p, a point s outside p, and one of the enumeration values LEFT or RIGHT indicating which vertex (ℓ or r) is being sought. It assumes that the vertex in p's window belongs to the near chain, which is why function leastVertex is called first. The function moves polygon p's window over the vertex it finds (ℓ or r):

```
void supportingLine(Point &s, Polygon *p, int side)
{
   int rotation = (side == LEFT) ? CLOCKWISE : COUNTER_CLOCKWISE;
   Vertex *a = p->v();
   Vertex *b = p->neighbor(rotation);
   int c = b->classify(s, *a);
```

```
while ((c == side) || (c == BEYOND) || (c == BETWEEN)) {
    p->advance(rotation);
    a = p->v();
    b = p->neighbor(rotation);
    c = b->classify(s, *a);
  }
}
```

Function `leastVertex`, which was defined in subsection 4.3.6, is used by program `insertionHull` to find the vertex of polygon p that is closest to the point stored in global variable `somePoint`. Comparison function `closestToPolygonCmp`, with which `leastVertex` is called, compares two points to decide which is closest to `somePoint`:

```
int closestToPolygonCmp(Point *a, Point *b)
{
    double distA = (somePoint - *a).length();
    double distB = (somePoint - *b).length();
    if (distA < distB) return -1;
    else if (distA > distB) return 1;
    return 0;
}
```

5.3.3 Analysis

As it proceeds, program `insertionHull` may build large current hulls which are disassembled by the time the program finishes. Consider the situation shown in Figure 5.7a, in which all the points except p, q, and r have been inserted. Each of the last three insertions removes a chain of vertices until only a triangular hull remains (Figures 5.7b–d). Clearly, had p, q, and r been inserted *first*, before the other points, the triangular hull would be constructed early and insertion of each remaining point would be faster, involving only the determination that the point lies in the triangle. Thus the order in which points are inserted affects efficiency.

Nonetheless, the cost of building the convex hull is in fact *not* dominated by the operations `insert` and `split` used to assemble and disassemble the current hulls. After all, every point can be inserted at most once and removed at most once. It follows that the total cost for all `insert` and `split` operations over the course of the algorithm is bounded above by $O(n)$.

Likewise, the calls to `supportingLine` are relatively inexpensive: The two calls to `supportingLine` performed in an iteration together take time proportional to the length of the near chain, and this work can be charged to the vertices of the near chain, which are then removed in the same iteration. Since a vertex can be removed at most once, the cost for all calls to `supportingLine` over the course of the algorithm is bounded above by $O(n)$.

It turns out that `insertionHull` spends most of its time executing `pointInConvexPolygon` and `leastVertex`. To process the ith point s_i, the call to each of the two functions takes time proportional to i in the worst case (when the convex

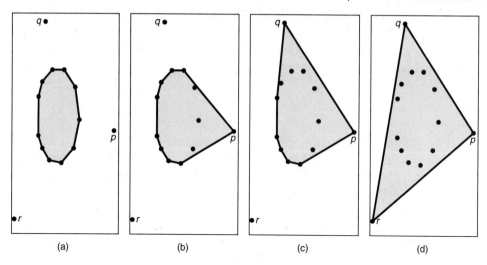

(a)	(b)	(c)	(d)

Figure 5.7:   Points p, q, and r are inserted last.

hull possesses i vertices). This case occurs *for every* point s_i if they are all extreme points because the current hull will then grow by one vertex per insertion. Hence `insertionHull`
runs in $O(n^2)$ time in the worst case.

  Later in this book we will cover two algorithms—*Graham scan* and *merge hull*—that
compute the convex hull of n points in optimal $O(n \log n)$ time.

5.4   Point Enclosure: The Ray-Shooting Method

In Chapter 4 we devised a simple algorithm for solving the point enclosure problem for
convex polygons: The algorithm decides whether a given point a lies inside, outside, or on
the boundary of a convex polygon p. It works by testing point a against each edge of p in
turn; if point a lies on the wrong side of some edge, the point has been shown to lie outside
polygon p; otherwise a has been shown to belong to p. The algorithm takes advantage of
the fact that the interior of a convex polygon lies entirely to one side of every edge—thus
a point which lies on the wrong side of some edge cannot lie in the polygon interior. The
algorithm, however, does not correctly solve the more general point enclosure problem,
which allows arbitrary (convex or nonconvex) polygons. In Figure 5.8, for example, the
interior of the polygon straddles both sides of the edge labeled e; since point a lies on the
"wrong" side of e, the algorithm mistakenly reports that a lies outside polygon.

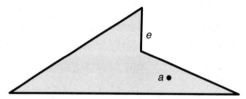

Figure 5.8:   How does one determine whether point a lies in the polygon?

The problem of point enclosure relative to a *convex* polygon is like deciding whether an unsorted list of numbers contains only numbers greater than or equal to zero. To solve the problem, we step through the list until reaching some negative number, at which time we report "no"; if none of the numbers turns out to be negative, we report "yes." The answer is yes only if every one of a set of distinct conditions holds true.

Point enclosure relative to an *arbitrary* polygon, on the other hand, is more like the problem of deciding whether the sum of an unsorted list of numbers is greater than or equal to zero. The problem cannot be decided until *all* the numbers have been added together. Adding just some of the numbers, or even all but one of them, cannot solve the problem since the remaining number may change everything. In the same manner, partial examination of a polygon may suggest that it does not contain some distant point, yet it may happen that the last several edges to be examined form a "finger" that protrudes far from the rest of the polygon, capturing the point. Deciding whether a point lies in an arbitrary polygon involves a single condition encompassing the polygon as a whole.

In this section we present the ray-shooting method for solving the point enclosure problem for arbitrary polygons. Imagine doing this to decide point enclosure for point a and polygon p: Starting from some point far from the polygon, move in a straight line toward a. Along the way we cross the polygon boundary zero or more times: the first time crossing into the polygon, the second time crossing back out, the third time crossing back in once again, and so forth, until arriving at a. In general, every odd-numbered crossing carries us into polygon p, and every even-numbered crossing carries us back out of p. If we arrive at a having undergone an odd number of crossings, a lies inside p; and if an even number of crossings, a lies outside p. For example, in Figure 5.9, ray $\overrightarrow{r_a}$ crosses the boundary once; since one is odd, a lies inside the polygon. We can conclude that point b lies outside the polygon since ray $\overrightarrow{r_b}$ crosses the boundary an even number of times (twice).

Transforming this idea into an algorithm turns on two key observations. First, *any* ray that originates at the point a to be classified will do (Figure 5.9). Being free to work with any ray originating at a, we can, for simplicity, work with the *right horizontal ray* $\overrightarrow{r_a}$ originating at a (the unique ray starting at a and directed parallel to the positive x-axis).

The second key observation is that the order of boundary crossings along ray $\overrightarrow{r_a}$ is irrelevant; all that matters is the parity (oddness or evenness) of their total number. Therefore, rather than simulate moving along ray $\overrightarrow{r_a}$, it is enough for the algorithm to

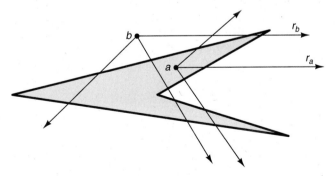

Figure 5.9: Every ray originating at a crosses the boundary an odd number of times, and every ray originating at b crosses an even number of times.

detect all edge crossings *in any order*, updating parity along the way. The easiest way to do this is to traverse the polygon boundary, toggling a parity bit whenever we visit an edge which ray $\overrightarrow{r_a}$ crosses.

Relative to the right horizontal ray $\overrightarrow{r_a}$, we distinguish three types of polygon edges: *touching edges*, which contain point a; *crossing edges*, which do not contain point a but which ray $\overrightarrow{r_a}$ crosses; and *inessential edges*, which ray $\overrightarrow{r_a}$ does not meet at all. For example, in Figure 5.10, edge c is a crossing edge, edge d is a touching edge, and edge e is an inessential edge.

Function `pointInPolygon` solves the point enclosure problem for point a and polygon p. The algorithm traverses the boundary of the polygon while toggling variable `parity` for each crossing edge it encounters. It returns the enumeration value `INSIDE` if the final value of `parity` is 1 (indicating odd), and `OUTSIDE` if its final value is 0 (indicating even). If a touching edge is discovered, the algorithm immediately returns the enumeration value `BOUNDARY`.

```
enum { INSIDE, OUTSIDE, BOUNDARY };       // point classifications
enum { TOUCHING, CROSSING, INESSENTIAL };// edge classifications

int pointInPolygon(Point &a, Polygon &p)
{
    int parity = 0;
    for (int i = 0; i < p.size(); i++, p.advance(CLOCKWISE)) {
        Edge e = p.edge();
        switch (edgeType(a, e)) {
          case TOUCHING:
            return BOUNDARY;
          case CROSSING:
            parity = 1 - parity;
        }
    }
    return (parity ? INSIDE: OUTSIDE);
}
```

Function call `edgeType(a,e)` classifies edge e with respect to right horizontal ray $\overrightarrow{r_a}$, returning one of the enumeration values `TOUCHING`, `CROSSING`, or `INESSENTIAL`. Definition of `edgeType` is somewhat tricky because function `pointInPolygon` must correctly handle the special cases that arise when ray $\overrightarrow{r_a}$ pierces vertices. Consider Figure 5.11. In case (a) the parity should be toggled—the ray crosses the boundary only once

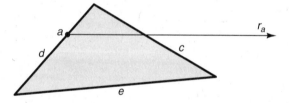

Figure 5.10:   Edge c is a crossing edge, edge d a touching edge, and edge e an inessential edge.

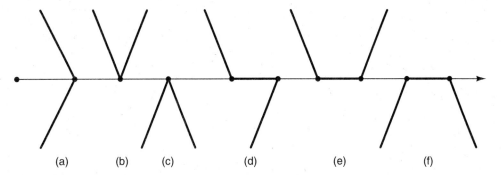

Figure 5.11:   Special cases: `parity` is toggled one time in cases (a) and (d), zero times in cases (b) and (e), and two times in cases (c) and (f).

even though, in doing so, it crosses two edges. In cases (b) and (c) the parity should not be changed. This can be achieved by polishing our scheme for classifying edges as follows:

- Edge e is a *touching* edge if e contains point a.

- Edge e is a *crossing* edge if (1) e is not horizontal and (2) ray $\vec{r_a}$ crosses e at some point other than e's lower endpoint.

- Edge e is an *inessential* edge if e is neither a crossing nor a touching edge.

Referring to Figure 5.11, we see that in case (a), variable `parity` is toggled once; in case (b), `parity` is not changed; and in case (c), `parity` is toggled twice with the net effect of remaining unchanged. Note that horizontal edges not containing point a are considered inessential and so are ignored by function `pointInPolygon`. Therefore, cases (d), (e), and (f) are handled the same as cases (a), (b), and (c), respectively.

Function `edgeType` classifies edge `e` as `CROSSING`, `TOUCHING`, or `INESSENTIAL` with respect to point `a`:

```
int edgeType(Point &a, Edge &e)
{
   Point v = e.org;
   Point w = e.dest;
   switch (a.classify(e)) {
   case LEFT:
     return ((v.y<a.y) && (a.y<=w.x)) ? CROSSING : INESSENTIAL;
   case RIGHT:
     return ((w.y<a.y) && (a.y<=v.y)) ? CROSSING : INESSENTIAL;
   case BETWEEN:
   case ORIGIN:
   case DESTINATION:
     return TOUCHING;
   default:
     return INESSENTIAL;
   }
}
```

Note how function edgeType detects crossing edges. If point a lies to the left of edge e, the edge is a crossing edge only if v (=e.org) lies below ray $\vec{r_a}$ and w (=e.dest) lies on or above the ray. For then the edge cannot be horizontal, and ray $\vec{r_a}$ must cross the edge at some point other than its lower endpoint. Alternatively, if a lies to the right of edge e, the roles of v and w are interchanged.

Program pointInPolygon runs in time proportional to the size of the polygon in the worst case (when point a does not lie on the polygon boundary).

5.5   Point Enclosure: The Signed Angle Method

Let us consider another approach to the point enclosure problem. This approach requires the notion of a *signed angle*. Given directed segment $\vec{bc}$ and some point a, suppose that the angle between vectors $\vec{ab}$ and $\vec{ac}$ measures θ. The *signed angle* at point a relative to $\vec{bc}$ then measures θ if c lies to the left of or is collinear with $\vec{ab}$, and −θ if c lies to the right of $\vec{ab}$. Note that the signed angle and the orientation of triangle △abc have the same sign.

We can extend the definition of signed angle to vertex chains. The signed angle at point a relative to a vertex chain is the sum of the signed angles at a relative to the chain's edges. Figure 5.12 gives some examples.

Function signedAngle computes and returns the signed angle at point a relative to edge e. After first treating the cases in which a is collinear with e, the function distinguishes between the configurations shown in Figure 4.6:

```
double signedAngle(Point &a, Edge &e)
{
    Point v = e.org - a;
    Point w = e.dest - a;
    double va = v.polarAngle();
    double wa = w.polarAngle();
    if ((va == -1.0) || (wa == -1.0))
        return 180.0;
    double x = wa - va;
    if ((x == 180.0) || (x == -180.0))
```

a

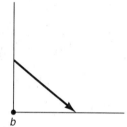

b

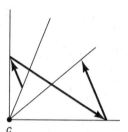

c

Figure 5.12:   (a) The signed angle at point a is 20; (b) the signed angle at b is −90; and (c) the signed angle at c is 20 − 90 + 40 = −30.

```
      return 180.0;
   else if (x < -180.0)
      return (x + 360.0);
   else if (x > 180.0)
      return (x - 360.0);
   else
      return x;
}
```

Let us consider how signed angles are used to classify a given point a with respect to a given polygon p. Assume that a does not lie in the boundary of p. Let A denote the signed angle at a relative to the boundary of p, where p has clockwise sense of rotation. A is useful for classifying the point: $A = -360$ degrees if a is inside the polygon, and $A = 0$ if a is outside the polygon. It is easy to see why this is true in the case of convex polygons. If a is inside convex polygon p, the boundary of p encircles a a full 360 degrees. Alternatively, if a is outside p, the boundary of p can be split into a near chain and a far chain, relative to point a. (Near and far chains were defined in Section 5.3.) Where A_n denotes the signed angle at p relative to the near chain and A_f the signed angle relative to the far chain, we have $A_n = -A_f$, from which it follows that $A = A_n + A_f = 0$.

That this also holds for *nonconvex* polygons is less obvious. Suppose first that a lies outside the polygon. Imagine casting a ray from point a through every vertex of the polygon, thereby partitioning the polygon into a number of triangles and convex quadrilaterals $p_1, p_2, \ldots, p_k$ (Figure 5.13a). Since a lies outside each p_i and each p_i is convex, the signed angle A_i at a relative to the boundary of p_i is zero (i.e., $A_i = 0$). But $A = A_1 + \cdots + A_k$ since the summation counts every edge of the original polygon p exactly once. Observe that new edges introduced by the rays contribute zero to A. It follows that $A = 0$ if point a is outside the polygon.

Figure 5.13b illustrates why $A = -360$ if a is inside polygon p. As before, imagine partitioning the polygon by rays originating from a, but this time preserve a small convex polygonal neighborhood around a (denoted p_0 in the figure). Since p_0 is convex and contains a, we know that $A_0 = -360$. Furthermore, since a lies outside the remaining

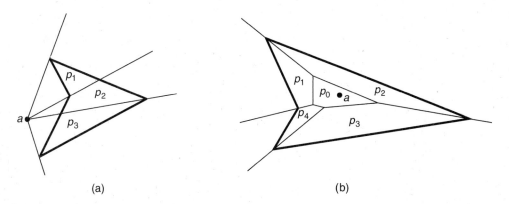

(a)   (b)

Figure 5.13:   (a) Point a is outside the polygon, so $A = A_1 + A_2 + A_3 = 0 + 0 + 0 = 0$; and (b) point b is inside the polygon, so $A = A_0 + A_1 + A_2 + A_3 + A_4 = -360 + 0 + 0 + 0 + 0 = -360$.

(convex) polygons p_i, we have $A_i = 0$ for each $i = 1, 2, \ldots, k$. It follows that $A = A_0 + A_1 + \cdots + A_k = -360 + 0 + \cdots + 0 = -360$.

Function `pointInPolygon2` solves the point enclosure problem for point a and polygon p. The signed angle at a relative to the polygon is accumulated in `total` as each edge is visited in turn. If a is found to lie on some edge (the signed angle relative to the edge equals 180), the function immediately returns the enumeration value BOUNDARY. Otherwise, when all polygon edges have been processed, it returns INSIDE or OUTSIDE depending on the final value of `total`.

```
int pointInPolygon2(Point &a, Polygon &p)
{
   double total = 0.0;
   for (int i = 0; i < p.size(); i++, p.advance(CLOCKWISE)) {
      Edge e = p.edge();
      double x = signedAngle(a, e);
      if (x == 180.0)
         return BOUNDARY;
      total += x;
   }
   return ((total < -180.0) ? INSIDE: OUTSIDE);
}
```

Program `pointInPolygon2` runs in time linear in the size of the polygon in the worst case.

5.6   Line Clipping: The Cyrus-Beck Algorithm

The process of discarding that portion of a geometric object that lies outside a given region is called *clipping*. Clipping is used for many purposes in computer graphics. In a windowing system, a window may serve as a small aperture into a panorama that extends far beyond. When drawing into the panorama, it is necessary to clip away those portions of objects that do not fall under the purview of the window. In some text editors, it is necessary to clip characters that do not fit on a line. In three-dimensional graphics, objects in space are clipped to a volume before being projected into the image plane, to avoid wasting time projecting things that will not be seen anyway.

In this section we present the Cyrus-Beck algorithm for clipping a line segment to a convex polygon. In the subsequent section we will cover the Sutherland-Hodgman algorithm for clipping an arbitrary polygon to a convex polygon.

Let s be a line segment and let p be a convex n-gon to which s is to be clipped. Here p is called a *clip polygon* and s the *subject*. We seek $s \cap p$, that portion of s which lies in p.

Let $\vec{s}$ denote one of the two directed infinite lines determined by s. Suppose we extend each of the n edges of polygon p to infinity, in both directions. Line $\vec{s}$ crosses all these extended edges of p in no more than n distinct intersection points. (If $\vec{s}$ is parallel to or collinear with some edge of p, the edge does not contribute an intersection point; moreover, if $\vec{s}$ passes through a vertex of polygon p, two intersection points coincide.)

The Cyrus-Beck clipping algorithm finds these intersection points and classifies each as either *potentially entering* (PE) or *potentially leaving* (PL). Suppose $\vec{s}$ crosses an extended edge e at intersection point i. Then point i is PE if $\vec{s}$ passes from the left of e to the right of e. Given our convention that the polygon interior lies to the right of each of its edges, $\vec{s}$ "potentially enters" the polygon at intersection point i. That is, if $s \cap p$ is nonempty, $s \cap p$ must lie *beyond* point i (see Figure 5.14). An intersection point i is PL if $\vec{s}$ passes from the right of e to the left of e. In this case, line $\vec{s}$ "potentially leaves" polygon p—if $s \cap p$ is nonempty, $s \cap p$ must lie *behind* point i.

Intersection points are easily classified as PE or PL. Let vector n be perpendicular to some edge e of the clip polygon, pointing to the right of e. Let vector $v = b - a$, where $\vec{s} = \vec{ab}$. Then intersection point i (at which $\vec{s}$ crosses e) is PE if the angle between n and v measures less than 90 degrees, and PL if this angle measures greater than 90 degrees. (If the angle measures 90 degrees, the intersection point does not exist since $\vec{s}$ must then be parallel to or collinear with edge e.) In terms of the dot product, point i is PE if $n \cdot v > 0$ and PL if $n \cdot v < 0$.

How is classification of the intersection points used? Suppose we order the intersection points along $\vec{s}$. Then line $\vec{s}$ intersects clip polygon p only if the intersection points comprise a sequence of PE intersection points followed by a sequence of PL intersection points. Moreover, the clipped line segment $s \cap p$ we seek extends from the last PE intersection point to the first PL intersection point (segments s_1 and s_2 of Figure 5.14).

On the other hand, if the PE and PL intersection points are interspersed along $\vec{s}$, clipped line segment $s \cap p$ is empty (s_3 of Figure 5.14). For in this case there must exist some point a along $\vec{s}$ such that some PL point lies behind a and some PE point lies beyond a. But since $s \cap p$ lies behind the PL point, $s \cap p$ must lie behind a; and since $s \cap p$ lies beyond the PE point, $s \cap p$ must lie beyond a. This is possible only if $s \cap p$ is empty.

Rather than work with intersection points directly, the Cyrus-Beck algorithm works with the parametric values (along $\vec{s}$) of these intersection points. The algorithm maintains

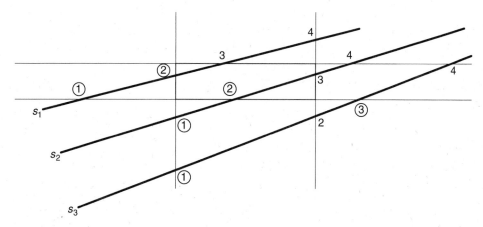

Figure 5.14:   Clipping line segments s_1, s_2, and s_3 to a square clip polygon. Intersection points are labeled according to their order along each s_i, and the labels of potentially entering (PE) intersection points are encircled; the remaining intersection points are potentially leaving (PL).

a range $[t_0, t_1]$ of parametric values corresponding to the *current line segment*, which converges to the clipped segment $s \cap p$ we seek as the algorithm proceeds. Initially, the current line segment is line segment s, represented by the range $[0, 1]$. As the algorithm processes each edge e of the clip polygon, the current range either remains unchanged or shrinks (its lower limit increases or its upper limit decreases). Specifically, whenever a PE intersection point with parametric value t is discovered, the lower limit t_0 of the current range is updated: $t_0 = \max(t_0, t)$. Similarly, finding a PL intersection point with parametric value t requires that we update the upper limit of the current range: $t_1 = \min(t_1, t)$. When all edges have been processed (and consequently all intersection points found), the current range $[t_0, t_1]$ represents the clipped segment $s \cap p$ we seek. If $t_0 \leq t_1$, this clipped segment is nonempty; otherwise ($t_0 > t_1$) it is empty.

The following function clips subject line segment s to clip polygon p and returns TRUE if the result is nonempty and FALSE otherwise. If nonempty, the clipped line segment is passed back through reference parameter `result`:

```
bool clipLineSegment(Edge &s, Polygon &p, Edge &result)
{
    double t0 = 0.0;
    double t1 = 1.0;
    double t;
    Point v = s.dest - s.org;
    for (int i = 0; i < p.size(); i++, p.advance(CLOCKWISE)) {
        Edge e = p.edge();
        if (s.intersect(e, t)==SKEW) { // s and e cross at a point
            Edge f = e;
            f.rot();
            Point n = f.dest - f.org;
            if (dotProduct(n, v) > 0.0) {
                if (t > t0)
                    t0 = t;
            } else {
                if (t < t1)
                    t1 = t;
            }
        } else {    // s and e are parallel or collinear
            if (s.org.classify(e) == LEFT)
                return FALSE;
        }
    }
    if (t0 <= t1) {
        result = Edge(s.point(t0), s.point(t1));
        return TRUE;
    }
    return FALSE;
}
```

Observe how function `clipLineSegment` handles the case where s is parallel to some edge e of the clip polygon. If s lies to the left of e, the function immediately returns

FALSE and exits. Otherwise the function ignores e and goes on to the next edge. The algorithm clearly runs in time proportional to the size of the clip polygon.

5.7   Polygon Clipping: The Sutherland-Hodgman Algorithm

Polygon clipping, the process of clipping a subject polygon to a clip polygon, is more interesting than line clipping, for what results from the process is not just a collection of line segments, but a collection of *polygons*. Moreover, the problem of polygon clipping challenges us to exploit the structure inherent in the subject polygon, to treat it as more than a mere collection of line segments. In this section we cover the Sutherland-Hodgman polygon clipping algorithm. Given a *convex* clip polygon p and an arbitrary subject polygon s, the algorithm constructs the region $s \cap p$, a collection of zero or more polygons.

The Sutherland-Hodgman algorithm clips the subject polygon to each edge of the convex clip polygon in turn. The subject polygon is first clipped to one edge of the clip polygon, then the polygon that results is clipped to the next edge, and so on: The polygon that results from each clip operation is "piped" into the next clip operation. We are done when the subject polygon has been clipped to every edge of the clip polygon. The algorithm is illustrated in Figure 5.15, where the clip polygon is a square.

The algorithm is implemented by function `clipPolygon`, which is passed a subject polygon s and a convex clip polygon p. The result is passed back through reference parameter `result`. The function returns TRUE only if the result is nonempty:

```
bool clipPolygon(Polygon &s, Polygon &p, Polygon* &result)
{
    Polygon *q = new Polygon(s);
    Polygon *r;
    int flag = TRUE;
```

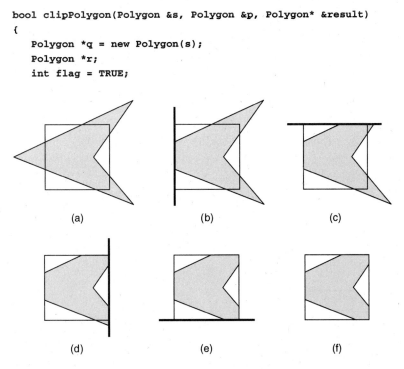

(a)   (b)   (c)

(d)   (e)   (f)

Figure 5.15:   The Sutherland-Hodgman clipping algorithm.

```
for (int i = 0; i < p.size(); i++, p.advance(CLOCKWISE)) {
   Edge e = p.edge();
   if (clipPolygonToEdge(*q, e, r)) {
      delete q;
      q = r;
   } else {
      delete q;
      flag = FALSE;
      break;
   }
}
if (flag) {
   result = q;
   return TRUE;
}
return FALSE;
}
```

In each iteration of `clipPolygon`, variable `q` points to the current subject polygon and variable `r` to the polygon that results from clipping `q` to edge `e` of the clip polygon. Initially, `q` is made to point to a copy of subject polygon `s` (it points to a *copy* of `s` so `s` is not destroyed). Clipping `q` to edge `e` is accomplished by the call to function `clipPolygonToEdge`, which returns `TRUE` if the polygon `r` which results is nonempty. If `r` turns out to be nonempty, it is piped into the next clip operation by the assignment instruction `q=r`; otherwise function `clipPolygon` exits, returning `FALSE`.

Function `clipPolygonToEdge` clips subject polygon `s` to the right side of an edge `e` of the clip polygon. An output polygon is grown incrementally into the clipped polygon we seek. The idea is to compare each edge of `s` to edge `e` in turn. Depending on the result of each comparison, zero, one, or two vertices are inserted into the output polygon under construction.

The four possible relationships between `e` and an edge of `s` are shown in Figure 5.16. Where $\overrightarrow{ab}$ is the current edge of `s`, the contribution to the output polygon resulting in each case is as follows:

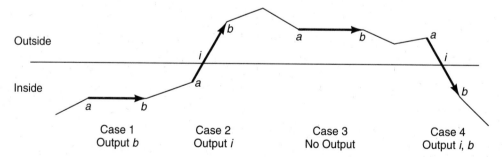

Figure 5.16:   Possible relationships between an edge and the clip half-plane: (Case 1) output b; (Case 2) output i; (Case 3) no output; (Case 4) output i, then b.

1. *Edge $\overrightarrow{ab}$ lies to the right of e.* Output vertex b.

2. *Edge $\overrightarrow{ab}$ crosses from the right of e to the left of e.* Output the point i where $\overrightarrow{ab}$ crosses e.

3. *Edge $\overrightarrow{ab}$ lies to the left of e.* No output.

4. *Edge $\overrightarrow{ab}$ crosses from the left of e to the right of e.* Output i, then b, where $\overrightarrow{ab}$ crosses edge e at point i.

Function `clipPolygonToEdge` clips subject polygon s to edge e. It returns the resulting polygon through reference parameter `result`, and returns TRUE only if polygon `result` is nonempty:

```
bool clipPolygonToEdge(Polygon &s, Edge &e, Polygon* &result)
{
    Polygon *p = new Polygon;
    Point crossingPt;
    for (int i = 0; i < s.size(); s.advance(CLOCKWISE), i++)
        Point org = s.point();
        Point dest = s.cw()->point();
        int orgIsInside = (org.classify(e) != LEFT);
        int destIsInside = (dest.classify(e) != LEFT);
        if (orgIsInside != destIsInside) {
            double t;
            e.intersect(s.edge(), t);
            crossingPt = e.point(t);
        }
        if (orgIsInside && destIsInside)            // case 1
            p->insert(dest);
        else if (orgIsInside && !destIsInside) {    // case 2
            if (org != crossingPt)
                p->insert(crossingPt);
        }
        else if (!orgIsInside && !destIsInside)     // case 3
            ;
        else {                                      // case 4
            p->insert(crossingPt);
            if (dest != crossingPt)
            p->insert(dest);
        }
    }
    result = p;
    return (p->size() > 0);
}
```

What happens if `clipPolygonToEdge` is handed a problem whose solution consists of *multiple* polygons? In this case, `clipPolygonToEdge` produces a single polygon that contains degenerate boundary edges. The situation is depicted in Figure 5.17.

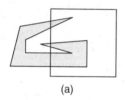   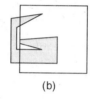   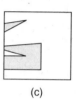

(a)   (b)   (c)

Figure 5.17:   (a) A clipping problem; (b) the resulting polygon with three degenerate edges (displaced horizontally in the figure); and (c) the collection of two polygons it represents.

To partition the polygon into non-degenerate pieces, we first sort the endpoints of the degenerate edges along the common line with which they are all collinear. We then apply `Vertex::splice` repeatedly to excise the degenerate edges. Since this refinement will not be needed for the applications in Chapter 8 that makes use of function `clipPolygonToEdge`, we will not pursue it further.

Let us analyze program `clipPolygon` in terms of the size $|s|$ of subject polygon s and the size $|p|$ of clip polygon p. Function `clipPolygonToEdge` runs in $O(|s|)$ time and is called at most once per edge of the clip polygon, or at most $|p|$ times. Hence program `clipPolygon` runs in $O(|s|\,|p|)$ time in the worst case.

5.8   Triangulating Monotone Polygons

A *triangulation* of a polygon is a decomposition of the polygon into a set of triangles. Triangulations are often used to reduce problems involving complicated regions to problems involving triangles, which, because triangles are among the simplest of regions, are generally easier to solve. For instance, to determine whether a given point lies in a nonconvex polygon, we can triangulate the polygon and then answer yes only if the point belongs to at least one of the triangles. Or to render a higher-order surface embedded in space, we can approximate the surface by a mesh of triangles, which can be rendered more easily.

In this section we present a linear-time algorithm to triangulate polygons of a special type, known as *monotone polygons*. With this algorithm's appearance in 1978, researchers achieved the first method for triangulating arbitrary n-gons in $O(n \log n)$ time:

1.   Decompose the polygon into monotone pieces in $O(n \log n)$ time.
2.   Triangulate the monotone pieces in total $O(n)$ time.

In Chapter 7 we will present an $O(n \log n)$-time algorithm for decomposing a polygon into monotone pieces.

An important question, which has been settled only recently, is whether a general triangulation algorithm faster than $O(n \log n)$ is possible. Faster triangulation algorithms have been developed, but some solve only special cases in which the input polygon is constrained, and the improved performance of others depends on additional properties of the polygon (such as the number of reflex vertices it possesses). Yet in recent years several general triangulation algorithms which run in $o(n \log n)$ time have been developed. In 1991 Bernard Chazelle devised an optimal $O(n)$-time algorithm.

5.8.1 What Are Monotone Polygons?

A vertex chain is said to be *monotone* if every vertical line crosses it in at most one point. When a monotone chain is traversed beginning from its leftmost vertex, its vertices are visited by increasing x-coordinates.

   A polygon is *monotone* if its boundary is composed of two monotone chains: the polygon's *upper* chain and *lower* chain. Each chain terminates at the polygon's leftmost vertex and rightmost vertex and contains zero or more vertices in between. Figure 5.18 gives some examples. Observe that the (nonempty) intersection of a vertical line and a monotone polygon consists of either a vertical line segment or a point.

5.8.2 The Triangulation Algorithm

Let p be a monotone polygon, and let us relabel its vertices as $v_1, v_2, \ldots, v_n$ by increasing x-coordinates since our algorithm will examine the vertices in this order. The algorithm produces a succession of monotone polygons $p = p_0, p_1, \ldots, p_n = \emptyset$. Polygon p_i, the result of examining vertex v_i, is obtained by splitting zero or more triangles from the previous polygon p_{i-1}. The algorithm is finished when we are left with p_n, the empty polygon—the collection of triangles accumulated along the way represents the triangulation of the original polygon p.

   The algorithm maintains a stack s of vertices that have been examined but not yet fully processed (some as yet undiscovered triangles may meet these vertices). As vertex v_i is about to be examined, the stack contains some of the vertices of polygon p_{i-1}. Certain stack invariants are maintained as the algorithm proceeds.[1] Specifically, where the vertices on the stack are labeled $s_1, s_2, \ldots, s_t$ from the bottom of the stack to the top, the following conditions are maintained:

1. $s_1, s_2, \ldots, s_t$ are ordered by increasing x-coordinates and includes every vertex of p_{i-1} that lies both to the right of s_1 and to the left of s_t,

2. $s_1, s_2, \ldots, s_t$ are consecutive vertices in either p_{i-1}'s upper chain or its lower chain,

3. vertices $s_2, s_3, \ldots, s_{t-1}$ are reflex vertices in p_{i-1} (the measure of each of their interior angles exceeds 180 degrees), and

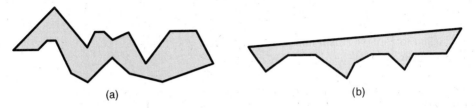

(a)   (b)

Figure 5.18:   Two monotone polygons. The upper chain of polygon (b) consists of a single edge only.

---

   [1]An *invariant* is a condition that holds true at specific points of the algorithm, such as at the start of every iteration of a given loop.

4. in polygon p_{i-1}, the next vertex v_i to be examined stands in one of these relations to vertices s_t and s_1:

    (a) v_i is adjacent to s_t but not to s_1, or

    (b) v_i is adjacent to s_1 but not to s_t, or

    (c) v_i is adjacent to both s_1 and s_t.

The three cases of condition 4 are shown in Figure 5.19.

The action taken when vertex v_i is examined depends on which one of stack conditions 4a, 4b, or 4c currently holds. The actions, illustrated in Figure 5.19, are as follows:

Case 4a *Vertex v_i is adjacent to s_t but not to s_1:* While $t > 1$ and internal angle $\angle v_i s_t s_{t-1}$ measures less than 180 degrees, split off triangle $\triangle v_i s_t s_{t-1}$, then pop s_t from the stack. Finally, push v_i. The algorithm uses the fact that $\angle v_i s_t s_{t-1} < 180$ only if either (1) s_{t-1} lies to the left of $\overrightarrow{v_i s_t}$ if v_i belongs to polygon p_{i-1}'s upper chain or (2) s_{t-1} lies to the right of $\overrightarrow{v_i s_t}$ if v_i belongs to the lower chain.

Case 4b *Vertex v_i is adjacent to s_1 but not to s_t:* Split off the polygon determined by vertices $v_i, s_1, s_2, \ldots, s_t$, then empty the stack, then push s_t followed by v_i. The polygon defined by the vertices $v_i, s_1, s_2, \ldots, s_t$ is in fact fan shaped with apex v_i (i.e., v_i belongs to its kernel). The algorithm then triangulates this polygon.

Case 4c *Vertex v_i is adjacent to both s_1 and s_t:* In this case $v_i = v_n$ and polygon p_{i-1}, determined by vertices $v_i, s_1, s_2, \ldots, s_t$, is fan shaped with apex v_n. The algorithm triangulates this polygon directly, and exits.

Figure 5.20 runs the algorithm on a small problem (the stages are ordered top to bottom, left to right). In each stage, the vertex being examined is circled, and the vertices on the stack are labeled $s_1, \ldots, s_t$.

The following program, `triangulateMonotonePolygon`, is passed a monotone polygon p and returns a list of triangles representing a triangulation of the polygon. The program assumes that polygon p's window is positioned over its leftmost vertex:

```
enum { UPPER, LOWER };

List<Polygon*> *triangulateMonotonePolygon(Polygon &p)
```

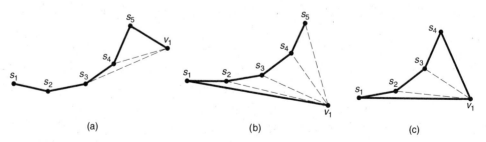

           (a)   (b)   (c)

Figure 5.19:   The three cases that occur while triangulating a monotone polygon: Vertex v is (a) adjacent to s_t but not to s_1, (b) adjacent to s_1 but not to s_t, or (c) adjacent to both s_1 and s_t.

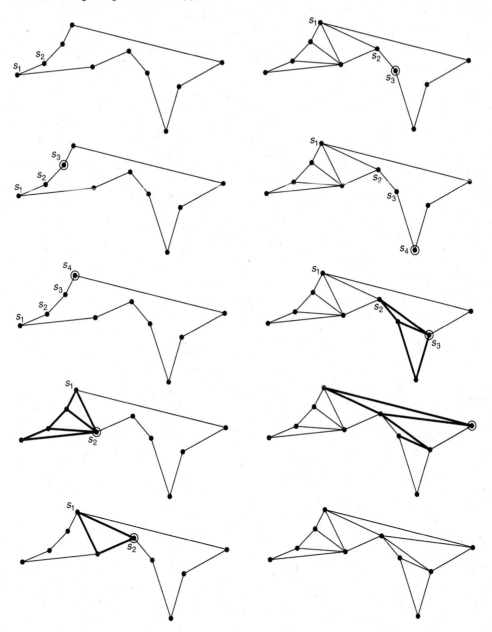

Figure 5.20:   Triangulating a small monotone polygon. The triangles discovered at each stage are highlighted. The stages proceed from top to bottom, left to right.

```
{
    Stack<Vertex*> s;
    List<Polygon*> *triangles = new List<Polygon*>;
    Vertex *v, *vu, *vl;
    leastVertex(p, leftToRightCmp);
```

```
    v = vu = vl = p.v();
    s.push(v);
    int chain = advancePtr(vl, vu, v);
    s.push(v);
    while (1) {    /* outer while loop */
        chain = advancePtr(vl, vu, v);
        if (adjacent(v, s.top()) &&
              !adjacent(v, s.bottom())) { // case 4a
            int side = (chain == UPPER) ? LEFT : RIGHT;
            Vertex *a = s.top();
            Vertex *b = s.nextToTop();
            while ((s.size() > 1) &&
                    (b->classify(v->point(),a->point()) == side)) {
                if (chain == UPPER) {
                    p.setV(b);
                    triangles->append(p.split(v));
                } else {
                    p.setV(v);
                    triangles->append(p.split(b));
                }
                s.pop();
                a = b;
                b = s.nextToTop();
            }
            s.push(v);
        } else if (!adjacent(v, s.top())) {    // case 4b
            Polygon *q;
            Vertex *t = s.pop();
            if (chain == UPPER) {
                p.setV(t);
                q = p.split(v);
            } else {
                p.setV(v);
                q = p.split(t);
                q->advance(CLOCKWISE);
            }
            triangulateFanPolygon(*q, triangles);
            while (!s.empty())
                s.pop();
            s.push(t);
            s.push(v);
        } else {    // case 4c
            p.setV(v);
            triangulateFanPolygon(p, triangles);
            return triangles;
        }
    } /* end of outer while */
}
```

Function `adjacent` returns TRUE just if the two vertices it is passed are adjacent:

```
bool adjacent(Vertex *v, Vertex *w)
{
   return ((w == v->cw()) || (w == v->ccw()));
}
```

Program `triangulateMonotonePolygon` merges the upper and lower chains of polygon p as it proceeds, thereby taking advantage of the fact that the vertices in each chain are already ordered by increasing x-coordinates [otherwise an $O(n \log n)$ time sort would be necessary]. In each iteration, variable v points to the vertex to be examined. The program maintains two variables, vu and vl, which point to the last vertex examined in p's upper and lower chains, respectively. As the program proceeds, these pointers are marched left to right by function `advancePtr`. Each time `advancePtr` is called, it advances either vu or vl and updates v to point to whichever is advanced:

```
int advancePtr(Vertex* &vu, Vertex* &vl, Vertex* &v)
{
   Vertex *vun = vu->cw();
   Vertex *vln = vl->ccw();
   if (vun->point() < vln->point()) {
      v = vu = vun;
      return UPPER;
   } else {
      v = vl = vln;
      return LOWER;
   }
}
```

Function `advancePtr` returns UPPER or LOWER, indicating which of the two chains v belongs to. Program `triangulateMonotonePolygon` uses this value to ensure that its subsequent call to `split` returns the piece detached from the main polygon, rather than the main polygon from which the piece was detached.

To triangulate a fan shaped polygon, we iteratively find the triangles which fan out from some common apex v. To do this, we traverse the polygon starting from v, and at each vertex w that is not adjacent to v, we split along the chord connecting v to w. This is performed by function `triangulateFanPolygon`, which destructively decomposes the n-gon p into $n - 2$ triangles and appends these to list `triangles`. The function assumes that polygon p is fan shaped, and its window is positioned over some apex:

```
void triangulateFanPolygon(Polygon &p, List<Polygon*> *triangles)
{
   Vertex *w = p.v()->cw()->cw();
   int size = p.size();
   for (int i = 3; i < size; i++) {
```

```
        triangles->append(p.split(w));
        w = w->cw();
    }
    triangles->append(&p);
}
```

Figure 5.21 depicts a triangulation produced by the algorithm. The monotone polygon contains 35 vertices.

5.8.3 Correctness

We must show two things: (1) that every diagonal the algorithm finds in iteration i is (a chord) internal to polygon p_{i-1}; (2) that the algorithm restores the four stack conditions from one iteration to the next. (That the chords which are found decompose the original polygon into *triangles* is apparent from Figure 5.19.)

First consider diagonal $\overline{v_i s_{t-1}}$ of Figure 5.19a (here $t = 5$). Letting triangle $T = \triangle s_{t-1} s_t v_i$, observe that no vertex of polygon p_{i-1} can lie in T: The vertices $s_0, \ldots, s_{t-2}$ lie to the left of T's leftmost vertex s_{t-1}, and vertices v_j for $j > i$ lie to the right of T's rightmost vertex v_i. Hence any edge that crosses diagonal $\overline{v_i s_{t-1}}$ must leave triangle T by one of the edges $\overrightarrow{s_{t-1} s_t}$ or $\overrightarrow{s_t v_i}$, which is impossible since these are boundary edges of p_{i-1}. Thus diagonal $\overline{v_i s_{t-1}}$ is a chord. Now split triangle T from p_{i-1}. The same argument shows that the remaining diagonals introduced in Case 4a are also chords.

Next consider Case 4b, depicted in Figure 5.19b. By stack conditions 2 and 3, polygon T, determined by vertices $v_i, s_1, \ldots, s_t$, is fan shaped with apex v_i. Observe that no vertex of p_{i-1} can lie in the interior of T—were one or more vertices to do so, the rightmost such vertex would currently be on the stack, and hence on the boundary of p_{i-1}. Since the interior of T is free of vertices, any edge which crosses $\overrightarrow{v_i s_t}$ must also cross one of the edges $\overrightarrow{v_i s_1}, \overrightarrow{s_1 s_2}, \ldots, \overrightarrow{s_{t-1} s_t}$, which is impossible since these are boundary edges of p_{i-1}. It is shown similarly that, in Case 4c (Figure 5.19c), p_{i-1} is fan shaped with apex v_i and interior free of vertices.

Next we argue that the stack conditions are maintained from one iteration to the next. At most v_i and s_t are pushed on the stack, and when they are both pushed, they are pushed in the correct horizontal order. Thus stack condition 1 is maintained. The vertices comprise a vertex chain in p_{i-1} by induction (in Case 4a) or by the fact that the stack is reset to two adjacent vertices (in Case 4b), so condition 2 is satisfied. The stack's vertices are reflex (except for top and bottom vertices) because v_i is pushed only when the vertex on the top

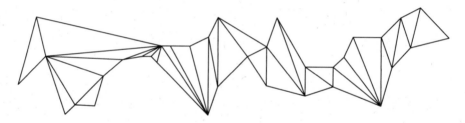

Figure 5.21: Triangulation of a monotone 35-gon.

of the stack (onto which it gets pushed) would become a reflex angle. Hence condition 3 is met (it is vacuously satisfied in Case 4b since the stack contains only two items.) Finally, v_i must be adjacent to at least one of s_1 or s_t because the monotonicity of p_{i-1} guarantees that v_i has a neighbor to its left, and all the stack's vertices except s_1 and s_t already have both neighbors accounted for. Hence stack condition 4 is satisfied.

5.8.4 Analysis

Program `triangulateMonotonePolygon` runs in $\Theta(n)$ time, where the input monotone polygon contains n vertices. To see the upper bound $O(n)$, observe that each iteration of the two inner `while` loops (in Cases 4a and 4b) pops a vertex from the stack. Yet every vertex is pushed onto the stack at most once (when it is first examined) and hence can be popped from the stack at most once. Since the algorithm (1) performs $O(n)$ constant-time stack operations and (2) spends constant time between successive stack operations, it runs in $O(n)$ time. The lower bound follows from the fact that each of the n vertices must be examined.

5.9 Chapter Notes

The need to sort arises in many settings and is ancient, predating computers and possibly even written language. Not surprisingly, many of the algorithms we cover in this book rely on sorting. During the course of this book, we present three sorting methods that belong to every computer scientist's repertoire—insertion sort, selection sort, and merge sort. These methods are so fundamental that they are all but unattributable. Yet despite their seeming simplicity, research continues to this day into the complexity of these and other basic sorting algorithms.

The number of polygonizations of a set of n points is exponential in n; however, the number of *star-shaped* polygonizations is bounded above by $O(n^4)$. If no three points in the point set are collinear, the kernels of the different star-shaped polygonizations partition the point set's convex hull. An algorithm for constructing this partition in $O(n^4)$ time is presented in [22], which leads to an $O(n^5)$-time algorithm for finding all star-shaped polygons. An algorithm for finding the kernel of any n-sided polygon in $O(n)$ time is presented in [53]; we present a simpler but less efficient $O(n \log n)$ algorithm in Chapter 8. The superb book *Art Gallery Theorems and Algorithms* by Joseph O'Rourke explores problems related to visibility inside a polygon [60].

The notion of convex hull makes sense for sets of points in d-dimensional space for any $d \geq 1$: The convex hull is the intersection of all convex polytopes that contain the points. Some methods for finding the convex hull of planar point sets are framed in terms of d-dimensional space. Insertion hull, for example, is a special case of the *beneath-beyond method* for finding the convex hull of points in d-dimensional space [45].

The line clipping method of section 5.6 is known as the Cyrus-Beck clipping algorithm, and the polygon clipping method of section 5.7 as the Sutherland-Hodgman algorithm [75]. Other well-known clipping methods include the Cohen-Sutherland and the midpoint subdivision [77] line clipping algorithms, and the Weiler-Atherton [88] polygon clipping algorithm. This last algorithm is general, allowing both subject and clip polygons to be nonconvex and to possess holes. This generality permits its use in an algorithm for performing hidden surface removal, also presented in [88].

The algorithm for triangulating monotone polygons is given in [31], which gives a more general definition of *monotone* than we have assumed: A vertex chain c is *monotone* relative to some line ℓ if every line perpendicular to ℓ intersects c in at most one point. A polygon is *monotone* if its boundary is composed of two vertex chains that are monotone relative to the same line. Our monotone polygons are actually polygons that are monotone relative to the horizontal axis. The article [67] presents a linear-time algorithm for deciding whether there exists a line relative to which a polygon is monotone.

Chazelle's [19] triangulation algorithm runs in optimal $O(n)$ time. A survey of polygon partitioning techniques is presented in [60, 61].

5.10   Exercises

1. Program `starPolygon` finds only fan-shaped polygons. Generalize the program so, when passed any point s lying in the convex hull of the set of points, it finds a star-shaped polygon containing s in its kernel.

2. Devise an $O(n \log n)$-time algorithm for finding a star-shaped polygon in a point set.

3. Prove that the kernel of a polygon is convex.

4. Write a version of insertion hull that runs in $O(n \log n)$ time. (Hint: Presort the points so the calls to `pointInConvexPolygon` and `closestVertex` are unnecessary.)

5. Show that $\Omega(n \log n)$ time is necessary to solve the convex hull finding problem. [Hint: Devise an efficient reduction from sorting to convex hull finding. Use the fact that $\Omega(n \log n)$ is a lower bound for sorting.]

6. Show that point p belongs to convex hull $\mathcal{CH}(S)$ if and only if there exist three points of S such that the triangle they determine contains p.

7. This question involves the Cyrus-Beck line clipping algorithm. Show that a line $\bar{s}$ intersects a convex polygon p only if the intersection points, when ordered along $\bar{s}$, consist of a subsequence of PE intersection points followed by a subsequence of PL intersection points.

8. Modify program `clipLineSegment` so it clips an infinite line, rather than a line segment, to a convex polygon.

9. Devise an algorithm to remove the degenerate edges which are sometimes produced by `clipPolygonToEdge`.

10. Given a polygon p and some point a inside p, devise a method for finding some ray that originates at a and crosses the minimum number of p's edges. (Hint: Consider sorting the vertices of p radially around a.)

11. Show that any triangulation of an n-gon uses $n - 3$ chords to decompose the polygon into $n - 2$ triangles.

6

Incremental Selection

Incremental selection methods solve problems incrementally, a little at a time. These methods, however, process the input in an order of their own making, rather than in the order in which the input is presented. Incremental selection involves scanning the input to "select" the best item to process next.

In some applications of incremental selection, the order in which items are to be processed can be determined in advance. In such cases the input can be *presorted*. In other applications the order cannot be anticipated, and each decision concerning which item to process next depends on what has been achieved so far.

In this chapter we will look at both kinds of applications. We will start with selection sort, an exemplar for incremental selection. We will then consider two more methods for constructing the convex hull of a finite point set: the gift-wrapping method and the Graham scan. The third geometric algorithm we will cover is the depth-sort method for performing hidden surface removal given a collection of triangles in space. Our next algorithm computes the intersection of two convex polygons in the plane. Our last algorithm constructs a special triangulation of a finite point set in the plane, known as the Delaunay triangulation.

6.1 Selection Sort

Selection sort, another sorting algorithm, repeatedly extracts the smallest item from a set until the set is empty. For sorting an array of items, it works as follows: Find the smallest item and exchange it with the item in the array's first position. Then find the smallest of the remaining items (to the right of the first position) and exchange it with the item in the second position. Continue in this manner until the array is sorted.

The function template `selectionSort` sorts the items in array `a[0..n-1]`. For each i from 0 through $n-1$, iteration i selects the smallest item from among `a[i..n-1]` and then exchanges this item with `a[i]`:

```
template<class T>
void selectionSort(T a[], int n, int (*cmp)(T,T))
{
   for (int i = 0; i < n-1; i++) {
      int min = i;
      for (int j = i+1; j < n; j++)
         if ((*cmp)(a[j], a[min]) < 0)
            min = j;
      swap(a[i], a[min]);
   }
}
```

The body of the inner `for` loop performs the selection for each increment of i. Variable `min` holds the index of the smallest item examined in the current scan. We maintain the *index* of the item, rather than the item itself, so the subsequent exchange can be performed.

Function `swap` exchanges its two arguments:

```
template <class T> void swap(T &a, T &b)
{
   T t = a;
   a = b;
   b = t;
}
```

The running time of selection sort is $T(n) = \sum_{i=1}^{n} I(i)$, where $I(i)$ time is needed to select the ith smallest item. Since selecting this item takes $n - i$ comparisons, the program performs $T(n) = (n - 1) + (n - 2) + \cdots + 1 = n(n - 1)/2$, or about $n^2/2$, comparisons in total. Although this running time is comparable to that of insertion sort, selection sort is generally preferable: Selection sort performs only n exchanges, whereas insertion sort performs about $n^2/2$ half-exchanges in the worst case (where shifting an item one position to the right counts as a half-exchange).

6.1.1 Off-Line and On-Line Programs

Selection sort is an example of an *off-line* method. This means that all its input data must be available from the start. It is easy to see why: If the smallest item were to arrive only after some other (larger) item were already selected, the opportunity to put the smallest item in the first position of the array would be lost. All incremental selection methods are in fact off-line since selection of the correct item at each stage cannot be guaranteed if all items are not accessible.

Insertion sort, like all incremental insertion methods, is an example of an *on-line* method. An on-line program does not look ahead at its input. This means that its input can arrive as a stream over time and does not have to be available in its entirety from the start. Although `insertionSort` happens to have access to the entire input array, it does not scan the array prior to inserting items; rather, it peels off one item at a time without looking ahead.

On-line programs are most useful in real-time settings, where the input data are generated on the fly. Text editors and flight simulators are on-line, since input to these programs is generated in real time by a user whose decisions cannot be anticipated. On the down side, on-line programs may do work which, on the basis of input data that arrives only later (too late), turns out to have been wasted effort. An example is the convex hull program `insertionHull` of the previous chapter, which sometimes assembles large current hulls only to disassemble them later. We now turn to a method for constructing convex hulls which avoids this sort of wasted work because it is based on the incremental selection approach.

6.2   Finding Convex Hulls: Gift Wrapping

One way to construct the convex hull of a finite point set S in the plane mimics how one would go about drawing it with straightedge and pencil. First select some point $a \in S$ that clearly belongs to the convex hull boundary—the leftmost vertex suffices. Then pivot a vertical ray clockwise around a until it first hits some other point b in S; segment $\overline{ab}$ is an edge of the convex hull. To find the next edge, continue pivoting the ray clockwise, this time around b, until the ray encounters some other point c; segment $\overline{bc}$ is the next edge of the convex hull. Continue in this fashion until returning to point a. Figure 6.1 depicts the process, which is known as the *gift-wrapping* method.

The process of pivoting the ray around each point is the "selection" part of the algorithm. To select the point that follows point a on the convex hull boundary, we seek point b such that no point lies to the left of ray $\overrightarrow{ab}$. The points are examined in turn, while the algorithm keeps track of the leftmost candidate encountered so far. Only those points not yet known to lie on the convex hull boundary need be examined.

The following program `giftwrapHull` returns a polygon representing the convex hull of the n points in array s. The array s should have length n + 1 since the program places a sentinel point in s[n]:

```
Polygon *giftwrapHull(Point s[], int n)
{
    int a, i;
    for (a = 0, i = 1; i < n; i++)
        if (s[i] < s[a])
            a = i;
    s[n] = s[a];
    Polygon *p = new Polygon;
    for (int m = 0; m < n; m++) {
        swap(s[a], s[m]);
```

```
        p->insert(s[m]);
        a = m + 1;
        for (int i = m + 2; i <= n; i++) {
            int c = s[i].classify(s[m], s[a]);
            if (c == LEFT || c == BEYOND)
                a = i;
        }
        if (a == n)
            return p;
    }
    return NULL;
}
```

Pivoting the ray around some point s[m] is simulated by the inner for loop. Point s[a] is the leftmost point the ray has encountered so far. If a new point s[i] lies to the left of the ray that originates at s[m] and passes through s[a], then the pivoting ray would hit s[i] before s[a], so a is updated. Variable a is also updated if s[i] lies *beyond* s[a]—point s[a] cannot be a vertex of the convex hull if it lies between points s[m] and s[i].

Observe that function giftwrapHull rearranges the points in array s. At the end of iteration m, subarray s[0..m] contains the known vertices of the convex hull in clockwise rotation, and s[m+1..n-1] contains the remaining points, which may or may not prove to be vertices of the convex hull. It is these latter points which must be examined in subsequent iterations.

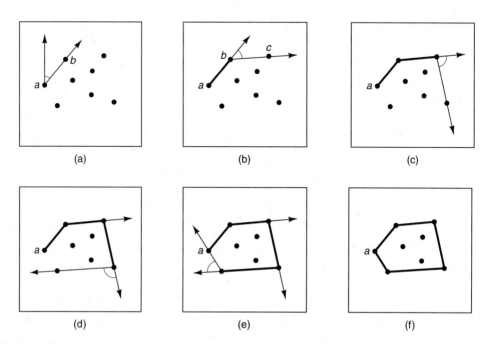

      (a)   (b)   (c)

      (d)   (e)   (f)

Figure 6.1:   Gift wrapping a set of points in the plane.

6.2.1 Analysis

To analyze the gift-wrapping method, note that pivoting around the mth point requires $n - m - 2$ (constant-time) point-line classifications. Since only h pivots are performed [where h is the number of vertices in convex hull $\mathcal{CH}(S)$], the total running time is $O(hn)$. If every one of the n points is a vertex of $\mathcal{CH}(S)$ (i.e., if $h = n$), the running time is $O(n^2)$, comparable to that of `insertionHull`. On the other hand, whenever h is small compared to n, the gift-wrapping method is faster than the insertion hull method.

A running time like $O(hn)$ is said to be *output sensitive* since it includes a factor h that depends on the size of the output. For analyzing programs which run more quickly the less output they produce (not all programs behave like this), output-sensitive bounds provide a tighter estimate of behavior than do bounds not sensitive to output size. In the case of gift wrapping, the $O(hn)$ running time indicates that the program is efficient when the convex hull is small; this fact is not captured by the $O(n^2)$ estimate of running time, which is sensitive only to input size but not to output size.

6.3   Finding Convex Hulls: Graham Scan

In this section we cover the Graham scan, a convex-hull finding method named for its inventor, R. L. Graham. The Graham scan finds the convex hull of a finite point set S in two phases. In the *presorting phase*, the algorithm selects an extreme point $p_0 \in S$ and sorts the remaining points of S radially around p_0. In the *hull finding phase*, the algorithm iteratively processes the sorted points, thereby producing a sequence of current hulls which converges to convex hull $\mathcal{CH}(S)$. Presorting simplifies the hull finding phase: Each point processed during the hull finding phase gets inserted into the current hull, no questions asked; moreover, the vertices to be removed from the current hull are easy to find. This compares favorably with the way that the insertion hull method of the previous chapter processes each point: It must decide whether to insert the point into the current hull and, if so, traverse the current hull boundary full circle to determine which vertices are to be removed.

Given point set S, Graham scan first finds some extreme point $p_0 \in S$. We will take p_0 to be the point of S with minimum y-coordinate, or the rightmost such point in the case of a tie. The remaining points are then sorted by polar angle around p_0. If two points have the same polar angle, the point closer to p_0 is considered less than the more distant point. This is the dictionary order relation for points based on their polar coordinates relative to p_0, realized by comparison function `polarCmp` of section 5.2. Let us relabel the remaining points $p_1, p_2, \ldots, p_{n-1}$ according to this ordering, as in Figure 6.2.

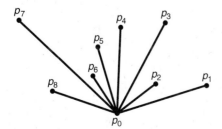

Figure 6.2: Labeling of points based on their polar coordinates relative to p_0.

During the hull finding phase, Graham scan maintains a current hull over those points that have already been inserted. Figure 6.3 illustrates the algorithm in action. Consider the insertion of point p_7 (Figure 6.3f). Because the points are ordered radially around p_0, it is

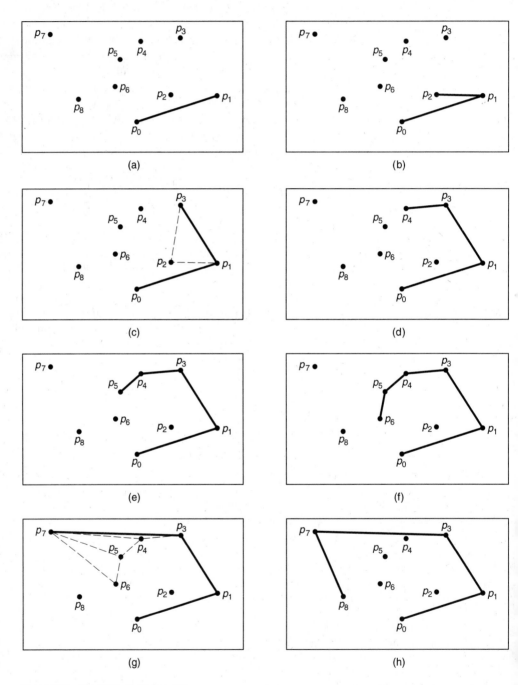

Figure 6.3:   The Graham scan in action.

clear that p_7 is to be inserted and that p_0 is to become its predecessor. But which point is to become p_7's successor? To answer this, we make use of the fact that every vertex must represent a left turn in a counterclockwise traversal of the convex hull boundary. Consider point p_6, our first candidate. Since the angle $\angle p_5 p_6 p_7$ represents a non-left turn (p_7 lies to the right of edge $\overrightarrow{p_5 p_6}$), we remove p_6 from the current hull. Next we consider p_5. Since angle $\angle p_4 p_5 p_7$ also represents a non-left turn, we similarly remove p_5 from the current hull. Similarly, we remove p_4 as well since angle $\angle p_3 p_4 p_7$ is also not a left turn. When we consider point p_3, things are different: Angle $\angle p_1 p_3 p_7$ does in fact represent a left turn, so we have found p_7's successor in the updated current hull (p_3).

Program grahamScan is passed an array pts of n points and returns a polygon representing pts's convex hull. The program works in five stages—the first two comprise the presorting phase, and the remaining three the hull finding phase:

1. Find extreme point p_0.

2. Sort the remaining sites by their polar coordinates relative to p_0.

3. Initialize the current hull.

4. Grow the current hull until it equals the convex hull of all n sites.

5. Convert the current hull to a Polygon object and return it.

The program is defined as follows:

```
Point originPt;

Polygon *grahamScan(Point pts[], int n)
{
// stage 1
  int m = 0;
  for (int i = 1; i < n; i++)
    if ((pts[i].y < pts[m].y) ||
        ((pts[i].y == pts[m].y) && (pts[i].x < pts[m].x)))
      m = i;
  swap(pts[0], pts[m]);
  originPt = pts[0];
// stage 2
  Point **p = new (Point*)[n];
  for (i = 0; i < n; i++)
    p[i] = &pts[i];
  selectionSort(&p[1], n-1, polarCmp); // or any sorting method
// stage 3
  for (i = 1; p[i+1]->classify(*p[0], *p[i]) == BEYOND; i++)
    ;
  Stack<Point*> s;
  s.push(p[0]);
  s.push(p[i]);
// stage 4
  for (i = i+1; i < n; i++) {
    while (p[i]->classify(*s.nextToTop(), *s.top()) != LEFT)
      s.pop();
```

```
      s.push(p[i]);
   }
// stage 5
   Polygon *q = new Polygon;
   while (!s.empty())
      q->insert(*s.pop());
   delete p;
   return q;
}
```

Stage 1 is straightforward. In stage 2 we allocate array p and initialize its elements to point to the `Points` in array `pts`. We require an array of *pointers* so we can employ one of our generalized sorting routines. Then we sort array p based on comparison function `polarCmp`, which was defined in section 5.2 in the context of finding star polygons in point sets. Recall that the global variable `originPt` is used to communicate the origin point—in this case point p_0—to function `polarCmp`.

Stages 3 and 4 maintain the current hull in a stack s. Letting set $S_i = \{p_0, p_1, \ldots, p_i\}$, the stack represents the current hull $\mathcal{CH}(S_i)$ as follows. Where the points in the stack are labeled $s_1, s_2, \ldots, s_t$ from the bottom of the stack to the top, the stack satisfies these two *stack conditions*:

1. $p_0 = s_1, s_2, \ldots, s_t = p_i$ are the vertices of current hull $\mathcal{CH}(S_i)$ in counterclockwise rotation, and

2. edge $\overrightarrow{s_1 s_2}$ is an edge of the final convex hull $\mathcal{CH}(S)$.

Stage 3 establishes these conditions initially. The `for` loop steps along ray $\overrightarrow{p_0 p_1}$ until arriving at the last (most distant) p_i along the ray; then it pushes p_0 and p_i onto the stack. Stack condition 1 is satisfied because line segment $\overline{p_0 p_i}$ *is* the convex hull of S_i since points $p_1, \ldots, p_{i-1}$ lie between p_0 and p_i. Stack condition 2 is satisfied because $\overline{p_0 p_i}$ is an edge of $\mathcal{CH}(S)$.

In stage 4, illustrated in Figure 6.4, point p_i is processed to produce current hull $\mathcal{CH}(S_i)$. Program `grahamScan` pops $s_t, s_{t-1}, \ldots, s_{k+1}$ from the stack until reaching s_k, the topmost point of the stack such that angle $\angle s_{k-1} s_k p_i$ represents a left turn. Since these points that are popped lie in the interior of triangle $\triangle p_0 p_i s_k$ or along one of the edges $\overline{p_0 p_i}$ or $\overline{p_i s_k}$, none of them can be a vertex of $\mathcal{CH}(S_i)$. Since only these points and none others are removed from the stack, the points that remain, together with p_i, are the vertices of $\mathcal{CH}(S_i)$. Because stack condition 1 ensures that $s_1, \ldots, s_k$ are ordered correctly within the stack and p_i follows these in the polar angle ordering, the new stack contents $(s_1, \ldots, s_k, p_i)$ are correctly ordered in counterclockwise rotation. It follows that stack condition 1 is maintained.

The purpose of stack condition 2 is to guarantee that s_k exists. Since edge $\overrightarrow{s_1 s_2}$ is an edge of $\mathcal{CH}(S)$, every p_i that gets processed lies to the left of $\overrightarrow{s_1 s_2}$. Since angle $\angle s_1 s_2 p_i$ represents a left turn, it follows that s_k exists for some $k \geq 2$. Moreover, since the original s_1 and s_2 are never popped from the stack, stack condition 2 is maintained.

Stage 5 of `grahamScan` grows a `Polygon` object q by iteratively popping a point from the stack and inserting it into q. By stack condition 1, the points are popped in clockwise order.

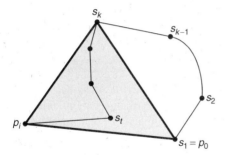

Figure 6.4:   Inserting point p_i to produce current hull $\mathcal{CH}(S_i)$.

With regard to running time, it is easy to see that stages 1, 3, and 5 each take $O(n)$ time. In stage 4, the body of the `while` loop is performed at most once per point (once popped from the stack, a point never returns to the stack a second time). Hence stage 4 also takes $O(n)$ time. Therefore, total running time is dominated by the initial sort (stage 2), so Graham scan runs in $O(n \log n)$ time if an appropriate sorting method is used. It is noteworthy that Graham scan runs in linear time if the point set is known to be sorted initially.

6.4   Removing Hidden Surfaces: The Depth-Sort Algorithm

6.4.1 Preliminaries

Three-dimensional computer graphics typically involves modeling a scene in space and then forming an image of the scene in a process known as *rendering*. To render, we select a position in space from which to view the scene and, based on this viewing position and several additional viewing parameters, project the scene into a plane, where the image is formed.

What makes rendering challenging is that some of the objects in the scene, and portions of other objects, are hidden from view and so should not appear in the final image. Some of the objects may lie outside the field of view (identifying these objects is the problem of clipping). In addition, some objects (and portions of objects) may be hidden by other opaque objects that lie between them and the viewing position. The problem of identifying these hidden objects is known as the *hidden surface removal* problem.

In this section we solve the hidden surface removal problem through *depth sorting*. The scene will be represented by a collection of triangles in space. This model is in wide use, in large part because it accommodates a wide range of scenes. For instance, any surface can be approximated by a mesh of triangles which, by making the mesh sufficiently fine, can be made to resemble the surface as closely as desired. Even relatively coarse meshes are useful in practice since shading methods applied during rendering can greatly enhance the impression of the surface's curvature.

The projection we will employ maps points in space along lines parallel to the z-axis: Point (x,y,z) projects to point $(x,y,0)$. This projection, known as *orthographic parallel projection*, can be assumed without loss of generality: Given the set of viewing parameters describing some desired view, a sequence of transformations can be performed which reduces the original rendering problem to one involving orthographic parallel projection.

By convention, we will assume that the viewing position is in the $-z$-half-space (behind the xy-plane), that the scene lies in the $+z$-half-space (beyond the xy-plane), and that depth increases—objects are farther away—as z increases.

We will further assume that the triangles in the scene are oriented such that they are viewed from their negative half-spaces—their normal vectors point away from the viewing position (Figure 6.5). This assumption is less limiting than might first appear. When using a mesh of triangles to model the surface of a solid, the triangles are oriented consistently, relative to the solid's interior: for example, the normals all point toward the interior of the solid. In a prerendering step known as *backface culling*, we discard those triangles whose normals point toward the viewing position since they cannot be seen—the solid's interior lies between each such triangle and the viewing position. We are left with only those triangles whose normals point away from the viewing position. Even when a mesh of triangles is used to represent a "free-floating" surface that is not the boundary of a solid (so there exists no solid to occlude triangles), the triangles can be reoriented to ensure that their normals point away from the viewing position.

6.4.2 The Depth-Sort Algorithm

Hidden surface removal is most easily performed on a set of triangles which do not overlap in z-coordinate. First sort the triangles by decreasing z (from far to near), and then paint them in this order. If a triangle is visible, it will paint over whatever it hides, and nothing will be painted over it. This approach is sometimes called the *painter's algorithm* since it is how a painter might first paint the background, then the scene at intermediate depth, and finally the foreground. Each layer is painted on top of the previous, more distant layer.

The painter's algorithm exploits the fact that it is safe to paint something if it does not hide anything to be painted later. We will say that a list of triangles is *visibility ordered* if it is safe to paint each one in the given order—that is, no triangle hides any that follow. More formally, a list of triangles $P_1 \prec P_2 \prec \cdots \prec P_n$ is visibility ordered with respect to viewpoint p if and only if this holds: If $P_i \prec P_j$, then P_i does not obscure P_j when viewed from p. *Depth sorting* is the process of arranging a set of triangles into visibility order.

Some sets of triangles admit more than one visibility ordering. A simple example is that of two triangles, neither of which obscures the other. Other sets admit a unique visibility ordering, and others, as we shall see shortly, admit none at all.

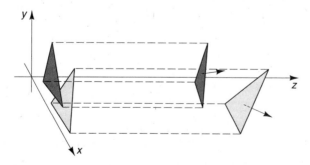

Figure 6.5:   The setting for hidden surface removal.

Hidden surface removal is more difficult to perform on a set of triangles which overlap in z-coordinate. Based on the painter's algorithm, we would like to determine which of two given triangles obscures the other by comparing canonical values selected from each triangle's z-extent. (A triangle's *z-extent* is the range of z-coordinates it spans; equivalently, it is the perpendicular projection of the triangle's bounding box into the z-axis.) However, this does not work. If, for example, we use z^M, the maximum value in each triangle's z-extent, the triangles in Figure 6.6 would be ordered $A \prec B$ since $z_A^M > z_B^M$. But this is not a visibility ordering since A obscures B and so cannot be safely painted first (their actual visibility ordering is $B \prec A$). This example illustrates that depth sorting generally requires that a given list of triangles be rearranged, even if the original list is tentatively ordered from far to near. The algorithm we will present rearranges the order of a tentatively ordered list by performing a sequence of *shuffle* operations.

Some sets of triangles admit no visibility ordering at all. If two triangles in the set interpenetrate each other as in Figure 6.7a, no visibility ordering is possible—neither triangle can precede the other in any legal visibility ordering since each obscures the other. A visibility ordering may be impossible even if the triangles are assumed not to interpenetrate each other. None of the triangles of Figure 6.7b can precede the other two in any legal visibility ordering since each obscures one of the remaining two.

The way out of this impasse involves *refining* the original set of triangles: splitting certain triangles into triangular pieces so the set of triangles which results *can* be depth sorted. If triangle A of Figure 6.7a is split by the plane of triangle B into pieces A_1, A_2, and A_3 (as in Figure 6.8a), the set of triangles that results is visibility ordered by $A_1 \prec B \prec A_2 \prec A_3$. If triangle C of Figure 6.7b is split by the plane of D into C_1, C_2, and C_3 (Figure 6.8b), we have the visibility ordering $C_1 \prec D \prec E \prec C_2 \prec C_3$. The set of

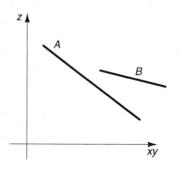

Figure 6.6: The visibility ordering of these triangles is $B \prec A$ even though $z_A^M > z_B^M$.

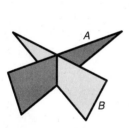

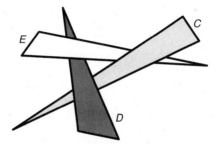

Figure 6.7:   No collection of triangles containing either of these configurations can be visibility ordered.

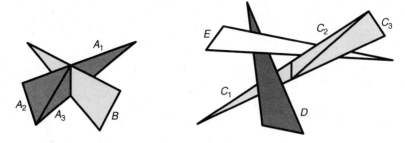

Figure 6.8: Refinements of Figure 6.7 are visibility ordered by (a) $A_1 \prec B \prec A_2 \prec A_3$ and (b) $C_1 \prec D \prec E \prec C_2 \prec C_3$.

triangles that results from splitting a set of triangles into pieces is known as a *refinement* of the original set.

The aforementioned ideas form the basis of our algorithm for depth sorting a set of triangles. First, we sort the triangles according to their maximum depths z^M from far to near. The resulting list represents a first approximation (or tentative) visibility ordering. Then we transform this into a true visibility ordering by incrementally shuffling the list and, whenever necessary, refining the list.

The algorithm works like this. Let S be the tentatively visibility ordered list, and let p be the first triangle in S. We wish to decide whether it is safe to paint p—that is, whether p does not obscure q for every $q \in S$. To do so, we compare p to each triangle q in list S whose z-extent overlaps that of p. For each triangle q, we ask whether it is possible for p to hide q. If it turns out that p obscures none of the triangles q, it is safe to paint p; hence we remove p from S and paint it, and then resume the algorithm using the first element in list S as the new p.

Alternatively, if it happens that p obscures some triangle q, we check whether q also obscures p or whether q has already been shuffled once. If either condition holds, we split q into pieces by the plane of p and then, within list S, replace q by its pieces (the refinement operation). (It is necessary to check whether q has already been shuffled in order to prevent an infinite loop to which configurations like those of Figure 6.7 would otherwise lead.) If neither condition holds, then the positions of p and q are interchanged in list S (the shuffle operation), and the algorithm resumes with q, now the first element of list S, serving as the new p.

Program depthSort depth sorts an array tri of n pointer-to-triangles and returns a visibility-ordered list of triangles. The tentatively ordered list of triangles is pointed to by local variable s, and the final depth-ordered list by variable result:

```
List<Triangle3D*> *depthSort(Triangle3D *tri[], int n)
{
    List<Triangle3D*> *result = new List<Triangle3D*>;
    Triangle3D **t = new (Triangle3D*)[n];
    for (int i = 0; i < n; i++)
        t[i] = new Triangle3D(*tri[i]);
    insertionSort(t, n, triangleCmp);
    List<Triangle3D*> *s = arrayToList(t, n);
    while (s->length() > 0) {    /* while */
```

```
        Triangle3D *p = s->first();
        Triangle3D *q = s->next();
        int hasShuffled = FALSE;
        for (; !s->isHead()&&overlappingExtent(p,q,2); q=s->next())
           if (mayObscure(p, q)) {
              if (q->mark || mayObscure(q, p))
                 refineList(s, p);
              else {
                 shuffleList(s, p);
                 hasShuffled = TRUE;
                 break;
              }
           }
        if (!hasShuffled) {
           s->first();
           s->remove();
           result->append(p);
        }
   }   /* while */
   return result;
}
```

Sorting is used to construct the initial tentatively ordered list. The comparison function `triangleCmp` compares two `Triangle3D`s according to their maximum depth:

```
int triangleCmp(Triangle3D *a, Triangle3D *b)
{
   if (a->boundingBox().dest.z > b->boundingBox().dest.z)
      return -1;
   else if (a->boundingBox().dest.z < b->boundingBox().dest.z)
      return 1;
   else
      return 0;
}
```

Function `arrayToList`, which was defined in Chapter 3, is then used to transform the sorted array of pointers into a list.

Function call `overlappingExtent(p,q,2)` returns TRUE if triangles p and q overlap in z-coordinate (the third argument specifies the coordinate via one of the indices 0, 1, or 2). The implementation of function `overlappingExtent` uses the fact that two intervals in the real number line intersect if and only if the left endpoint of one of the intervals is contained in the other interval:

```
bool overlappingExtent(Triangle3D *p, Triangle3D *q, int i)
{
   Edge3D pbox = p->boundingBox();
   Edge3D qbox = q->boundingBox();
   return (((pbox.org[i] <= qbox.org[i]) &&
```

```
                    (qbox.org[i] <= pbox.dest[i])) ||
                  ((qbox.org[i] <= pbox.org[i]) &&
                   (pbox.org[i] <= qbox.dest[i])));
}
```

We shuffle list s with function shuffleList, which exchanges the first item p in
the list with the item q occurring in the list's window:

```
void shuffleList(List<Triangle3D*> *s, Triangle3D *p)
{
    Triangle3D *q = s->val();
    q->mark = TRUE;
    s->val(p);
    s->first();
    s->val(q);
}
```

6.4.3 Comparing Two Triangles

The depthSort program uses the function call mayObscure(p,q) to determine whether
triangle p potentially hides triangle q. Function mayObscure performs five tests in order
of increasing complexity. As soon as one of these tests succeeds, p has been shown not to
obscure q. Alternatively, if none of the five tests succeeds, then p potentially obscures q.
The five tests are as follows:

1. Do the x-extents of p and q not overlap?
2. Do the y-extents of p and q not overlap?
3. Is p entirely behind or on the plane of q?
4. Is q entirely in front of or on the plane of p?
5. Do the projections of p and q not overlap?

Tests 3 and 4 are shown in Figure 6.9.

Most of the machinery for performing the tests is already in place. Tests 1 and 2
make use of the triangles' bounding boxes to compare x-extents and y-extents, respectively.

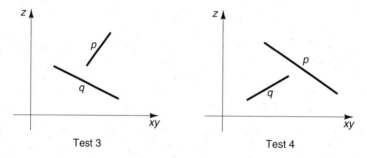

Test 3   Test 4

Figure 6.9:   Two of the tests checked by mayObscure: (Test 3) p is behind the plane of q; (test 4)
q is in front of the plane of p.

Test 3 classifies the three vertices of p with respect to the plane of q, and it succeeds if none of the vertices lies in front of the plane (in q's negative half-space). Similarly, test 4 succeeds if none of q's vertices lies behind the plane of p (in p's positive half-space). Test 5 is performed using function `projectionsOverlap`, which returns TRUE if the two triangles it is passed overlap in their projection.

Function `mayObscure` applies the tests to triangles p and q until one of the tests succeeds. If none succeeds, the function returns TRUE, indicating that it is possible for p to obscure q.

```
bool mayObscure(Triangle3D *p, Triangle3D *q)
{
    int i;
 // case 1
    if (!overlappingExtent(p, q, 0))
       return FALSE;
 // case 2
    if (!overlappingExtent(p, q, 1))
       return FALSE;
 // case 3
    for (i = 0; i < 3; i++)
       if ((*p)[i].classify(*q) == NEGATIVE)
          break;
    if (i == 3) return FALSE;
 // case 4
    for (i = 0; i < 3; i++)
       if ((*q)[i].classify(*p) == POSITIVE)
          break;
    if (i == 3) return FALSE;
 // case 5
    if (!projectionsOverlap(p, q))
       return FALSE;
    return TRUE;
}
```

Let us focus on test 5. To decide whether the projections of triangles p and q overlap, we first project the triangles into the xy-plane, producing the plane triangles P and Q. We then apply three tests to P and Q to see if they overlap. If any of the tests succeed, the projections of p and q overlap; otherwise they do not. The three tests are as follows:

1. Does some vertex of P lie in Q?

2. Does some vertex of Q lie in P?

3. Does some edge of P intersect some edge of Q?

The first test detects the case that P is contained in the interior of Q, and the second test detects the case that Q is contained in the interior of P. Overlap due to any remaining configuration is detected by the third test (although some of these configurations will first be picked up by the first or second test).

Function `projectionsOverlap` is passed triangles p and q and returns TRUE if and only if their projections overlap. It uses function `project` (defined in section 4.6) to obtain the projections of *p* and *q*:

```
bool projectionsOverlap(Triangle3D *p, Triangle3D *q)
{
    int answer = TRUE;
    Polygon *P = project(*p, 0, 1);
    Polygon *Q = project(*q, 0, 1);
    for (int i = 0; i < 3; i++, P->advance(CLOCKWISE))
        if (pointInConvexPolygon(P->point(), *Q))
            goto finish;
    for (i = 0; i < 3; i++, Q->advance(CLOCKWISE))
        if (pointInConvexPolygon(Q->point(), *P))
            goto finish;
    for (i = 0; i < 3; i++, P->advance(CLOCKWISE)) {
        double t;
        Edge ep = P->edge();
        for (int j = 0; j < 3; j++, Q->advance(CLOCKWISE)) {
            Edge eq = Q->edge();
            if (ep.cross(eq, t) == SKEW_CROSS)
                goto finish;
        }
    }
    answer = FALSE;
 finish:
    delete P;
    delete Q;
    return answer;
}
```

6.4.4 Refining a List of Triangles

In the depth-sort algorithm, refining list s involves splitting triangle q by the plane of candidate polygon p and then replacing q (within list s) by the two or three pieces into which it has been split. This is accomplished by function `refineList`, which is passed the current list s and the candidate triangle p. Triangle q is assumed to be the current item of list s:

```
void refineList(List<Triangle3D*> *s, Triangle3D *p)
{
    Triangle3D q = s->val();
    Triangle3D *q1, *q2, *q3;
    int nbrPieces = splitTriangleByPlane(*q, *p, q1, q2, q3);
    if (nbrPieces > 1) {
        delete s->remove();
        s->insert(q1);
        s->insert(q2);
```

```
      if (nbrPieces == 3)
         s->insert(q3);
   }

}
```

Triangle splitting is performed by function `splitTriangleByPlane`, defined next. Input parameters consist of triangle q to be split and splitter triangle p. The pieces of q produced by the function are passed back through the reference parameters q1, q2, and q3. (Parameter q3 is not used if q is split into only two pieces.) The function returns the number of pieces it yields:

```
int splitTriangleByPlane(Triangle3D &q, Triangle3D &p,
      Triangle3D* &q1, Triangle3D* &q2, Triangle3D* &q3)
{
   Point3D crossingPts[2];
   int edgeIds[2], cl[3];
   double t;
   int nbrPts = 0;
   for (int i = 0; i < 3; i++)
      cl[i] = q[i].classify(p);
   for (i = 0; i < 3; i++)
      if (((cl[i]==POSITIVE) && (cl[(i+1)%3]==NEGATIVE)) ||
          ((cl[i]==NEGATIVE) && (cl[(i+1)%3]==POSITIVE))) {
         Edge3D e(q[i], q[(i+1)%3]);
         e.intersect(p, t);
         crossingPts[nbrPts] = e.point(t);
         edgeIds[nbrPts++] = i;
      }
   if (nbrPts == 0)
      return 1;
   Point3D a = q[edgeIds[0]];
   Point3D b = q[(edgeIds[0]+1) % 3];
   Point3D c = q[(edgeIds[0]+2) % 3];
   if (nbrPts == 1) {
      Point3D d = crossingPts[0];
      q1 = new Triangle3D(d, b, c, q.id);
      q2 = new Triangle3D(a, d, c, q.id);
   } else {
      Point3D d = crossingPts[0];
      Point3D e = crossingPts[1];
      if (edgeIds[1] == (edgeIds[0]+1)%3) {
         q1 = new Triangle3D(d, b, e, q.id);
         q2 = new Triangle3D(a, d, e, q.id);
         q3 = new Triangle3D(a, e, c, q.id);
      } else {
         q1 = new Triangle3D(a, d, e, q.id);
         q2 = new Triangle3D(b, e, d, q.id);
         q3 = new Triangle3D(c, e, b, q.id);
      }
```

```
        }
        return (nbrPts + 1);
    }
```

In the first of two phases, function `splitTriangleByPlane` computes the points at which the plane of p crosses the edges of q. These crossing points are stored in array `crossingPts`, and the edges of q which contain the crossing points are stored in array `edgeIds`. Here an edge is identified by the identifier of its origin vertex (0, 1, or 2) within triangle q.

In its second phase, `splitTriangleByPlane` computes the pieces of q. The vertices of triangle q are labeled a, b, and c relative to the first crossing point d, as in Figure 6.10. Under this labeling scheme, triangle q is then split according to diagram (a) of Figure 6.10 if there is one crossing point d, and according to diagram (b) or (c) if there are two crossing points d and e.

With regard to performance of depth sorting, some configurations of n triangles in space require the algorithm to split the list into as many as $\Theta(n^2)$ pieces. Since the list s can become as long as $\Theta(n^2)$ and processing each candidate triangle p can take time proportional to the length of the list, depth sorting runs in $O(n^4)$ time at worst. However, such configurations are rare, and the algorithm performs well in practice. Furthermore, the list of polygons produced by depth sorting can be piped into any graphics system for display; the same cannot be said of all hidden surface removal methods, for some methods depend on the resolution of the display device.

6.5   Intersection of Convex Polygons

In this section we consider the problem of forming the intersection polygon $P \cap Q$ of two convex polygons P and Q. Except where noted, we will assume that the two polygons intersect non-degenerately: When two edges intersect, they do so at a single point which is not a vertex of either polygon. Given this assumption of non-degeneracy, intersection polygon $P \cap Q$ consists of alternating chains of P and Q. Each pair of consecutive chains is joined at an *intersection point*, at which the boundaries of P and Q cross (Figure 6.11).

There are several solutions to this problem that run in time linear in the total number of vertices. The algorithm we present here is especially clever and easy to implement. Given two convex polygons P and Q as input, the algorithm maintains a window over an edge of P and one over an edge of Q. The idea is to advance these windows around the polygon boundaries while growing the intersection polygon $P \cap Q$: The windows chase each other

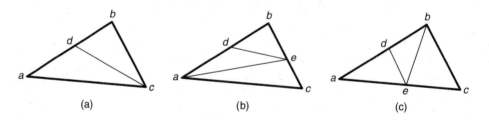

Figure 6.10:   Splitting a triangle into (a) two pieces and (b and c) three pieces.

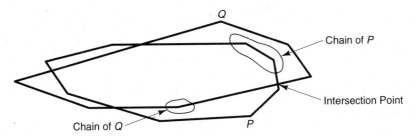

Figure 6.11:   Structure of the intersection polygon $P \cap Q$.

clockwise around their respective polygons in search of intersection points. Since intersection points are discovered in the order they occur around $P \cap Q$, the intersection polygon is complete when some intersection point is discovered for the second time. Alternatively, if not a single intersection point is found after so many iterations, then the polygon boundaries do not intersect. In this case, simple tests are used to determine whether one of the polygons contains the other in its interior or if they do not intersect at all.

The notion of a *sickle* is handy for explaining the algorithm. In Figure 6.12, the sickles are the six shaded regions. Each is bounded by a chain from P and a chain from Q, and each terminates in two consecutive intersection points. The *inner chain* of a sickle is that chain which lies along the boundary of the intersection polygon. Observe that an intersection polygon is encircled by an even number of sickles whose inner chains alternate between P and Q.

In terms of sickles, the algorithm for finding the intersection polygon proceeds in two phases. In phase 1, P's window p and Q's window q are advanced clockwise until positioned over edges that belong to the same sickle. Each window starts off in arbitrary position. (For brevity, we will use p to denote both P's window as well as the edge in the window. Thus "the origin of p" refers to the origin of the edge in P's window, and the instruction "advance p" means we are to advance P's window to the next edge. Similarly, q denotes both Q's window as well as the edge in the window. We will also sometimes refer to edges p and q as *current edges*.)

In phase 2, p and q continue to be advanced clockwise, but this time moving in unison from sickle to adjacent sickle. Before either window leaves the current sickle for the next, edges p and q cross at the intersection point where the two sickles meet.

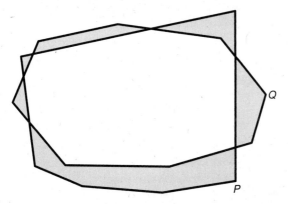

Figure 6.12:   The sickles encircling the intersection polygon.

The intersection polygon is grown during this second phase. Whenever p is about to be advanced, edge p's destination endpoint is inserted into the intersection polygon *if edge p belongs to the current sickle's inner chain*. Similarly, when q is to be advanced, edge q's destination endpoint is inserted if q belongs to the current sickle's inner chain. Whenever p and q cross, the intersection point at which they cross is inserted into the intersection polygon.

The algorithm employs *advance rules* to decide which window to advance in each iteration. The advance rules depend on the following notion: An edge a is said to *aim* at edge b if the infinite line determined by b lies in front of a (Figure 6.13). Edge a aims at b if either of these conditions hold:

- $\vec{a} \times \vec{b} \geq 0$ and point a.dest does not lie to the right of $\vec{b}$, or
- $\vec{a} \times \vec{b} < 0$ and point a.dest does not lie to the left of $\vec{b}$.

Note that $\vec{a} \times \vec{b} \geq 0$ corresponds to the case in which the counterclockwise angle from vector $\vec{a}$ to $\vec{b}$ measures less than 180 degrees.

Function aimsAt returns TRUE if and only if edge a aims at edge b. The parameter aclass indicates the classification of endpoint a.dest relative to edge b. The parameter crossType equals COLLINEAR if and only if edges a and b are collinear:

```
bool aimsAt(Edge &a, Edge &b, int aclass, int crossType)
{
     Point2 va = a.dest - a.org;
     Point2 vb = b.dest - b.org;
     if (crossType != COLLINEAR) {
        if ((va.x * vb.y) >= (vb.x * va.y))
           return (aclass != RIGHT);
        else
           return (aclass != LEFT);
     } else {
        return (aclass != BEYOND);
     }
}
```

If edges a and b are collinear, a aims at b if endpoint a.dest does not lie beyond b. This is used to ensure that a is advanced, rather than b, when the two edges intersect degenerately

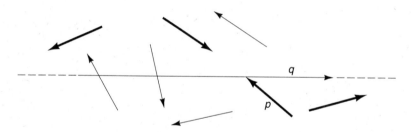

Figure 6.13:   Only the thickened edges aim at edge q; the other edges do not.

in more than one point. By allowing a to "catch up" with b, we ensure that no intersection points are skipped over.

Let us return to our discussion of the advance rules. The advance rules are designed so that the intersection point which should be found next is not skipped over. They distinguish between the current edge which *may* contain the next intersection point and the current edge which *cannot possibly* contain the next intersection point; the window over the latter edge is then (safely) advanced. The advance rules distinguish between the following four cases, illustrated in Figure 6.14. In this account, edge a is considered *outside* edge b if endpoint a.dest lies to the left of b.

1. *p and q aim at each other*: Advance the window over whichever edge, p or q, is outside the other. In Figure 6.14a, we advance the window over p. The next intersection point cannot lie on edge p since p is outside the intersection polygon.

2. *p aims at q but q does not aim at p*: Insert p's destination endpoint into the intersection polygon if p is not outside q, and then advance window p. In Figure 6.14b, p cannot contain the *next* intersection point (although it may contain *some* intersection point if p is not outside q). The figure shows the situation in which edge p, whose window is to be advanced, *is not* outside edge q.

3. *q aims at p but p does not aim at q*: Insert q's destination endpoint into the intersection polygon if q is not outside p, and then advance window q (Figure 6.14c). This case is symmetric to the previous case. The figure shows the situation in which edge q, whose window is to be advanced, *is* outside edge p.

4. *p and q do not aim at each other*: Advance the window over whichever current edge is outside the other. In Figure 6.14d we advance window p since edge p is outside edge q.

Figure 6.15 illustrates the algorithm at work. Each edge bears label i if reached in iteration i (some edges bear two labels since they are reached twice). The two initial edges are labeled 0. In this figure, phase 2—when the two current edges belong to the same sickle—begins after three iterations.

Program convexPolygonIntersect implements the algorithm. The program is passed polygons P and Q and returns a pointer to the resulting intersection polygon R. The call to function advance is used to advance one of the two current edges and to insert

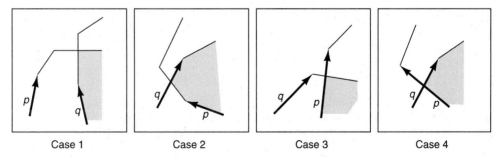

| Case 1 | Case 2 | Case 3 | Case 4 |

Figure 6.14:   The four advance rules: (Case 1) Advance p, (Case 2) advance p, (Case 3) advance q, and (Case 4) advance p.

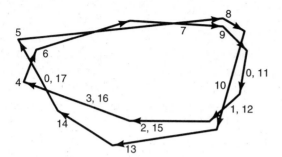

Figure 6.15:   Finding the intersection polygon. An edge bears label i if it is reached in iteration i. The two initial edges are labeled 0.

conditionally the edge's destination endpoint into polygon R. The windows built into class Polygon are used.

```
enum { UNKNOWN, P_IS_INSIDE, Q_IS_INSIDE };

Polygon *convexPolygonIntersect(Polygon &P, Polygon &Q)
{
    Polygon *R;
    Point iPnt, startPnt;
    int inflag = UNKNOWN;
    int phase = 1;
    int maxItns = 2 * (P.size() + Q.size());
    for (int i = 1; (i<=maxItns) || (phase==2); i++) { // for
        Edge p = P.edge();
        Edge q = Q.edge();
        int pclass = p.dest.classify(q);
        int qclass = q.dest.classify(p);
        int crossType = crossingPoint(p, q, iPnt);
        if (crossType == SKEW_CROSS) {
            if (phase == 1) {
                phase = 2;
                R = new Polygon;
                R->insert(iPnt);
                startPnt = iPnt;
            } else if (iPnt != R->point()) {
                if (iPnt != startPnt)
                    R->insert(iPnt);
                else
                    return R;
            }
            if (pclass==RIGHT) inflag = P_IS_INSIDE;
            else if (qclass==RIGHT) inflag = Q_IS_INSIDE;
            else inflag = UNKNOWN;
        } else if ((crossType==COLLINEAR) &&
                    (pclass!=BEHIND) &&
                    (qclass!=BEHIND))
```

```
        inflag = UNKNOWN;
    bool pAIMSq = aimsAt(p, q, pclass, crossType);
    bool qAIMSp = aimsAt(q, p, qclass, crossType);
    if (pAIMSq && qAIMSp) {
        if ((inflag==Q_IS_INSIDE) ||
            ((inflag==UNKNOWN) && (pclass==LEFT)))
            advance(P, *R, FALSE);
        else
            advance(Q, *R, FALSE);
    } else if (pAIMSq) {
        advance(P, *R, inflag==P_IS_INSIDE);
    } else if (qAIMSp) {
        advance(Q, *R, inflag==Q_IS_INSIDE);
    } else {
        if ((inflag==Q_IS_INSIDE) ||
            ((inflag==UNKNOWN) && (pclass==LEFT)))
            advance(P, *R, FALSE);
        else
            advance(Q, *R, FALSE);
    }
}    // for
if (pointInConvexPolygon(P.point(), Q))
    return new Polygon(P);
else if (pointInConvexPolygon(Q.point(), P))
    return new Polygon(Q);
return new Polygon;
}
```

If $2(|P|+|Q|)$ iterations are performed without some intersection point being found, the main loop is exited since the polygon boundaries are then known not to cross. The subsequent calls to pointInConvexPolygon are used to determine whether $P \subset Q$, $Q \subset P$, or $P \cap Q = \emptyset$. Alternatively, if some intersection point iPnt is found, then the algorithm proceeds to grow the intersection polygon R, stopping only when iPnt is reached for the second time.

Variable inflag indicates which of the two input polygons is currently inside the other—that is, the polygon whose current edge lies in the inner chain of the current sickle. Moreover, inflag is set to UNKNOWN during phase 1, and whenever the two current edges are collinear and overlap. It is updated whenever a new intersection point is discovered.

Procedure advance advances the current edge of polygon A, representing either P or Q. The procedure also inserts the edge's destination endpoint x into intersection polygon R, if A is inside the other polygon and x was not the last point inserted into R:

```
void advance(Polygon2 &A, Polygon2 &R, int inside)
{
    A.advance(CLOCKWISE);
    if (inside && (R.point() != A.point()))
        R.insert(A.point());
}
```

6.5.1 Analysis and Correctness

The correctness proof bears out what is most remarkable about this algorithm: that the same set of advance rules works for *both* phases. The advance rules get p and q into the same sickle, and then they advance p and q in unison from sickle to sickle.

Correctness of the algorithm follows from two assertions:

1. If current edges p and q belong to the same sickle, then the next intersection point—at which the sickle terminates—will be found, and it will be found next.

2. If the boundaries of P and Q intersect, current edges p and q will cross at some intersection point after no more than $2(|P| + |Q|)$ iterations.

Assertion 2 ensures that the algorithm will find some intersection point, if one exists. Since edges p and q belong to the same sickle if they cross, assertion 1 then ensures that the remaining intersection points will be found in order.

Let us show assertion 1 first. Suppose that p and q belong to the same sickle and that q reaches the next intersection point first, before p. We will show that q then remains stationary while p catches up to the intersection point via a sequence of advances. Two cases can occur. First, assume that p is outside q (Figure 6.16a). In this case, q remains fixed while p is advanced by zero or more applications of rule 4, then by zero or more applications of rule 1, and then by zero or more applications of rule 2. In the second case, assume that p is not outside q (Figure 6.16b). In this case, q remains fixed while p is advanced by zero or more applications of rule 2. In the symmetric situation, where p reaches the next intersection point before q, edge q remains stationary while p catches up. This is shown as before, where the roles of p and q are swapped, and rule 3 replaces rule 2. Assertion 1 follows.

To show assertion 2, let us assume that the boundaries of P and Q intersect. After $|P| + |Q|$ iterations, either p or q must have traversed full circle around its polygon. Let us assume that p has. At some time, p must have been positioned such that it contains an intersection point at which polygon Q passes from the outside of P to its inside. This is the case because there are at least two intersection points and they alternate in direction of crossing. Let q be the edge in Q's window when p was so positioned.

In Figure 6.17, the boundary of Q is partitioned into two chains C_r and C_s. The first chain, C_r, terminates in edge q_r, the edge of Q that enters P through edge p. The other chain, C_s, terminates in edge q_s, whose destination vertex both lies to the right of, and

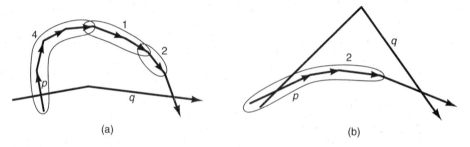

(a)   (b)

Figure 6.16:   Advancing to the next intersection point.

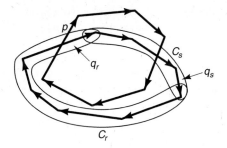

Figure 6.17: Illustrations for the proof that an intersection point is found if the boundaries of P and Q intersect.

is farthest from, the infinite line determined by edge p. There are two cases to consider, depending on which of the two chains edge q belongs to:

Case 1 $[q \in C_r]$ In this case, p remains fixed while q advances by zero or more applications of rule 3, then rule 4, then rule 1, and finally rule 3, at which time the intersection point is found.

Case 2 $[q_j \in C_s]$ In this case, q remains fixed while p advances by zero or more applications of rule 2, then rule 4, then rule 1, and finally rule 2, at which time p will be inside q. At this point, p and q may both be advanced a number of times—however, q cannot advance beyond its next intersection point until p first reaches q's previous intersection point (if p has not done so already). Since p and q end up in the same sickle, assertion 1 guarantees that after some number of additional advances, they will cross at the intersection point at which this sickle terminates.

To see why $2(|P|+|Q|)$ iterations are enough to find some intersection point, observe that the initial positions of p and q used to show assertion 2—the boundary of Q entering P through p, and q situated anywhere—were arrived at after no more than $|P|+|Q|$ iterations. (Actually, either this situation or the symmetric situation, in which the roles of p and q are swapped, is achieved after this many iterations.) Since neither p nor q then advances full circle around its polygon before reaching the first intersection point, no more than $|P|+|Q|$ additional iterations are needed.

6.5.2 Robustness

Our algorithm for finding the intersection of two convex polygons is most susceptible to round-off error when the two polygons intersect at a point that is a vertex of one or both polygons. One problem is that intersection points may be missed. In Figure 6.13, edges p and q intersect at point x, the destination endpoint of p. Using exact arithmetic, the parametric value of x along edge p equals one. However, using floating-point arithmetic, the parametric value actually calculated might exceed one by a slight amount, locating x *beyond* edge p. The intersection point would go undetected.

Function `crossingPoint`, used by program `convexPolygonIntersect` to compute the intersection point of two edges, attempts to resolve these sort of difficulties. Given two edges e and f, the function first computes the point at which *infinite lines* e and f intersect. If this point lies in the vicinity of one of the edges' four endpoints, the endpoint is taken to be the point of intersection. As implemented, the function works with parametric values rather than points. By extending the range of parametric values along edge f, the edge is lengthened by distance EPSILON2 in both directions. If the intersection point which would be computed lies within EPSILON2 of one of f's endpoints, the intersection point is "snapped back" to the endpoint. Otherwise the same is done for edge e.

Function crossingPoint returns one of the values COLLINEAR, PARALLEL, SKEW_NO_CROSS, or SKEW_CROSS to indicate the relationship between edges e and f. If SKEW_CROSS is returned, indicating that the edges intersect at a point, their point of intersection is passed back through reference paramter p:

```
#define EPSILON2    1E-10

int crossingPoint(Edge &e, Edge &f, Point &p)
{
    double s,t;
    int classe= e.intersect(f, s);
    if ((classe==COLLINEAR) || (classe==PARALLEL))
        return classe;
    double lene = (e.dest-e.org).length();
    if ((s < -EPSILON2*lene) || (s > 1.0+EPSILON2*lene))
        return SKEW_NO_CROSS;
    f.intersect(e, t);
    double lenf = (f.org-f.dest).length();
    if ((-EPSILON2*lenf <= t) && (t <= 1.0+EPSILON2*lenf)) {
        if (t <= EPSILON2*lenf) p = f.org;
        else if (t >= 1.0-EPSILON2*lenf) p = f.dest;
        else if (s <= EPSILON2*lene) p = e.org;
        else if (s >= 1.0-EPSILON2*lene) p = e.dest;
        else p = f.point(t);
        return SKEW_CROSS;
    } else
        return SKEW_NO_CROSS;
}
```

If it relies on function crossingPoint to calculate points of intersection, our program for finding the intersection of convex polygons works even when the polygons intersect at vertices. This is important to us, for in Chapter 8 we will use the program in applications which unavoidably give rise to this special case. However, note that our program can fail if a vertex of one polygon lies very close—within EPSILON2—to the boundary of the other polygon, without actually touching the boundary.

6.6   Finding Delaunay Triangulations

A *triangulation* of a finite point set S is a triangulation of the convex hull $CH(S)$ that uses all the points of S. The line segments of the triangulation may not cross—they may meet only at shared endpoints, points of S. Since the line segments enclose triangles, we usually refer to them as edges. Figure 6.18 depicts two triangulations of the same set of points (ignore the circles in the figure for the moment).

Given a point set S, we have seen that the points of S can be partitioned into *boundary points*—those points of S which lie on the boundary of the convex hull $CH(S)$—and *interior points*—those points which lie in the interior of $CH(S)$. The edges of a triangulation of S can be classified similarly, as *hull edges* and *interior edges*. The hull edges are those edges that lie along the boundary of the convex hull $CH(S)$, and the interior edges are the remaining edges, those that pierce the convex hull interior. Note that every hull edge connects two boundary points, whereas an interior edge can connect two points of either type; in particular, if an interior edge connects two boundary points, it is a chord of $CH(S)$. Observe also that every edge of the triangulation is met by two *faces*: each interior edge by two triangles, and each hull edge by one triangle and the unbounded plane.

All point sets except the most trivial ones admit more than one triangulation. Remarkably, every triangulation of a given point set contains the same number of triangles, as the following theorem indicates:

Theorem 3 (Point-Set Triangulation Theorem)   *Suppose point set S contains $n \geq 3$ points, not all collinear. Suppose further that i of the points are interior [lying in the interior of $CH(S)$]. Then every triangulation of S contains exactly $n + i - 2$ triangles.*

To see why this theorem is true, first consider triangulating the $n - i$ boundary points. Since they are the vertices of a convex polygon, any such triangulation contains $(n - i) - 2$ triangles. (This is not hard to see; in Chapter 8 we will show that every triangulation of *any* m-sided polygon—convex or nonconvex—consists of $m - 2$ triangles.) Now consider incorporating the remaining i interior points into the triangulation, one at a time. We claim that adding each such point increases the number of triangles by two. The two cases illustrated in Figure 6.19 can occur. First, if the point falls in the interior of some triangle, the triangle is replaced by three new triangles. Second, if the point falls on some edge of the triangulation, each of the two triangles that meet the edge is replaced by two new triangles. It follows that after all i points are inserted, the total number of triangles is $(n-i-2)+(2i)$, or simply $n + i - 2$.

In this section we present an algorithm to construct a special kind of triangulation known as a *Delaunay triangulation*. Such triangulations are well balanced in the sense that the triangles tend toward equiangularity. In Figure 6.18, for example, triangulation (a) is

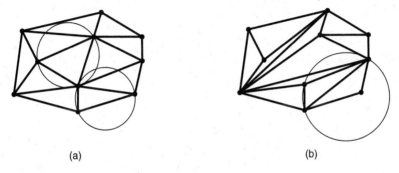

(a)   (b)

Figure 6.18:   Two triangulations of the same set of points.

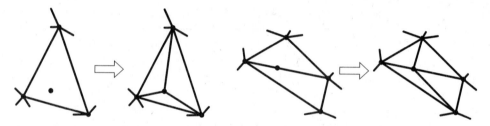

Figure 6.19:   The two ways in which an interior site can be incorporated into a triangulation.

Delaunay whereas triangulation (b), which contains some long "slivers," is not Delaunay. Figure 6.20 shows the Delaunay triangulation of a large point set.

To define *Delaunay triangulation*, we need some new definitions. A set of points is *cocircular* if there exists some circle on whose boundary all the points lie. If the circle is unique, it is called the *circumcircle* of the points. The circumcircle of a triangle is simply the circumcircle of its three (non-collinear) vertices. A circle is said to be *point free* with respect to a given point set S if none of the points of S lies in the circle's interior. Points of S may, however, lie along the boundary of a point-free circle.

A triangulation of point set S is a *Delaunay triangulation* if the circumcircle of every triangle is point free. In triangulation (a) of Figure 6.18, the two circumcircles which have been drawn are clearly point free (you might want to draw the remaining circumcircles to verify that they are also point free). Since the circumcircle shown in triangulation (b) is not point free, the triangulation is not Delaunay.

We will make two assumptions about point set S to simplify the triangulation algorithm. First, to ensure that some triangulation exists, we will assume that S contains at least three points, not all collinear. Second, to ensure that the Delaunay triangulation is unique, we will assume that no four points of S are cocircular. It is easy to see that without this latter assumption, the Delaunay triangulation need not be unique: Four cocircular points admit two different Delaunay triangulations.

Our algorithm works by growing a current triangulation, triangle by triangle. Initially the current triangulation consists of a single hull edge, and at completion the current triangulation equals the Delaunay triangulation. In each iteration, the algorithm seeks a new triangle which attaches to the *frontier* of the current triangulation.

The definition of *frontier* depends on the following scheme, which classifies the edges of the Delaunay triangulation relative to the current triangulation. Every edge is either *dormant*, *live*, or *dead*:

- *Dormant edges*: An edge of the Delaunay triangulation is dormant if it has not yet been discovered by the algorithm.
- *Live edges*: An edge is live if it has been discovered but only one of its faces is known.
- *Dead edges*: An edge is dead if it has been discovered and both of its faces are known.

Initially only a single hull edge is live—the unbounded plane is known to meet it—and all the remaining edges are dormant. As the algorithm proceeds, edges transition from dormant to live, then from live to dead. The *frontier* at each stage consists of the set of live edges.

In each iteration, we select any edge e of the frontier and process it, which consists of seeking edge e's unknown face. If this face turns out to be some triangle t determined

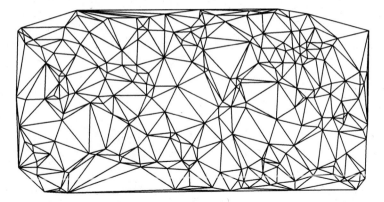

Figure 6.20:   A Delaunay triangulation of 250 points chosen at random within a rectangle.   The triangulation contains 484 triangles.

by the endpoints of e and some third vertex v, edge e dies since both of its faces are now known.   Moreover, each of the other two edges of triangle t transition to the next state: from dormant to live, or from live to dead.   Here vertex v is called the *mate* of edge e. Alternatively, if the unknown face turns out to be the unbounded plane, edge e simply dies. In this case e has no mate.

Figure 6.21 illustrates the algorithm.   In the figure, the action proceeds top to bottom, then left to right.   The frontier in each stage is darkened.

The following program, `delaunayTriangulate`, implements the algorithm.   The program is handed an array `s` of `n` points and returns a list of triangles representing its Delaunay triangulation:

```
List<Polygon*> *delaunayTriangulate(Point s[], int n)
{
    Point p;
    List<Polygon*> *triangles = new List<Polygon*>;
    Dictionary<Edge*> frontier(edgeCmp);
    Edge *e = hullEdge(s, n);
    frontier.insert(e);
    while (!frontier.isEmpty()) {
        e = frontier.removeMin();
        if (mate(*e, s, n, p)) {
            updateFrontier(frontier, p, e->org);
            updateFrontier(frontier, e->dest, p);
            triangles->insert(triangle(e->org, e->dest, p));
        }
        delete e;
    }
    return triangles;
}
```

The triangles which make up the triangulation are maintained in the list `triangles`. The frontier is represented by the dictionary `frontier` of live edges.   Each edge is directed such that its unknown face (yet to be sought) lies to the right of the edge.   The comparison

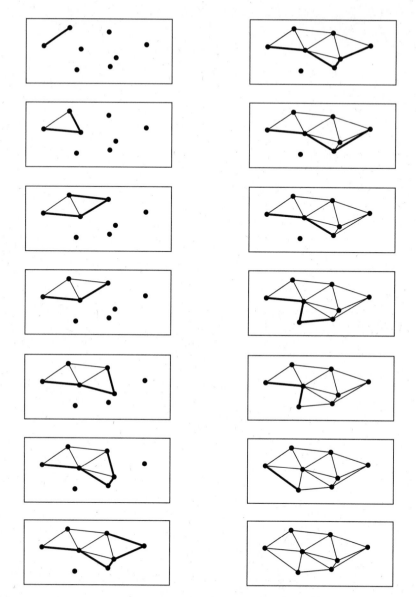

Figure 6.21:   Growing a Delaunay triangulation. The edges of the frontier are highlighted.

function `edgeCmp` is used to perform look-up in the dictionary. It compares two edges'
origins and, if these are the same, then compares their destinations:

```
int edgeCmp(Edge *a, Edge *b)
{
    if (a->org < b->org) return -1;
    if (a->org > b->org) return 1;
    if (a->dest < b->dest) return -1;
```

```
    if (a->dest > b->dest) return 1;
    return 0;
}
```

How does the frontier change from one iteration to the next, and how does function `updateFrontier` update the dictionary to reflect these changes? When a new triangle t attaches to the frontier, the state of the triangle's three edges changes. The edge of t which attaches to the frontier changes from live to dead. Function `updateFrontier` can ignore this edge since it will already have been removed from the dictionary by the call to `removeMin`. Each of the two remaining edges of t changes state from dormant to live if the edge is not already in the dictionary, or from live to dead if the edge is already in the dictionary. Figure 6.22 illustrates both cases. In the figure, we process the live edge $\overrightarrow{af}$ and, upon discovering that point b is its mate, add triangle $\triangle afb$ to the current triangulation. Then we look up edge $\overrightarrow{fb}$ in the dictionary—since it is not present, it has just been discovered for the first time, so its state changes from dormant to live. To update the dictionary, we flip $\overrightarrow{fb}$ so its unknown face lies to its right and then insert the edge into the dictionary. Next we look up edge $\overrightarrow{ba}$ in the dictionary—since it is present, it is already live (its known face is triangle $\triangle abc$). Since its unknown face, triangle $\triangle afb$, has just been discovered, we then remove the edge from the dictionary.

Function `updateFrontier` updates dictionary `frontier`, where the edge from point a to point b changes state:

```
void updateFrontier(Dictionary<Edge*> &frontier,
                    Point &a, Point &b)
{
    Edge *e = new Edge(a, b);
    if (frontier.find(e))
        frontier.remove(e);
    else {
        e->flip();
        frontier.insert(e);
    }
}
```

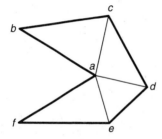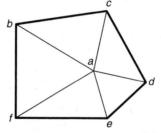

Figure 6.22:   Attaching triangle $\triangle afb$ to live edge $\overline{af}$.

Function `hullEdge` returns a hull edge from among the n points of array s. The function essentially implements the initialization and first iteration of the gift-wrapping method:

```
Edge *hullEdge(Point s[], int n)
{
    int m = 0;
    for (int i = 1; i < n; i++)
        if (s[i] < s[m])
            m = i;
    swap(s[0], s[m]);
    for (m = 1, i = 2; i < n; i++) {
        int c = s[i].classify(s[0], s[m]);
        if ((c == LEFT) || (c == BETWEEN))
            m = i;
    }
    return new Edge(s[0], s[m]);
}
```

Function `triangle` simply constructs and returns a polygon over the three points it is passed:

```
Polygon *triangle(Point &a, Point &b, Point &c)
{
    Polygon *t = new Polygon;
    t->insert(a);
    t->insert(b);
    t->insert(c);
    return t;
}
```

6.6.1 Finding the Mate of an Edge

Let us turn our attention to the problem solved by function `mate`, that of determining whether a given live edge has a mate and, if so, finding it. Consider this: Any edge $\overrightarrow{ab}$ determines the infinite family of circles whose boundaries contain both endpoints a and b. Let $C(a,b)$ denote this family of circles (Figure 6.23).

The centers of the circles in $C(a,b)$ lie along edge $\overrightarrow{ab}$'s perpendicular bisector and can be put into one-to-one correspondence with the points of this bisector. To specify circles of the family, we parameterize the perpendicular bisector and identify each circle by the parametric value of the circle's center. The machinery of Chapter 4 provides a natural parameterization: Rotate edge $\overrightarrow{ab}$ 90 degrees into its perpendicular bisector and then use the parameterization along this edge. In Figure 6.23, we use C_r to denote the circle corresponding to parametric value r.

How do we find the mate of some live edge $\overrightarrow{ab}$ from among the points of S? Suppose that C_r is the circumcircle of $\overrightarrow{ab}$'s known face (in Figure 6.24, triangle $\triangle abc$ is the known

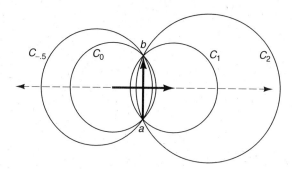

Figure 6.23:   Four circles of the family $C(a,b)$ determined by edge $\overline{ab}$, and their parametric values.

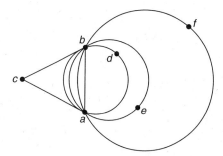

Figure 6.24:   Finding the mate (d) of edge $\overline{ab}$.

face). If $\overrightarrow{ab}$'s known face is unbounded, then $r = -\infty$ and C_r is the half-plane to the left of $\overrightarrow{ab}$. We seek the smallest value $t > r$ such that some point of S (other than a or b) lies in the boundary of C_t. If no such value t exists, then edge $\overrightarrow{ab}$ has no mate. More picturesquely, this is like blowing a two-dimensional bubble through edge $\overrightarrow{ab}$. If the bubble eventually reaches some point of S, this point is the mate of edge $\overrightarrow{ab}$ (point d of Figure 6.24). Alternatively, if no point of S is reached and the bubble expands to fill the half-plane to the right of edge $\overrightarrow{ab}$, then $\overrightarrow{ab}$ has no mate.

Why does this work? Let C_r denote the circumcircle of edge $\overrightarrow{ab}$'s known face, and C_t the circumcircle of edge $\overrightarrow{ab}$'s unknown face. Here $t > r$, and $t = \infty$ if $\overrightarrow{ab}$ has no mate. Is circle C_t point free, as desired? To the left of $\overrightarrow{ab}$, C_t must be point free since C_r is point free and the portion of C_t which lies to the left of $\overrightarrow{ab}$ is contained in C_r. To the right of edge $\overrightarrow{ab}$, C_t must also be point free because, were some point q to lie in its interior, q would lie in the boundary of some circle $C_s \in C(a,b)$, where $r < s < t$, contradicting our choice of t. In our bubble analogy, the expanding bubble would reach point q before reaching the mate of edge $\overrightarrow{ab}$.

To find the mate of edge $\overrightarrow{ab}$, we consider only those points $p \in S$ that lie to the right of $\overrightarrow{ab}$. The center of the circle circumscribing any three points a, b, and p lies at the intersection of the perpendicular bisectors of $\overrightarrow{ab}$ and $\overrightarrow{bp}$. (Here we use the fact that the perpendicular bisectors of a triangle's edges intersect at the center of the triangle's circumcircle.) Rather than compute the center point of the circle, we compute its parametric

value along the perpendicular bisector of edge $\overrightarrow{ab}$. This way we can keep track of the smallest parametric value found so far.

This method is implemented by function `mate`, which returns `TRUE` if edge e has a mate and `FALSE` if it does not. If the mate exists, it is passed back through reference parameter p:

```
bool mate(Edge &e, Point s[], int n, Point &p)
{
    Point *bestp = NULL;
    double t, bestt = FLT_MAX;
    Edge f = e;
    f.rot();    // f is the perpendicular bisector of e
    for (int i = 0; i < n; i++)
        if (s[i].classify(e) == RIGHT) {
            Edge g(e.dest, s[i]);
            g.rot();
            f.intersect(g, t);
            if (t < bestt) {
                bestp = &s[i];
                bestt = t;
            }
        }
    if (bestp) {
        p = *bestp;
        return TRUE;
    }
    return FALSE;
}
```

In function `mate`, variable `bestp` points to the best point examined so far, and `bestt` holds the parametric value of the circle whose boundary contains the point. Note that only those points to the right of edge e are considered.

This algorithm for computing the Delaunay triangulation of a set of n points runs in $O(n^2)$ time because one edge leaves the frontier in each iteration. Since every edge leaves the frontier exactly once—every edge enters the frontier once and later leaves it, never to return—the number of iterations equals the number of edges in the Delaunay triangulation. Now the point-set triangulation theorem implies that any triangulation contains no more than $O(n)$ edges, so the algorithm performs $O(n)$ iterations. Because it spends $O(n)$ time per iteration, the algorithm runs in $O(n^2)$ time.

6.7   Chapter Notes

The gift-wrapping method, also known as Jarvis's march after the manner in which it marches around the convex hull boundary, is presented in [43]. The same basic idea can be

used to find the convex hull of points in higher dimensions [17]; in three dimensions, the method reminds us of how we would go about wrapping a gift. Graham scan is presented in [33].

There are numerous algorithms for finding convex hulls, and this book covers several: insertion hull, which runs in $O(n^2)$ time, where n is the number of points; plane sweep in $O(n \log n)$ time; Graham scan in $O(n \log n)$ time; gift wrapping in $O(nh)$ time, where the convex hull contains $h \leq n$ vertices; and merge hull in $O(n \log n)$ time. One interesting algorithm we will not cover is called *quick hull*. Like the quicksort algorithm after which it is modeled, quick hull takes $O(n^2)$ time in the worst case but $O(n \log n)$ time in the expected case [14, 25, 34]. An optimal convex hull finding algorithm was developed by Kirkpatrick and Seidel [46]. Where the convex hull it produces contains h vertices, the algorithm runs in $O(n \log h)$ time in the worst case.

Because hidden surface removal is usually indispensable for realistic three-dimensional graphics, the problem has been the focus of much research, leading to numerous solutions. Solutions vary with regard to the types of scene models they accommodate, efficiency, degree of realism, and other factors. The depth-sorting method presented in this chapter is from [59]. Other well-known methods include z-buffering [16], Warnock's area subdivision method [86], the Weiler-Atherton "cookie-cutter" method [88], scanline methods [50, 87], and ray tracing. (The computer graphics texts [28, 39, 68] also provide accounts of these algorithms.) In z-*buffering*, the depth of the object displayed by each pixel is maintained in a buffer of depth values (the z-*buffer*). When a new object is to be painted, pixels are selectively updated—only those pixels displaying a more distant object are overwritten by the new object. The z-buffer is also updated with the new (closer) depth values. Because it is both simple and general (in the sense of accommodating a wide range of scene models), z-buffering has been implemented in hardware in several recent graphics systems. In ray tracing, another hidden surface removal method, simulated rays of light are cast into the scene. Ray tracing can be used to create images which include such features as transparency, reflection, specular highlights, and shadows.

The algorithm for finding the intersection of two convex polygons P and Q is presented in [62, 61], although our presentation more closely follows [66]. An earlier algorithm for the same problem is given in [75]. In this method, a vertical line is drawn through every vertex, thereby partitioning the plane into vertical slabs and each polygon into triangles and trapezoids. The intersection problem is then solved within each slab in turn, and the resulting polygonal pieces assembled. Since the intersection of two polygons of bounded size can be computed in constant time and there are no more than $|P| + |Q|$ slabs, this algorithm, like the one we have presented, runs in $O(|P| + |Q|)$ time.

The Delaunay triangulation is dual to the Voronoi diagram, a polygonal decomposition of the plane which assumes a central role in computational geometry. The connection will be explored in Chapter 8, where an algorithm for constructing Voronoi diagrams will be presented. The Delaunay triangulation algorithm presented in this chapter is based on [5, 55]. The algorithm is lifted to three-dimensional space in [24], and a data structure appropriate for lifting it to d-dimensional space is given in [12]. An $O(n \log n)$-time algorithm for constructing Delaunay triangulations in the plane using divide and conquer is presented in [36]. A survey of Voronoi diagrams and Delaunay triangulations is provided by [4].

6.8 Exercises

1. Modify program `giftwrapHull` so the vertices of the convex hull $CH(S)$ it produces consist of all boundary points of set S, not just the extreme points.

2. Modify `grahamScan` to do as described in the previous question.

3. The *depth* of a point p in finite point set S is the number of convex hulls that must be removed until p becomes a boundary point. For instance, the boundary points of S are at depth zero, and those points that become boundary points when the boundary points of S are removed are at depth one. The brute-force approach to determine the depth of all points repeatedly finds the convex hull of the point set and removes the boundary points from the set, until the set is empty. Modify `giftwrapHull` so it computes the depth of every point in $O(n^2)$ time.

4. The *diameter* of a point set is the maximum distance between any pair of points.

   (a) Show that the diameter is realized by a pair of extreme points.

   (b) Give an $O(n \log n)$-time algorithm for computing the diameter of a set of n points in the plane.

5. Describe a configuration of n triangles in space which `depthSort` splits into $\Omega(n^2)$ pieces.

6. In the program `depthSort`, the function call `mayObscure(p,q)` returns TRUE if it is possible for triangle p to obscure triangle q. What is the effect on `depthSort` of making `mayObscure` stronger, such that it returns TRUE if *and only if* p obscures q? What are the advantages and disadvantages of making `mayObscure` stronger?

7. In the program `depthSort`, note that the second call to function `mayObscure` is inefficient, since tests 1, 2, and 5 are repeated unnecessarily. Rewrite the program to remove this inefficiency.

8. Consider this claim concerning the algorithm for finding the intersection polygon of two convex polygons P and Q: If the boundaries of P and Q intersect, then the algorithm finds *all* their intersection points in no more than $2(|P|+|Q|)$ iterations. Either prove this claim and modify program `convexPolygonIntersect` accordingly, or disprove the claim by giving a counterexample.

9. Characterize the inputs for which program `convexPolygonIntersect` fails, in terms of `EPSILON2`.

10. Show how the correctness proof for `convexPolygonIntersect` uses the assumption that input polygons P and Q are convex.

11. Show that if no four points of point set S are cocircular ($|S| \geq 3$), then the Delaunay triangulation of S is unique.

12. Show that any triangulation of a finite point set S contains $3|S|-3-h$ edges, where the boundary of $CH(S)$ contains h edges. [From this it follows that a triangulation contains $O(|S|)$ edges, a fact used in our proof that the Delaunay triangulation algorithm runs in $O(n^2)$ time.]

13. Show that, over all triangulations of finite point set S, the Delaunay triangulation maximizes the minimum measure of the internal angles.

7

Plane-Sweep Algorithms

Plane sweep is a powerful approach for solving problems involving geometric objects in the plane. An imaginary vertical *sweepline* moves from left to right across the objects. As the sweepline proceeds, the problem restricted to the left of the sweepline is solved. A *sweepline structure*, which represents the state of the algorithm for each position of the sweepline, captures whatever information about the problem to the left of the sweepline is needed to extend the solution to the right of the sweepline. When the sweepline has advanced far enough, usually beyond all the objects, the original problem is solved in its entirety.

The sweepline advances in increments, halting at positions known as *event points*. Event points are points in the plane which, when reached by the advancing sweepline, cause the state of the algorithm to change. They may, for instance, be vertices of polygons, endpoints of line segments, or points of intersection, depending on the problem being solved. Event points are maintained in an *event-point schedule*, which is ordered by increasing x-coordinates and is used to decide which event point the sweepline will encounter next. In some applications the event-point schedule is static since all event points can be anticipated prior to sweeping; in others it is dynamic since future event points detected only as the sweep proceeds must be scheduled.

The algorithm undergoes a *transition* at each event point. Transitions encompass three kinds of actions:

1. Update the event-point schedule: Insert just-detected event points, and remove the current event point as well as any others that have become obsolete.

2. Update the sweepline structure to represent state changes in the algorithm due to the new position of the sweepline.

3. Solve more of the problem.

   Plane sweep reduces a problem in two dimensions (the plane) to a series of similar problems in one dimension (the sweepline). The approach is powerful because the one-dimensional problems which result are generally easier to solve than the original two-dimensional problem. Moreover, since the one-dimensional problems change incrementally, in only small, predictable ways from one position of the sweepline to the next, the one-dimensional problems can be treated as a series of related problems amenable to solution by (often standard) abstract data types.

   In this chapter we present several applications of plane sweep. The first application finds all pairs of line segments that intersect, given a collection of line segments in the plane. The second application finds the convex hull of a planar point set using a method similar to, but more efficient than, insertion hull of section 5.3. The third application computes the boundary of the union of a set of rectangles whose sides are parallel to the two axes. The fourth and final application decomposes an arbitrary polygon into monotone subpolygons. If this last application is used together with the algorithm of section 5.8 for triangulating monotone polygons, an efficient method for triangulating *arbitary* polygons results.

7.1   Finding the Intersections of Line Segments

In this section we will tackle the following problem: Given a collection of n line segments in the plane, report all pairs of line segments that intersect. The brute-force solution tests all pairs of line segments for intersection. This takes $\Theta(n^2)$ time, since there are $\frac{n(n-1)}{2}$ pairs and each intersection test can be performed in constant time. In this section we will use plane sweep to solve the problem in $O((r + n) \log n)$ time, where r equals the number of pairs reported. Plane sweep outperforms the brute-force approach (when r is small) by performing fewer intersection tests: It avoids testing pairs of line segments that lie so far apart that they cannot possibly intersect.

   We will make these assumptions to simplify the discussion: First, no line segment is vertical (any problem instance can be made to satisfy this assumption by rotating the plane). Second, any two line segments which intersect do so at a single point. Third, no three line segments intersect at the same point.

7.1.1 Representing Event Points

Under plane sweep, the sweepline advances from left to right across the n line segments, halting at event points. There are three kinds of event points: *left endpoints*, *right endpoints*, and *crossings* (or points of intersection). We will represent event points by three classes derived from a common base class, the abstract class `EventPoint`:

```
class EventPoint {
 public:
   Point p;
```

```
    virtual void handleTransition(Dictionary<Edge*>&,
                                  Dictionary<EventPoint*>&,
                                  List<EventPoint*>*) = 0;
};
```

Data member p contains the event point. Abstract member function handleTransition
will be overridden in the classes derived from EventPoint.

Class LeftEndpoint stores the left endpoint of a line segment in data member p
inherited from the base class. The line segment itself is stored in data member e:

```
class LeftEndpoint : public EventPoint {
 public:
    Edge e;
    LeftEndpoint(Edge*);
    void handleTransition(Dictionary<Edge*>&,
                          Dictionary<EventPoint*>&,
                          List<EventPoint*>*);
};
```

The constructor LeftEndpoint initializes the data members:

```
LeftEndpoint::LeftEndpoint(Edge *_e) :
    e(*_e)
{
    p = (e.org < e.dest) ? e.org : e.dest;
}
```

Class RightEndpoint is defined analogously:

```
class RightEndpoint : public EventPoint {
 public:
    Edge e;
    RightEndpoint(Edge*);
    void handleTransition(Dictionary<Edge*>&,
                          Dictionary<EventPoint*>&,
                          List<EventPoint*>*);
};
```

```
RightEndpoint::RightEndpoint(Edge *_e) :
    e(*_e)
{
    p = (e.org < e.dest) ? e.dest : e.org;
}
```

Class Crossing stores in data members e1 and e2 the two line segments that cross,
and in data member p their point of intersection:

```
class Crossing : public EventPoint {
 public:
    Edge e1, e2;
```

```
   Crossing(Edge*, Edge*, Point&);
   void handleTransition(Dictionary<Edge*>&,
                         Dictionary<EventPoint*>&,
                         List<EventPoint*>*);
};
```

Its constructor initializes the data members:

```
Crossing::Crossing(Edge *_e1, Edge *_e2, Point &_p) :
   e1(*_e1), e2(*_e2)
{
   p = _p;
}
```

7.1.2 The Top-Level Program

The problem as a whole is solved by program intersectSegments. The program is passed an array s of n line segments and returns a list of Crossing objects representing the intersection points it discovers. The program uses the global variable curx to hold the current x-coordinate of the sweepline:

```
double curx;    // current x-coordinate of the sweepline

List<EventPoint*> *intersectSegments(Edge s[], int n)
{
   Dictionary<EventPoint*> schedule = buildSchedule(s, n);
   Dictionary<Edge*> sweepline(edgeCmp2);
   List<EventPoint*> *result = new List<EventPoint*>;
   while (!schedule.isEmpty()) {
      EventPoint *ev = schedule.removeMin();
      curx = ev->p.x;
      ev->handleTransition(sweepline, schedule, result);
   }
   return result;
}
```

Program intersectSegments initializes the event-point schedule and sweepline structure and then iteratively performs transitions. Since function handleTransition was declared virtual, the version of handleTransition invoked in each iteration of the while loop depends on the type of event ev.

We represent the event-point schedule by a dictionary because the schedule changes dynamically: Intersection points must be inserted into and removed from the event-point schedule as the sweepline advances. However, the n left endpoints and n right endpoints can be anticipated prior to sweeping. Function buildSchedule inserts these 2n event points into the event-point schedule, which it then returns:

```
Dictionary<EventPoint*> &buildSchedule(Edge s[], int n)
{
```

```
Dictionary<EventPoint*> *schedule =
    new Dictionary<EventPoint*>(eventCmp);
for (int i = 0; i < n; i++) {
  schedule.insert(new LeftEndpoint(&s[i]));
  schedule.insert(new RightEndpoint(&s[i]));
}
return *schedule;
}
```

Comparison function `eventCmp`, used by function `buildSchedule` to initialize the event-point schedule, orders event points by increasing x-coordinates and, in the case of ties, by increasing y-coordinates:

```
int eventCmp(EventPoint *a, EventPoint *b)
{
  if (a->p < b->p) return -1;
  else if (a->p > b->p) return 1;
  return 0;
}
```

7.1.3 The Sweepline Structure

The set of all line segments can be classified relative to any given position of the sweepline: *Dormant segments* have both endpoints to the right of the sweepline; *active segments* have one endpoint on either side of the sweepline; and *dead segments* have both endpoints to the left of the sweepline. The sweepline structure `sweepline` is a dictionary containing the *active* line segments—those that the sweepline currently crosses—ordered by the y-coordinates of their intersections with the sweepline. For example, in Figure 7.1 the active segments are ordered $a < b < c$ when the sweepline is in position x_1 (since line segment d is not active, it is ignored for now).

Dictionary `sweepline` is initialized with the comparison function `edgeCmp2`, which implements this vertical ordering. As noted, the global variable `curx` holds the current x-coordinate of the sweepline:

```
#define EPSILON3    1E-10

int edgeCmp2(Edge *a, Edge *b)
{
  double ya = a->y(curx - EPSILON3);
  double yb = b->y(curx - EPSILON3);
  if (ya < yb) return -1;
  else if (ya > yb) return 1;
  double ma = a->slope();
  double mb = b->slope();
  if (ma > mb) return -1;
  else if (ma < mb) return 1;
  return 0;
}
```

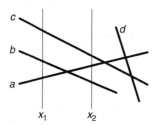

Figure 7.1:   The vertical ordering of the active segments is $a < b < c$ when the sweepline is in position x_1, and $b < a < c$ when it is in position x_2.

Comparison function `edgeCmp2` is unexpectedly complicated because it is capable of comparing all pairs of line segments, even those that happen to cross the sweepline at the same point. When this occurs, the function compares the slopes of the line segments and considers the line segment whose slope is greater to be below the other line segment. This simulates shifting the sweepline an infinitesimal distance to the left. `EPSILON3` is used to avoid errors due to round-off.

7.1.4 Transitions

The following observation is the crux of our algorithm: Suppose that line segments a and b cross at point p, where p lies to the right of the sweepline. Then if no endpoint or intersection point lies between p and the sweepline—that is, if p is the next event point that the sweepline will reach—then line segments a and b must be vertically adjacent in the sweepline structure.

Why is this true? It is easy to see that both a and b must be active segments. To see why a and b must be vertically adjacent in the sweepline structure, suppose to the contrary that the sweepline will encounter their intersection point p next, yet a and b are *not* vertically adjacent. In this case some active line segment c must cross the sweepline between a and b. Either the right endpoint of c occurs between p and the sweepline (Figure 7.2a), or c crosses a or b at some point which lies between p and the sweepline (Figure 7.2b). In either case, the sweepline will reach an endpoint or a crossing before reaching p, contradicting our assumption.

The algorithm employs this observation in the form of an invariant involving the event-point schedule: For every pair of vertically adjacent edges which cross to the right of the sweepline, the event-point schedule contains their point of intersection. This ensures that when the sweepline is about to reach an intersection point, the point will be present

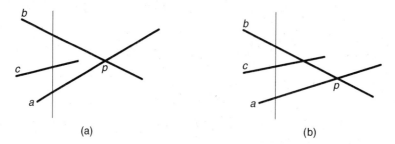

(a)   (b)

Figure 7.2:   (a) The right endpoint of line segment c lies between the sweepline and point p, and (b) line segment c crosses line segment a between the sweepline and point p.

in the event-point schedule. No intersection point will be skipped over. Most of the work involved in transitions is aimed at maintaining this invariant.

Let us consider the three kinds of transitions, starting with left endpoint transitions (Figure 7.3a). When the sweepline reaches the left endpoint of line segment *b*, active segments *a* and *c* (below and above *b*, respectively) cease to be vertically adjacent along the sweepline. If *a* and *c* both exist (they may not) and they cross to the right of the sweepline, we remove their intersection point from the event-point schedule. Moreover, since *a* and *b* have now become vertically adjacent, we check whether they cross—if they do, we insert their intersection point into the event-point schedule (note that their intersection point must lie to the right of the sweepline). Similarly, if *b* and *c* cross, we insert their intersection point into the event-point schedule. Function `LeftEndpoint::handleTransition` results:

```
void LeftEndpoint::handleTransition(Dictionary<Edge*> &sweepline,
                              Dictionary<EventPoint*> &schedule,
                              List<EventPoint*> *result)
{
    Edge *b = sweepline.insert(&e);
    Edge *c = sweepline.next();
    sweepline.prev();
    Edge *a = sweepline.prev();
    double t;
    if (a && c && (a->cross(*c, t)==SKEW_CROSS)) {
        Point p = a->point(t);
        if (curx < p.x) {
            Crossing cev(a, c, p);
            delete schedule.remove(&cev);
        }
    }
    if (c && (b->cross(*c, t)==SKEW_CROSS))
        schedule.insert(new Crossing(b, c, b->point(t)));
    if (a && (b->cross(*a, t)==SKEW_CROSS))
        schedule.insert(new Crossing(a, b, b->point(t)));
}
```

Let us turn our attention to crossing transitions. When the sweepline reaches the intersection point of line segments *b* and *c*, the two line segments must be transposed within the vertical ordering (Figure 7.3b). Since *b* crosses above *c*, we check whether *b* and

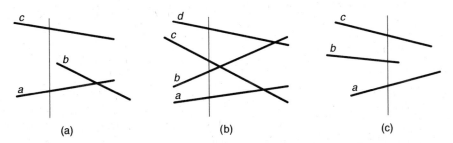

Figure 7.3:   Configurations for (a) left endpoint events, (b) crossing events, and (c) right endpoint events.

active segment d (now above b) cross to the right of the sweepline and, if so, we schedule their point of intersection. Similarly, if c and active segment a (now below c) cross to the right of the sweepline, we schedule their point of intersection as well. In addition, we remove from the event-point schedule the intersection points of a and b and of c and d, if they are present. This leads to the following function definition:

```
void Crossing::handleTransition(Dictionary<Edge*> &sweepline,
                                Dictionary<EventPoint*> &schedule,
                                List<EventPoint*> *result)
{
   Edge *b = sweepline.find(&e1);
   Edge *a = sweepline.prev();
   Edge *c = sweepline.find(&e2);
   Edge *d = sweepline.next();
   double t;
   if (a && (a->cross(*c, t)==SKEW_CROSS)) {
      Point p = a->point(t);
      if (curx < p.x)
         schedule.insert(new Crossing(a, c, p));
   }
   if (d && (d->cross(*b, t)==SKEW_CROSS)) {
      Point p = d->point(t);
      if (curx < p.x)
         schedule.insert(new Crossing(b, d, p));
   }
   if (a && (a->cross(*b, t)==SKEW_CROSS)) {
      Point p = a->point(t);
      if (curx < p.x) {
         Crossing cev(a, b, p);
         delete schedule.remove(&cev);
      }
   }
   if (d && (d->cross(*c, t)==SKEW_CROSS)) {
      Point p = d->point(t);
      if (curx < p.x) {
         Crossing cev(c, d, p);
         delete schedule.remove(&cev);
      }
   }
   sweepline.remove(b);
   curx += 2*EPSILON3;
   sweepline.insert(b);
   curx -= 2*EPSILON3;
   result->append(this);
}
```

The last several lines of the function swap the positions of edges b and c within the sweepline structure. This is done by removing b and then reinserting b after first shifting the sweepline an infinitesimal distance to the right.

Finally, we consider right endpoint transitions. When the sweepline reaches the right endpoint of line segment b, active segments a and c (below and above b, respectively) become vertically adjacent along the sweepline (Figure 7.3c). If a and c exist and cross to the right of the sweepline, their intersection point is scheduled. Function `RightEndpoint::handleTransition` takes care of this:

```
void RightEndpoint::handleTransition(Dictionary<Edge*> &sweepline,
                           Dictionary<EventPoint*> &schedule,
                           List<EventPoint*> *result)
{
    Edge *b = sweepline.find(&e);
    Edge *c = sweepline.next();
    sweepline.prev();
    Edge *a = sweepline.prev();
    double t;
    if (a && c && (a->cross(*c, t)==SKEW_CROSS)) {
        Point p = a->point(t);
        if (curx < p.x)
            schedule.insert(new Crossing(a, c, p));
    }
}
```

7.1.5 Analysis

Where r equals the total number of intersection points among the n line segments, a total of $r + 2n$ transitions are performed. Each transition involves a (small) constant number of operations involving the sweepline structure and the event-point schedule. The sweepline structure operations each take $O(\log n)$ time since at most n line segments can be active at a time. The event-point schedule operations each run in $O(\log n)$ time as well. To see why, observe that the event-point schedule contains at most $n - 1$ crossing event points at any given time, since there are no more than $n - 1$ pairs of vertically adjacent active segments. The event-point schedule may also contain up to $2n$ endpoints. Hence the event-point schedule contains $O(n)$ items, so its operations run in $O(\log n)$ time. Since each of the $r + 2n$ transitions takes $O(\log n)$ time, the algorithm as a whole runs in $O((r+n)\log n)$ time.

This algorithm's performance reflects its broad strategy: to spend extra time avoiding pairs of line segments which cannot possibly cross, in order to save the time of testing them. Pairs that are distant horizontally—whose x-extents fail to overlap—are not tested because they are never active at the same time. Pairs that are distant vertically—in the sense that one or more line segments are interposed between them—are not tested because they are never adjacent within the sweepline structure. But the penalty for avoiding unpromising pairs of line segments is a factor of $\log n$ slowdown. The strategy pays off when r is sufficiently small: If $r \in o(\frac{n^2}{\log n})$, the algorithm runs in $o(n^2)$ time, outperforming the brute-force approach to the problem. However, when many line segments do in fact cross [e.g., $r \in \Omega(n^2)$)], the algorithm is less efficient than the brute-force approach because the cost of avoiding unpromising pairs of line segments proves too expensive and unproductive.

7.2   Finding Convex Hulls: Insertion Hull Revisited

In section 5.3 we presented program `insertionHull`, which finds the convex hull of a set of n points in the plane by incorporating them one at a time into a current hull. Our analysis of the program revealed that its performance is dominated by two operations: (1) deciding whether each point p to be inserted lies inside—is "absorbed" by—the current hull, and (2) finding some vertex of the current hull's near chain, whenever p lies outside the current hull. Since each of the two operations takes time proportional to the size of the current hull and, in the worst case, the current hull grows by one vertex per iteration, we concluded that `insertionHull` runs in $O(n^2)$ time. In this section we briefly consider an *off-line* version of the insertion hull algorithm which does not require these two operations and which, as a result, is more efficient, taking $O(n \log n)$ time.

The idea is to presort the points from left to right and then insert them into the current hull in this order. This obviates the need to test whether each point p to be inserted lies in the current hull: Since p lies to the right of all previously inserted points (or at least above the previously inserted point), p necessarily lies outside the current hull. Having determined that p lies outside the current hull, we must then insert p into the current hull, which requires that we locate some vertex of the current hull's near chain. But due to the order in which points are inserted, such a vertex is already at hand: The last point inserted into current hull is just such a vertex.

Program `insertionHull2` returns the convex hull of the n points of array `pts`. It is worthwhile to compare this program to program `insertionHull` of section 5.3.

```
Polygon *insertionHull2(Point pts[], int n)
{
    Point **s = new (Point*)(n);
    for (int i = 0; i < n; i++)
        s[i] = &pts[i];
    selectionSort(s, n, leftToRightCmp);
    Polygon *p = new Polygon;
    p->insert(new Vertex(*s[0]));
    for (i = 1; i < n; i++) {
        if (*s[i] == *s[i-1])
            continue;
        supportingLine(*s[i], p, LEFT);
        Vertex *l = p->v();
        supportingLine(*s[i], p, RIGHT);
        delete p->split(l);
        p->insert(new Vertex(*s[i]));
    }
    return p;
}
```

Observe that this new version of insertion hull is an example of plane sweep, although we explained it without recourse to plane-sweep terminology. To spell out the connection, the sorted array of points serves as the (static) event-point schedule and the current hull serves as the sweepline structure. As each point gets processed, the current hull is updated; thus both the sweepline structure and the solution to the problem to the left of the sweepline are implicitly updated.

7.2.1 Analysis

Let us analyze `insertionHull2`. Within a single iteration of the `for` loop, only the two calls to `supportingLine` take more than constant time—together they take time proportional to the length of the current hull's near chain. Let us charge one unit of work to each of the near chain's vertices to pay for the two calls to `supportingLine`. Since these vertices are removed by the `split` operation that follows, every point accrues at most one such charge—once removed from the current hull, a point is never reinserted. Because there are only n points, the total cost for all calls to `supportingLine`, over all $n - 1$ iterations, is $O(n)$ time.

Hence `insertionHull2` is dominated by the initial sort. If we use an optimal sorting method such as `mergeSort` (to be described in the next chapter), `insertionHull2` runs in $O(n \log n)$ time.

7.3   Contour of the Union of Rectangles

An *axes-parallel rectangle* is a rectangle whose sides are aligned with the axes of the plane—two sides are vertical and two are horizontal. In this section we will use plane sweep to solve the *contour finding* problem: Compute the boundary (or *contour*) of the region formed by the union of a collection of axes-parallel rectangles. This problem arises in the design of integrated circuits (IC) using axes-parallel rectangles known as *IC masks*. Algorithms are used in the layout of IC masks to ensure certain constraints, such as economic (minimizing total area of the circuit) and electrical (insulation and contact) constraints.

A contour is made up of one or more loops, each composed of alternating horizontal and vertical *contour segments*. The loops do not cross one another and may be nested to any depth. Figure 7.4 depicts six rectangles and the contour of their union. The contour consists of four loops: One encloses a second, which in turn encloses a third; the fourth loop lies outside the others. Figure 7.5 shows the contour of 120 rectangles positioned randomly within a rectangular region of the plane.

To solve the contour finding problem using plane sweep, we advance the sweepline from left to right across the n rectangles while maintaining the following invariant: At each position of the sweepline, all contour segments lying entirely to the left of the sweepline will have been discovered. (A horizontal contour segment that crosses the sweepline is not discovered until the sweepline reaches its right endpoint.) The invariant must be restored whenever the sweepline reaches each of the $2n$ vertical edges, meaning that we must find

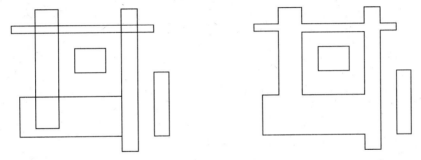

Figure 7.4:   The contour of the union of six axes-parallel rectangles.

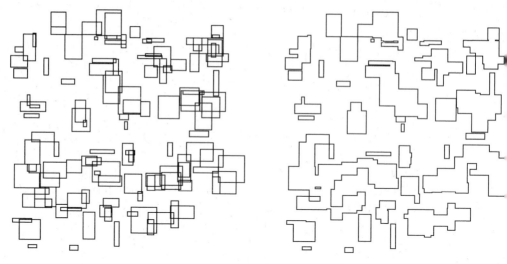

Figure 7.5:   The contour of the union of 120 rectangles.

those contour segments which now for the first time lie to the left of the sweepline. Thus the left and right edges of the rectangles serve as event points. Figure 7.6, which depicts a problem involving two rectangles, highlights the contour segments discovered at successive positions of the sweepline. The sweepline is offset to the right in each diagram for clarity.

7.3.1 Representing Rectangles

We will represent a rectangle by the following class:

```
class Rectangle {
 public:
    Point sw;     // south-west (lower left) corner
    Point ne;     // north-east (upper right) corner
    int id;       // identifier
    Rectangle(Point &_sw, Point &_ne, int _id = -1);
    Rectangle(void) { }
};
```

A rectangle is determined by two opposing corners sw and ne and is assigned an identifier id. The class constructor is defined thus:

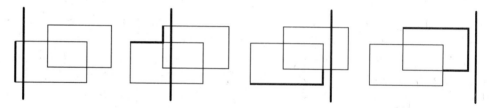

Figure 7.6:   The contour segments discovered at each position of the sweepline are darkened.

```
Rectangle::Rectangle(Point &_sw, Point &_ne, int _id) :
   sw(_sw), ne(_ne), id(_id)
{
}
```

We will represent the sides of a rectangle using class `AxisParallelEdge`:

```
enum { LEFT_SIDE, RIGHT_SIDE, BOTTOM_SIDE, TOP_SIDE };

class AxisParallelEdge {
 public:
   Rectangle *r;   // rectangle that owns the edge
   int count;
   double m;
   int type;        // LEFT_SIDE, RIGHT_SIDE, BOTTOM_SIDE, TOP_SIDE
   AxisParallelEdge(Rectangle*, int);
   double pos(void);
   double min(void);
   double max(void);
   void setMin(double);
   void handleLeftEdge(Dictionary<AxisParallelEdge*>&, List<Edge*>*);
   void handleRightEdge(Dictionary<AxisParallelEdge*>&, List<Edge*>*);
};
```

The class constructor is defined like this:

```
AxisParallelEdge::AxisParallelEdge(Rectangle *_r, int _type) :
   r(_r), count(0), m(-DBL_MAX), type(_type)
{
}
```

Member function `pos` returns the position of this edge along the axis to which it is perpendicular, and functions `min` and `max` return the minimum and maximum extents of the edge along the axis to which it is parallel. For example, for the vertical edge with endpoints (1,2) and (1,4), `pos` returns 1, `min` returns 2, and `max` returns 4. The functions are defined as follows:

```
double AxisParallelEdge::pos(void)
{
   switch (type) {
      case LEFT_SIDE:
         return r->sw.x; break;
      case RIGHT_SIDE:
         return r->ne.x; break;
      case TOP_SIDE:
         return r->ne.y; break;
      case BOTTOM_SIDE:
      default:
         return r->sw.y; break;
   }
}
```

```
double AxisParallelEdge::min(void)
{
    if (m > -DBL_MAX)
        return m;
    switch (type) {
        case LEFT_SIDE:
        case RIGHT_SIDE:
            return r->sw.y; break;
        case TOP_SIDE:
        case BOTTOM_SIDE:
        default:
            return r->sw.x; break;
    }
}


double AxisParallelEdge::max(void)
{
    switch (type) {
        case LEFT_SIDE:
        case RIGHT_SIDE:
            return r->ne.y; break;
        case TOP_SIDE:
        case BOTTOM_SIDE:
        default:
            return r->ne.x; break;
    }
}
```

When a top or bottom edge is initialized, it coincides with the top or bottom side of the rectangle which owns the edge. However, our algorithm must sometimes reposition the left endpoints of horizontal edges. Member function setMin accommodates this. It is used to update the value returned by subsequent calls to member function min. The member function is defined thus:

```
void AxisParallelEdge::setMin(double f)
{
    m = f;
}
```

7.3.2 The Top-Level Program

Program findContour solves the contour finding problem for array r of n rectangles. The function accumulates the contour segments it discovers in list segments, which it returns upon completion:

```
List<Edge*> *findContour(Rectangle r[], int n)
{
    AxisParallelEdge **schedule = buildSchedule(r, n);
    List<Edge*> *segments = new List<Edge*>;
    Dictionary<AxisParallelEdge*> sweepline(axisParallelEdgeCmp);
```

```
Rectangle *sentinel = new Rectangle(Point(-DBL_MAX,-DBL_MAX),
                                    Point(DBL_MAX,DBL_MAX), -1);
sweepline.insert(new AxisParallelEdge(sentinel, BOTTOM_SIDE));
for (int i = 0; i < 2*n; i++)
   switch (schedule[i]->type) {
     case LEFT_SIDE:
       schedule[i]->handleLeftEdgeTransition(sweepline, segments);
       break;
     case RIGHT_SIDE:
       schedule[i]->handleRightEdgeTransition(sweepline, segments);
       break;
   }
   return segments;
}
```

Function `buildSchedule` creates the event-point schedule, an array of $2n$ vertical edges sorted by increasing x-coordinates. The function is passed array `r` of n rectangles and returns the event-point schedule:

```
AxisParallelEdge **buildSchedule(Rectangle r[], int n)
{
    AxisParallelEdge **schedule = new AxisParallelEdgePtr[2*n];
    for (int i = 0; i < n; i++) {
        schedule[2*i] = new AxisParallelEdge(&r[i], LEFT_SIDE);
        schedule[2*i+1] = new AxisParallelEdge(&r[i], RIGHT_SIDE);
    }
    insertionSort(schedule, 2*n, axisParallelEdgeCmp);
    return schedule;
}
```

Function `buildSchedule` sorts the event-point schedule using the comparison function `axisParallelEdgeCmp`:

```
int axisParallelEdgeCmp(AxisParallelEdge *a, AxisParallelEdge *b)
{
    if (a->pos() < b->pos()) return -1;
    else if (a->pos() > b->pos()) return 1;
    else if (a->type < b->type) return -1;
    else if (a->type > b->type) return 1;
    else if (a->r->id < b->r->id) return -1;
    else if (a->r->id > b->r->id) return 1;
    return 0;
}
```

Comparison function `axisParallelEdgeCmp` compares two vertical edges with respect to their x-coordinates, and if these are the same, it then compares the edges with respect to their types (left edges are considered less than right edges). Finally, if their types are the same, the edges are compared with respect to the identifiers of their respective rectangles. Horizontal edges are compared analogously, where y-coordinates play the role of x-coordinates, and bottom edges are considered less than top edges. (The algorithm never compares a vertical edge with a horizontal edge.)

If the left edge e_1 of some rectangle R_1 and the right edge e_2 of rectangle R_2 have the same x-coordinate, why is edge e_1 is considered less than edge e_2? The reason is to ensure that e_1 gets scheduled before e_2, so the sweepline enters rectangle R_1 before leaving R_2. Were we not to do this, the algorithm would mistakenly report as a contour segment the vertical edge along which the two rectangles meet.

The sweepline structure is a dictionary containing active horizontal edges, those horizontal edges that cross the sweepline in its current position. Comparison function `axisParallelEdgeCmp` is used not only to create the event-point schedule, but also to create and maintain the sweepline structure.

7.3.3 Transitions

Transitions, which occur whenever the sweepline encounters a vertical edge, are handled differently for left edges and right edges. In both cases, however, we must make use of the `count` field of the active horizontal edges. The *count* of an edge equals the number of rectangles which cover the interval of the sweepline extending from the edge to the next edge just above. Counts are indicated in Figures 7.7 and 7.8.

Let us first consider left edge events, when the sweepline enters some rectangle R. We will refer to Figure 7.7a to explain what takes place. To begin, we insert the two horizontal edges a and h of rectangle R into the sweepline structure. Next we use the sweepline structure to visit the sequence of active horizontal edges extending from a up to h. Three kinds of contour segments may be discovered along the way. First, we find a horizontal contour segment along each bottom edge whose count equals 1 (edges b and d in the figure). Second, we find a horizontal contour segment along each top edge whose count equals 0 (edges c and g). Since both types of contour segments our now hidden by R, the sweepline has reached their right endpoints. Third, we may find vertical contour segments which terminate in a bottom horizontal edge with count 1 (between edges a and b), or which terminate in a top edge with count 0 (between edges g and h), or which terminate

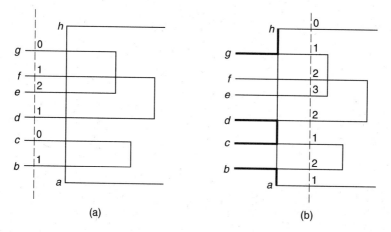

(a)   (b)

Figure 7.7: Processing a left edge event, with counts indicated. The contour segments that are found are darkened.

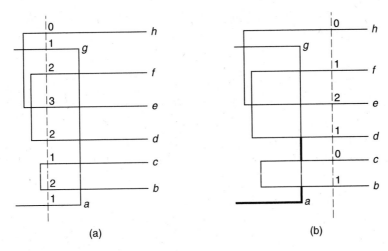

Figure 7.8:   Processing a right edge event, with counts indicated. The contour segments are darkened.

in both (between edges c and d). Such edges lie along the left edge of R. Figure 7.7b results.

In addition to finding contour segments, we must update the counts associated with the active horizontal edges. We increment the counts of all active horizontal edges lying between a and h, to account for the arrival of rectangle R. We initialize the counts of a and h based on the count of the active horizontal edge that lies just below each.

Left edge events are processed by member function `handleLeftEdge`. The function is passed the sweepline structure and the list of already known contour segments, to which it appends the new contour segments it discovers:

```
void AxisParallelEdge::handleLeftEdge(
                Dictionary<AxisParallelEdge*> &sweepline,
                List<Edge*> *segs)
{
   sweepline.insert(new AxisParallelEdge(r, TOP_SIDE));
   AxisParallelEdge *u = sweepline.val();
   sweepline.insert(new AxisParallelEdge(r, BOTTOM_SIDE));
   AxisParallelEdge *l = sweepline.val();
   AxisParallelEdge *p = sweepline.prev();
   float curx = pos();
   l->count = p->count + 1;
   p = sweepline.next();
   l = sweepline.next();
   for ( ; l != u; p = l, l = sweepline.next()) {
      if ((l->type == BOTTOM_SIDE) && (l->count++ == 1)) {
         segs->append(new Edge(Point(curx, p->pos()),
                               Point(curx, l->pos())));
         segs->append(new Edge(Point(l->min(), l->pos()),
                               Point(curx, l->pos())));
      } else if ((l->type == TOP_SIDE) && (l->count++ == 0))
         segs->append(new Edge(Point(l->min(), l->pos()),
                               Point(curx, l->pos())));
   }
}
```

```
        if ((1->count = p->count - 1) == 0)
          segs->append(new Edge(Point(curx, p->pos()),
                                Point(curx, 1->pos()))));
    }
```

Next we consider how to process right edge events, when the sweepline exits some
rectangle R (Figure 7.8). First we look up R's horizontal edges in the sweepline structure
(a and g in the figure). Next we visit the sequence of active horizontal edges from a up
to g while looking out for two kinds of contour segments. First, the horizontal edges of R
may contain contour segments—R's bottom edge if its count is 1, and R's top edge if its
count is 0 (a is a contour segment, but g is not). Second, we find a vertical contour segment
connecting each top horizontal edge whose count equals 1 to a bottom horizontal edge
whose count equals 2 (between edges a and b, and edges c and d). The count of each
edge visited (between a and g) is decremented along the way to account for rectangle R's
departure.

We perform an additional task while traversing the list from a up to g: For top horizontal edges with (decremented) count 0 and for bottom horizontal edges with (decremented)
count 1, we use function `setMin` to shift the left endpoint rightward to the sweepline. In
Figure 7.8, the left endpoints of horizontal edges b, c, and d are updated in this way. To see
why this is necessary, observe that b, c and d each contains a contour segment that is yet to
be discovered, and that each of these contour segments has its left endpoint along the right
edge of rectangle R, the current position of the sweepline.

To finish processing the right edge event, we remove the horizontal edges of rectangle R (a and g) from the sweepline structure to account for rectangle R's departure.

Member function `handleRightEdge` processes right edge events. The contour
segments it finds are appended to list `segs`:

```
void AxisParallelEdge::handleRightEdge(
                Dictionary<AxisParallelEdge*> &sweepline,
                List<Edge*> *segs)
{
    AxisParallelEdge uedge(r, TOP_SIDE);
    AxisParallelEdge ledge(r, BOTTOM_SIDE);
    AxisParallelEdge *u = sweepline.find(&uedge);
    AxisParallelEdge *1 = sweepline.find(&ledge);
    float curx = pos();
    if (1->count == 1)
        segs->append(new Edge(Point(1->min(), 1->pos()),
                              Point(curx, 1->pos()))));
    if (u->count == 0)
        segs->append(new Edge(Point(u->min(), u->pos()),
                              Point(curx, u->pos()))));
    AxisParallelEdge *init1 = 1;
    AxisParallelEdge *p = 1;
    1 = sweepline.next();
    for ( ; 1 != u; p = 1, 1 = sweepline.next()) {
        if ((1->type == BOTTOM_SIDE) && (--1->count == 1)) {
            segs->append(new Edge(Point(curx, p->pos()),
                                  Point(curx, 1->pos()))));
```

```
          l->setMin(curx);
      } else if ((l->type == TOP_SIDE) && (--l->count == 0))
          l->setMin(curx);
  }
  if (l->count == 0)
      segs->append(new Edge(Point(curx, p->pos()),
                            Point(curx, l->pos())));
  sweepline.remove(u);
  sweepline.remove(initl);
}
```

7.3.4 Analysis

Given n rectangles, consider the cost of performing a transition involving some rectangle R. A transition of either type requires a (small) constant number of operations involving the sweepline structure, taking at most $O(\log n)$ time, plus time proportional to the number of active horizontal edges that lie between rectangle R's lower and upper edges. Since there may be as many as $\Omega(n)$ such edges, visiting these active horizontal edges dominates total cost in the worst case. Hence each transition takes up to $O(n)$ time. Since there are $2n$ transitions, the algorithm as a whole runs in $O(n^2)$ time in the worst case.

In one worst-case scenario, $\frac{n}{2}$ tall rectangles and $\frac{n}{2}$ wide rectangles form a mesh—every tall rectangle intersects every wide rectangle. Since the contour of this mesh contains $\Omega(n^2)$ contour segments, $\Omega(n^2)$ time is required if only to report every contour segment.

We might attempt to express running time as an output-sensitive function of both n and the size of the contour that is produced. However, even contours composed of very few contour segments may require $\Omega(n^2)$ time. Consider running findContour on this input: the mesh of n rectangles described in the previous paragraph, plus a large rectangle R which encloses the mesh. Although the contour of the union of these $n + 1$ rectangles consists only of the four edges of R, the algorithm requires $\Omega(n^2)$ time to discover this. As the sweepline advances from left to right, the algorithm must update the sweepline structure in response to the mesh even though the mesh is covered by R. For were the sweepline to reach the right edge of R abruptly before passing entirely beyond the mesh, the state of the algorithm with respect to the mesh would become critical. Although in this example the sweepline in fact passes beyond the mesh before leaving R, the algorithm does not know this to be the case in advance.

7.4   Decomposing Polygons into Monotone Pieces

In this section we present an algorithm to decompose an arbitrary polygon into monotone subpolygons, a process known as *regularization*. (Recall from section 5.8 that a polygon is monotone if its boundary is composed of a monotone upper chain and a monotone lower chain.) The algorithm employs plane sweep to regularize an n-gon in $O(n \log n)$ time. Using this algorithm together with the linear-time method of section 5.8 for triangulating monotone polygons, we obtain an $O(n \log n)$-time algorithm for triangulating an arbitrary polygon: First, decompose the polygon into monotone subpolygons; then triangulate each of these in turn.

To simplify the presentation, we will assume throughout this section that no two vertices of a polygon have the same x-coordinate.

Our algorithm hinges on the notion of a cusp. A reflex vertex—a vertex whose interior angle exceeds 180 degrees—is a *cusp* if its two neighbors either both lie to the left of v or both lie to the right of v (Figure 7.9). It is easy to see that a polygon that is monotone cannot contain any cusps. Yet it is the converse, expressed by the following theorem, which lies at the heart of the algorithm:

Theorem 4 (Monotone Polygon Theorem) *Any polygon that contains no cusps is monotone.*

We prove the theorem by showing the contrapositive: If polygon P is non-monotone, then P contains a cusp. Assume that P is non-monotone, and suppose that this is due to its upper chain being non-monotone. Label the vertices along P's upper chain $v_1, v_2, \ldots, v_k$, and let v_i be the first vertex along the chain such that v_{i+1} lies to the left of v_i (Figure 7.10). If v_{i+1} lies above edge $\overrightarrow{v_{i-1}v_i}$, then v_i is a cusp, so we will assume that v_{i+1} lies below $\overrightarrow{v_{i-1}v_i}$. Let v_j be the leftmost vertex of the chain from v_i to v_k before the chain crosses above edge $\overrightarrow{v_iv_k}$. Vertex v_j is reflex because it is locally leftmost and the polygon interior lies to its left, and v_j is a cusp because it is reflex and both its neighbors lie to its right. The theorem follows.

7.4.1 The Top-Level Program

Our algorithm works by decomposing P into subpolygons without cusps. In the first of two phases, the algorithm removes leftward-pointing cusps as it sweeps across P from left to right, producing a set of subpolygons $P_1, P_2, \ldots, P_m$, none of which contains leftward-pointing cusps. In the second phase the algorithm removes rightward-pointing cusps as it sweeps from right to left across each P_i in turn. The collection of polygons that results represents a decomposition of the original polygon P into subpolygons which possess neither leftward- nor rightward-pointing cusps, and hence no cusps at all.

Program `regularize` is passed a polygon p, and it returns a list of monotone polygons representing the regularization of p. Polygon p is destroyed in the process:

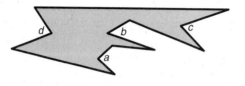

Figure 7.9: Vertices a, b, and c are leftward-pointing cusps, and d is a rightward-pointing cusp.

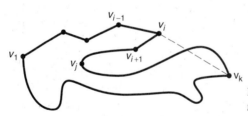

Figure 7.10: Illustration that a non-monotone polygon must possess cusps.

```
enum { LEFT_TO_RIGHT, RIGHT_TO_LEFT };

List<Polygon*> *regularize(Polygon &p)
{
 // phase 1
   List<Polygon*> *polys1 = new List<Polygon*>;
   semiregularize(p, LEFT_TO_RIGHT, polys1);
 // phase 2
   List<Polygon*> *polys2 = new List<Polygon*>;
   polys1->last();
   while (!polys1->isHead()) {
      Polygon *q = polys1->remove();
      semiregularize(*q, RIGHT_TO_LEFT, polys2);
   }
   return polys2;
}
```

In the program, the polygons produced in the first phase are accumulated in list `polys1`, and those produced in the second phase in list `polys2`.

The goal of function `semiregularize` is to remove all cusps that point in the same direction. For example, the call `semiregularize(p,LEFT_TO_RIGHT,polys1)` sweeps from left to right across polygon p to remove leftward-pointing cusps and appends to list `polys1` the subpolygons that result. Whenever the sweepline reaches a leftward-pointing cusp v, we split the polygon along the chord which connects v to some vertex w to the left of v. To ensure that line segment $\overline{vw}$ is in fact a chord (i.e., an *interior* diagonal) of the polygon, our choice of vertex w is critical. Where vertex v lies between active edges a and d, we choose as w the rightmost vertex from among those vertices which lie between edges a and d and to the left of the sweepline (Figure 7.11a).

Another way to view our choice of vertex w is as follows: Consider the trapezoid bounded by the sweepline, edge a, edge d, and the line parallel to the sweepline and passing through point x. Here x is the left endpoint of either a or d, whichever endpoint lies to the right of the other. Vertex w is the rightmost vertex lying in this trapezoid's interior; however, if the trapezoid's interior is free of vertices, then w is vertex x. We will refer to w as the *target vertex* of edge pair a–d (the vertically adjacent pair of edges a and d).

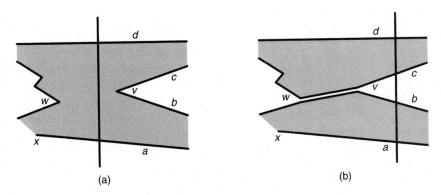

(a)   (b)

Figure 7.11:   The action taken when the sweepline reaches leftward-pointing cusp v.

Figure 7.11b illustrates the action taken when the sweepline encounters cusp v: The polygon is split along chord $\overline{vw}$. Vertex v is not a cusp in either of the two polygons that result—in both polygons, one of v's neighbors lies to the left of v and the other lies to its right. Indeed, the following invariant is maintained as the sweep proceeds from left to right: None of the vertices to the left of the sweepline are leftward-pointing cusps.

A transition occurs as the sweepline reaches each polygon vertex. The type of transition depends on the type of vertex, where a vertex is classified according to the position of its two neighbors relative to the sweep direction:

- *Start vertex:* Both neighbors of v lie beyond the sweepline—that is, in the direction in which the sweepline is moving.
- *Bend vertex:* One neighbor of v lies behind the sweepline and the other neighbor of v lies beyond the sweepline.
- *End vertex:* Both neighbors of v lie behind the sweepline.

The three corresponding transitions—start transitions, bend transitions, and end transitions—are depicted in Figure 7.12, where we assume that the sweep proceeds from left to right. The transition types are framed in terms of the sweep direction so function semiregularize can be used to sweep in either direction.

Function semiregularize is passed an arbitrary polygon p and a sweep direction: LEFT_TO_RIGHT to resolve leftward-pointing cusps, or RIGHT_TO_LEFT to resolve rightward-pointing cusps. The subpolygons that result are appended to list polys. The function relies on three global variables:

```
int sweepdirection;    // current sweep direction
double curx;           // current position of sweepline
int curtype;           // current transition type

void semiregularize(Polygon &p,
                     int direction,
                     List<Polygon*> *polys)
{
    sweepdirection = direction;
    int (*cmp)(Vertex*, Vertex*);
    if (sweepdirection==LEFT_TO_RIGHT) cmp = leftToRightCmp;
    else cmp = rightToLeftCmp;
    Vertex **schedule = buildSchedule(p, cmp);
    Dictionary<ActiveElement*> sweepline = buildSweepline();
```

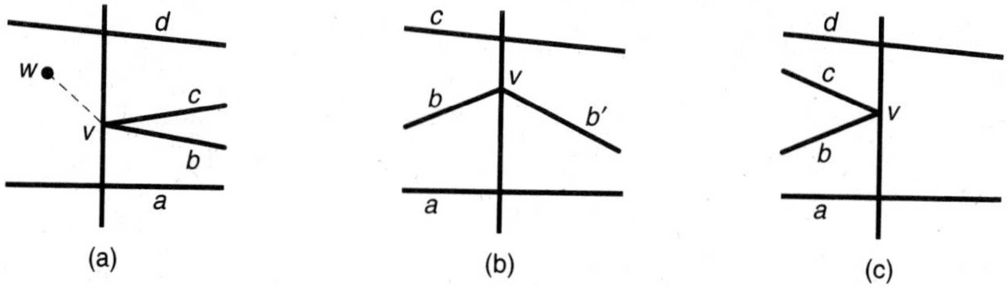

Figure 7.12:   The three types of transitions that occur when the sweepline is moving left to right.

```
for (int i = 0; i < p.size(); i++) {
    Vertex *v = schedule[i];
    curx = v->x;
    switch (curtype = typeEvent(v, cmp)) {
        case START_TYPE:
            startTransition(v, sweepline);
            break;
        case BEND_TYPE:
            bendTransition(v, sweepline);
            break;
        case END_TYPE:
            endTransition(v, sweepline, polys);
            break;
    }
}
p.setV(NULL);
}
```

The event points are the polygon's vertices. Since these are all known in advance, the event-point schedule is an array of the vertices presorted by increasing x-coordinates (the dynamic support of a dictionary is not needed). The schedule is created by function buildSchedule, which is passed one of the point comparison functions leftToRightCmp or rightToLeftCmp, depending on the sweep direction:

```
Vertex **buildSchedule(Polygon &p, int(*cmp)(Vertex*, Vertex*))
{
    Vertex **schedule = new (Vertex*)[p.size()];
    for (int i = 0; i < p.size(); i++, p.advance(CLOCKWISE))
        schedule[i] = p.v();
    insertionSort(schedule, p.size(), cmp);
    return schedule;
}
```

Function semiregularize uses function typeEvent to classify vertices, in order to determine what type of transition to perform. To classify vertex v, function type tests the position of v's two neighbors relative to the sweep direction:

```
int typeEvent(Vertex *v, int(*cmp)(Vertex*,Vertex*))
{
    int a = (*cmp)(v->cw(), v);
    int b = (*cmp)(v->ccw(), v);
    if ((a <= 0) && (b <= 0)) return END_TYPE;
    else if ((a > 0) && (b > 0)) return START_TYPE;
    else return BEND_TYPE;
}
```

7.4.2 The Sweepline Structure

The sweepline structure is a dictionary of active edges—those polygon edges which currently cross the sweepline—ordered by increasing y-coordinates. In addition, the sweepline structure contains a point with minimal *y*-coordinates (below all the edges) to serve as sentinel. We will represent the sweepline structure as a dictionary of `ActiveElement` objects:

```
class ActiveElement {
 public:
    int type;    // ACTIVE_EDGE or ACTIVE_POINT
    ActiveElement(int type);
    virtual double y(void) = 0;
    virtual Edge edge(void) { return Edge(); };
    virtual double slope(void) { return 0.0; };
};
```

The constructor `ActiveElement` initialized data member `type`, which indicates whether the element is an edge or a point:

```
ActiveElement::ActiveElement(int t) :
    type(t)
{
}
```

The remaining member functions of class `ActiveElement` are virtual and will be discussed shortly, in the context of the two derived classes.

An active edge is represented by an `ActiveEdge` object:

```
class ActiveEdge : public ActiveElement {
 public:
    Vertex *v;
    Vertex *w;
    int rotation;
    ActiveEdge(Vertex *_v, int _r, Vertex *_w);
    Edge2 edge(void);
    double y(void);
    double slope(void);
};
```

Data member `v` points to one of this edge's endpoints, and `v->cw()` points to the other. Data member `w` is the target vertex of the edge pair consisting of this edge and the active edge just above. Data member `rotation` is used to traverse from this edge to the edge that meets it *beyond* the sweepline: If such an edge exists, `v->neighbor(rotation)` is a window over the edge.

The constructor `ActiveEdge` is straightforward:

```
ActiveEdge::ActiveEdge(Vertex *_v, int _r, Vertex *_w) :
    ActiveElement(ACTIVE_EDGE), v(_v), rotation(_r), w(_w)
{
}
```

Member function y returns the *y*-coordinate at which this edge crosses the sweepline. Member functions edge and slope return this edge and the slope of this edge, respectively. The three functions are defined as follows:

```
double ActiveEdge::y(void)
{
    return edge().y(curx);
}

Edge ActiveEdge::edge(void)
{
    return Edge(v->point(), v->cw()->point());
}

double ActiveEdge::slope(void)
{
    return edge().slope();
}
```

The sweepline structure is designed to accommodate points as well as edges, because it must support *point location* operations of this form: Given a point on the sweepline, find the pair of active edges between which the point lies. This is why we have defined class ActiveElement and derived from it one class to represent edges and a second class to represent points. For the purpose of searching within the sweepline structure, we represent a point as an ActivePoint object:

```
class ActivePoint : public ActiveElement {
 public:
    Point p;
    ActivePoint(Point&);
    double y(void);
};
```

The class constructor is defined like this:

```
ActivePoint::ActivePoint(Point &_p) :
    ActiveElement(ACTIVE_POINT), p(_p)
{
}
```

Member function y simply returns this point's *y*-coordinate:

```
double ActivePoint::y(void)
{
    return p.y;
}
```

Having defined the necessary classes, we turn our attention to the sweepline structure itself. The sweepline structure is created with function buildSweepline. The function initializes a new dictionary and inserts an active point to serve as sentinel—the point lies below any edge to be inserted later into the dictionary:

```
Dictionary<ActiveElement*> &buildSweepline()
{
   Dictionary<ActiveElement*> *sweepline =
         new Dictionary<ActiveElement*>(activeElementCmp);
   sweepline->insert(new ActivePoint(Point(0.0, -DBL_MAX)));
   return *sweepline;
}
```

The comparison function `activeElementCmp` is used to compare two active elements:

```
int activeElementCmp(ActiveElement *a, ActiveElement *b)
{
   double ya = a->y();
   double yb = b->y();
   if (ya < yb) return -1;
   else if (ya > yb) return 1;
   if ((a->type == ACTIVE_POINT) && (b->type == ACTIVE_POINT))
      return 0;
   else if (a->type == ACTIVE_POINT) return -1;
   else if (b->type == ACTIVE_POINT) return 1;
   int rval = 1;
   if ((sweepdirection == LEFT_TO_RIGHT && curtype == START_TYPE) ||
      (sweepdirection == RIGHT_TO_LEFT && curtype == END_TYPE))
         rval = -1;
   double ma = a->slope();
   double mb = b->slope();
   if (ma < mb) return rval;
   else if (ma > mb) return -rval;
   return 0;
}
```

Function `activeElementCmp` initially compares active elements a and b based on the y-coordinates of their respective crossings with the sweepline. If they cross at the same point, an active point is considered below an active edge. If both a and b are active edges, their respective slopes are used to decide which is below the other. If we assume the sweep is left to right, the edge with lesser slope is below the other edge if the event point is a start vertex, and above the other edge if the event point is an end vertex. If we assume the sweep is right to left, the roles of *start vertex* and *end vertex* are interchanged (e.g., a start vertex under left-to-right sweep is an end vertex under right-to-left sweep).

7.4.3 Transitions

Let us consider how to process transitions, beginning with start transitions (Figure 7.12a). When the sweepline reaches a start vertex v, we first look up in the sweepline structure the two active edges a and d between which vertex v lies. Where vertex v is met by edges b and c, we insert b and c into the sweepline structure and then make v the target vertex for edge pairs a–b, b–c, and c–d. In addition, if vertex v is reflex (implying v is a cusp), we split v's polygon along the chord which connects v to w. Function `startTransition` results:

```
void startTransition(Vertex* v,
                     Dictionary<ActiveElement*> &sweepline)
{
   ActivePoint ve(v->point());
   ActiveEdge *a = (ActiveEdge*)sweepline.locate(&ve);
   Vertex *w = a->w;
   if (!isConvex(v)) {
      Vertex *wp = v->split(w);
      sweepline.insert(new ActiveEdge(wp->cw(),CLOCKWISE,wp->cw()));
      sweepline.insert(new ActiveEdge(v->ccw(),COUNTER_CLOCKWISE,v));
      a->w = (sweepdirection == LEFT_TO_RIGHT) ? wp->ccw() : v;
   } else {
      sweepline.insert(new ActiveEdge(v->ccw(),COUNTER_CLOCKWISE,v));
      sweepline.insert(new ActiveEdge(v, CLOCKWISE, v));
      a->w = v;
   }
}
```

Function `startTransition` splits v's polygon using function `Vertex::split`, rather than `Polygon::split`, so it does not need to know which polygon v belongs to. As the sweepline advances toward v and new polygons are produced by `split` operations, vertex v may migrate from polygon to polygon. By working at the level of vertices rather than polygons, we avoid having to keep track of the polygon to which each vertex belongs.

Function call `isConvex(v)` returns TRUE if vertex v is a convex vertex, and FALSE otherwise (v is reflex). The function is defined as follows:

```
bool isConvex(Vertex *v)
{
   Vertex *u = v->ccw();
   Vertex *w = v->cw();
   int c = w->classify(*u, *v);
   return ((c == BEYOND) || (c == RIGHT));
}
```

To process a bend transition at bend vertex v, we first locate edges a, b, and c in the sweepline structure and then make vertex v the target vertex of edge pairs a–b and b–c (Figure 7.12b). Finally, we replace edge b in the sweepline structure by the edge b', which meets edge b at vertex v. Thus we have function `bendTransition`:

```
void bendTransition(Vertex *v,
                    Dictionary<ActiveElement*> &sweepline)
{
   ActivePoint ve(v->point());
```

```
ActiveEdge *a = (ActiveEdge*)sweepline.locate(&ve);
ActiveEdge *b = (ActiveEdge*)sweepline.next();
a->w = v;
b->w = v;
b->v = b->v->neighbor(b->rotation);
}
```

To process an end transition at end vertex v, we first find active edges a, b, c, and d in the sweepline structure (Figure 7.12c). On the one hand, if vertex v is convex, then v must be the rightmost vertex in its polygon. Were it not so, v's polygon would possess a leftward-pointing cusp to the left of v, contradicting the sweep invariant. Since v is its polygon's rightmost vertex, we append the polygon to the list `polys` at this time. On the other hand, if vertex v is reflex, v is made the target vertex of edge pair a–d. Finally, we remove edges b and c from the sweepline structure. Function `endTransition` results:

```
void endTransition(Vertex *v,
                   Dictionary<ActiveElement*> &sweepline,
                   List<Polygon*> *polys)
{
   ActivePoint ve(v->point());
   ActiveElement *a = sweepline.locate(&ve);
   ActiveEdge *b = (ActiveEdge*)sweepline.next();
   ActiveEdge *c = (ActiveEdge*)sweepline.next();
   if (isConvex(v))
      polys->append(new Polygon(v));
   else
      ((ActiveEdge*)a)->w = v;
   sweepline.remove(b);
   sweepline.remove(c);
}
```

Figure 7.13 depicts the regularization of a 25-gon. The left-to-right sweep removes four leftward-pointing cusps and one rightward-pointing cusp (one of the `split` operations removes two cusps at once). The subsequent right-to-left sweep removes the two remaining rightward-pointing cusps. Seven monotone polygons result. Finally, we triangulate each of these using the algorithm of section 5.8.

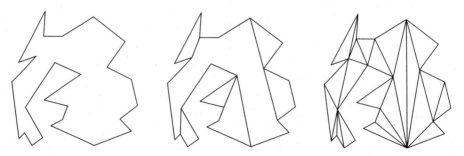

Figure 7.13:   Regularizing a 25-gon into seven monotone pieces and then triangulating these.

7.4.4 Analysis

Let us analyze program `regularize` for an input polygon of n vertices. As the program proceeds through successive calls to function `semiregularize`, the total number of vertices increases by two for every `split` that is performed. However, since at most $\frac{n}{2}$ vertices of the original polygon are cusps, no more than $2(\frac{n}{2}) = n$ vertices are added, making a total of at most $2n$ vertices. Since each vertex prompts at most two transitions (one in each sweep direction), no more than $4n$ transitions are performed in total.

Each type of transition is dominated by a (small) constant number of dictionary operations taking $O(\log n)$ time. Since $O(n)$ transitions are performed, the algorithm runs in $O(n \log n)$ time.

7.5 Chapter Notes

The algorithm of section 7.1 for finding the intersection points of n line segments was presented in [9].

The basic idea behind our algorithm for finding the contour of the union of n axes-parallel rectangles is from [54]. However, by representing the sweepline with a more sophisticated search structure (the *segment tree*), Lipski and Preparata obtain an algorithm that runs in $O(n \log n + r \log(n^2/r))$ time, where the contour consists of r edges. They use the segment tree to represent the "gaps" along the sweepline, those intervals not covered by any rectangles. (In our terminology, a gap is an interval between an active horizontal edge with count 0 and one with count 1.) The time it takes to search within the sweepline structure is thus a function of the number of vertical contour edges that are discovered. Güting [37] subsequently devised an optimal algorithm which runs in $O(r + n \log n)$ time.

Our polygon regularization algorithm is from [52], and the statement and proof of the monotone polygon theorem is from [31]. Hertel and Mehlhorn [40] present a plane-sweep algorithm for triangulating an arbitrary polygon in $O(n + r \log r)$ time, where r equals the number of reflex vertices in the polygon. The sweepline proceeds from left to right in pieces (rather than as a single vertical line) and stops at no more than $O(r)$ vertices. Other polygon triangulation methods include Tarjan and van Wyk's [84], which runs in $O(n \log \log n)$ time, and more recently Chazelle's [19], which runs in optimal $O(n)$ time. A survey of polygon partitioning techniques is presented in [60, 61].

7.6 Exercises

1. Modify our program for finding the intersection points among a collection of line segments so it remains correct even if we drop the assumption that no more than two line segments intersect at a single point.

2. Devise a plane-sweep algorithm for computing the area of the union of a collection of axes-parallel rectangles.

3. Using Big-Oh notation, express the *space* complexity of our line-segment intersection algorithm as a function of the number of line segments and the number of intersections reported. What would the space complexity be if the functions handling transitions

were modified so an event point is removed from the event-point schedule only when it is to be processed, and not otherwise? Would the algorithm's time complexity change?

4. Design an algorithm to report all intersection points among a set of n horizontal and vertical lines segments in the plane. The algorithm should run in $O(n \log n + r)$ time, where r intersections are reported.

5. Given two convex polygons P and Q, devise a plane-sweep algorithm to compute the intersection of P and Q in time proportional to $|P| + |Q|$. (Hint: Let the boundaries of P and Q together serve as the event-point schedule. As intersection points are discovered, they can be used to piece together the boundary of $P \cap Q$.)

6. What purpose does member `Rectangle::id` serve in the contour finding algorithm?

7. Show that the contour finding problem on n rectangles has lower bound $\Omega(n \log n)$. [Hint: Reduce SORTING to the problem. Given numbers $x_1, x_2, \ldots, x_n$ to be sorted, map x_i to the axes-parallel rectangle with corners $(0, 0)$ and (x_i, M), where $M = \max_j \{x_j\}$.]

8. Devise an $O(n \log n)$-time plane-sweep algorithm for triangulating an arbitrary polygon. (Hint: Triangulate the polygon while regularizing it.)

9. Given a polygon P, a triangulation of P's vertex set is a triangulation of the vertices regarded as points in the plane, subject to the constraint that every edge of P must belong to the triangulation. Devise an $O(n \log n)$-time plane-sweep algorithm for triangulating the vertex set of any polygon. (Hint: Modify the algorithm of the previous exercise.)

10. Given a set of n variable-radius disks in the plane, design a plane-sweep algorithm to decide in $O(n \log n)$ time whether any two disks intersect.

11. A point $p = (p_x, p_y)$ is said to *dominate* point $q = (q_x, q_y)$ if $p_x \geq q_x$ and $p_y \geq q_y$. Where p belongs to some point set S, p is called a *maximum* if no point in S dominates p. Devise a plane-sweep algorithm to report all maxima among a set of n points in $O(n \log n)$ time.

8

Divide-and-Conquer Algorithms

A divide-and-conquer approach divides a problem into several subproblems, solves these problems recursively, and then combines their solutions into a solution for the original problem. The subproblems are similar in kind to the original problem, but smaller in size—indeed, the sum of their sizes equals the size of the original problem. When a problem is sufficiently small or easy, it is solved directly without being divided further, and this is the base case which terminates the process. In its most common form, divide and conquer divides a problem into two subproblems, each half as large as the original.

Consider a divide-and-conquer algorithm for finding the smallest value in an array of integers. The idea is to divide the array into left and right subarrays, apply the algorithm recursively to these to obtain the smallest value in each, and then return the smaller of these two values. The base case occurs when a subarray has length one—the sole value it contains is returned. The algorithm is implemented by function fMin, which returns the smallest integer in subarray a[1..r]. Function findMin is a driver function which makes the top-level call to fMin:

```
int findMin(int a[], int n)
{
    return fMin(a, 0, n-1);
}



int fMin(int a[], int l, int r)
```

```
{
    if (l == r)
        return a[l];
    else {
        int m = (l + r) / 2;
        int i = fMin(a, l, m);
        int j = fMin(a, m+1, r);
        return (i < j) ? i : j;
    }
}
```

With respect to the number of comparisons that are performed, findMin is as efficient as scanning the array from left to right while keeping track of the smallest integer seen so far (both methods perform $n - 1$ comparisons). Although the recursive approach is less efficient in practice due to the overhead for the recursive function calls, it serves as a good example of divide and conquer.

We begin this chapter with merge sort, a classic divide-and-conquer sorting algorithm. We then present a method for forming the intersection of a collection of half-planes and apply this method to the problems of constructing the kernel of a polygon and of constructing Voronoi polygons (to be defined in due course). In our next application, we return to the problem of computing the convex hull of a planar point set. Next we will use divide and conquer in an efficient algorithm for finding a pair of closest points from a set of points in the plane. Finally, we present a divide-and-conquer method for triangulating an arbitrary polygon.

8.1   Merge Sort

Merge sort is the only sorting algorithm we will cover with optimal $O(n \log n)$ worst-case running time. Given an array of items to be sorted, merge sort divides the array into left and right subarrays of roughly equal size, recursively sorts each of the two subarrays, and then merges the two now-sorted subarrays into a single sorted array (Figure 8.1). Because the sorted subarrays can be merged in linear time, the running time is expressed by the recurrence $T(n) = 2T(\frac{n}{2}) + an$, which is solved by $T(n) \in O(n \log n)$.

Function template mSort merge sorts subarray a[l..m] using comparison function cmp. Function template mergeSort is the driver function:

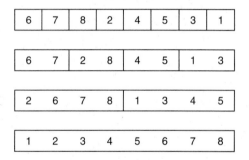

Figure 8.1:   Merge sort.

```
template<class T>
void mergeSort(T a[], int n, int (*cmp)(T,T))
{
    mSort(a, 0, n-1, cmp);
}


template<class T>
void mSort(T a[], int l, int r, int (*cmp)(T,T))
{
    if (l < r) {
        int m = (l + r) / 2;
        mSort(a, l, m, cmp);
        mSort(a, m+1, r, cmp);
        merge(a, l, m, r, cmp);
    }
}
```

The function call merge(a,l,m,r,cmp) merges sorted subarrays a[l..m] and a[m+1..r]. Let us consider how to merge two sorted arrays a and b into a third array c of sufficient length. To do this, we maintain an index aindx, which indexes the smallest (leftmost) item in array a not yet copied into array c, an index bindx defined similarly for array b, and an index cindx indexing the next (leftmost) free position in array c. In each step, we copy the smaller of a[aindx] and b[bindx] into c[cindx] and then increment cindex, as well as either aindx or bindx (whichever indexes the item just copied). If aindx advances past the rightmost element of array a, then the remaining items in array b (starting at bindx) are copied into the remaining positions of array c. Similarly, if bindx advances beyond the rightmost element of array b, the remaining items in array a are copied to array c.

The following template function merges sorted subarrays x[l..m] and x[m+1..r] into a separate array c, which is then copied back into x[l..r]:

```
template<class T>
void merge(T x[], int l, int m, int r, int (*cmp)(T,T))
{
    T *a = x+l;
    T *b = x+m+1;
    T *c = new T[r-l+1];
    int aindx = 0, bindx = 0, cindx = 0;
    int alim = m-l+1, blim = r-m;
    while ((aindx < alim) && (bindx < blim))
        if ((*cmp)(a[aindx], b[bindx]) < 0)
            c[cindx++] = a[aindx++];
        else
            c[cindx++] = b[bindx++];
    while (aindx < alim)    // copy rest of a
        c[cindx++] = a[aindx++];
    while (bindx < blim)    // copy rest of b
        c[cindx++] = b[bindx++];
```

```
for (aindx=cindx=0; aindx <= r-1; a[aindx++] = c[cindx++])
    ;    // copy back
delete c;
}
```

Merge sort is efficient because two sorted arrays are merged in time proportional to the sum of their sizes. Function `merge` runs in $O(r - l)$ time since each of the $r - l + 1$ items to be merged is moved only twice: first into array c, then back into array x. Where $T(n)$ represents the time to merge sort an array of n items, the program takes time

$$T(n) = \begin{cases} 2T(\frac{n}{2}) + an & \text{if } n > 1 \\ b & \text{if } n = 1 \end{cases}$$

for suitable constants a and b. Here $2T(\frac{n}{2})$ represents the time to sort two subarrays recursively, and an the time to merge them subsequently. Thus we have $T(n) \in O(n \log n)$.

8.2   Computing the Intersection of Half-Planes

A line subdivides a plane into two *half-planes*, one to either side of the line. Although half-planes are among the simplest of convex planar regions, any polygon whatsoever can be formed by combining suitably chosen half-planes by intersection and union operations. In this section we will restrict our attention to the problem of forming the intersection of a collection of half-planes.

Let H be a collection of half-planes, and let $I(H)$ denote their intersection. If nonempty, $I(H)$ is called a *convex polytope*. $I(H)$ is indeed convex because the intersection of convex regions is convex. Figure 8.2 depicts two convex polytopes formed by the intersection of half-planes. Figure 8.2a is a convex polygon, whereas Figure 8.2b is an unbounded convex polytope. A half-plane in H is *redundant* if its removal does not change $I(H)$. In Figure 8.2, only the half-plane determined by line e is redundant.

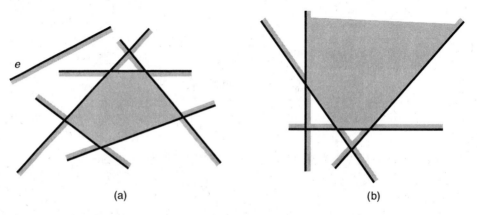

(a)   (b)

Figure 8.2:   Two convex polytopes formed by the intersection of half-planes.

One way to form the intersection of n half-planes is to process them one at a time. The most straightforward implementation of this approach runs in $O(n^2)$ time. Yet the divide-and-conquer approach is also feasible because set intersection is associative—the intersection of n half-planes can be obtained by applying pairwise intersections *in any order*. Hence for any partition of H into nonempty subsets H_1 and H_2, we have $I(H) = I(H_1) \cap I(H_2)$. To compute $I(H)$ using divide and conquer, we partition the collection H of half-planes into two nonempty subsets H_1 and H_2 of approximately equal size, and then recursively compute $I(H_1)$ and $I(H_2)$ and combine them to form $I(H_1) \cap I(H_2)$. In the base case ($n = 1$) we simply return the sole half-plane in H.

Let us turn our attention to implementation. We need a way of representing the boundaries of the convex polytopes produced as the algorithm proceeds, as well as the final one $I(H)$. Unfortunately, we cannot use `Polygon` objects to do this since the boundaries of the *unbounded* convex polytopes are not closed. Rather than define a new class, we will clip $I(H)$ to a convex bounding box B. This ensures that every polytope produced as the algorithm proceeds is bounded: the intersection of some convex polytope and bounding box B.

In program `halfplaneIntersect`, we represent a half-plane by an `Edge` object: The half-plane lies to the right of the edge. The program is passed an array H of n edges and a convex bounding box `box`. It returns the convex polygon equal to the intersection of `box` and the n half-planes of H:

```
Polygon *halfplaneIntersect(Edge H[], int n, Polygon &box)
{
    Polygon *c;
    if (n == 1)
        clipPolygonToEdge(box, H[0], c);
    else {
        int m = n / 2;
        Polygon *a = halfplaneIntersect(H, m, box);
        Polygon *b = halfplaneIntersect(H+m, n-m, box);
        c = convexPolygonIntersect(*a, *b);
        delete a;
        delete b;
    }
    return c;
}
```

The program uses two functions defined earlier. Function `clipPolygonToEdge` of section 5.7 is used to clip the bounding box to the right side of an edge (a single half-plane). Function `convexPolygonIntersect` of section 6.5 is used to form the intersection of two convex polygons.

The bounding box passed to program `halfplaneIntersect` should be large enough that no information is lost. Ideally, the half-planes determined by the bounding box's edges are redundant so the solution returned by the program equals $I(H)$. When this is not possible, such as when $I(H)$ is unbounded, the bounding box should contain all the vertices of $I(H)$ so only the uninteresting portion of $I(H)$ is clipped away. The application program that calls function `halfplaneIntersect` is responsible for setting up the bounding box.

8.2.1 Analysis

On input size n, program `halfplaneIntersect`'s running time $T(n)$ is expressed by the recurrence

$$T(n) = \begin{cases} 2T(\frac{n}{2}) + an & \text{if } n > 1 \\ b & \text{otherwise } (n = 1) \end{cases}$$

Here the term an represents the time function `convexPolygonIntersect` takes to form the intersection of two convex polygons. Hence `halfplaneIntersect` runs in $O(n \log n)$ time.

This algorithm is optimal because this problem has lower bound $\Omega(n \log n)$. To show this, we exhibit a linear-time reduction from sorting to this problem of convex polytope formation. Given numbers $x_1, x_2, \ldots, x_n$ to be sorted, map each x_i to the point (x_i, x_i^2) along the parabola $y = x^2$. Let H_i be the half-plane bounded below by the line tangent to the parabola at (x_i, x_i^2). Then form the convex polytope $I(H)$ equal to the intersection of the half-planes $H_1, H_2, \ldots, H_n$. Here the edges of $I(H)$ are ordered by slope, and their points of contact (x_i, x_i^2) with the parabola are ordered by abscissa. Finally, report the x_is in edge order around $I(H)$.

8.3 Finding the Kernel of a Polygon

Recall from section 5.2 that the the kernel of a polygon is defined as the locus of points which see all the points in a polygon. If nonempty, the kernel of polygon P is a convex polygon contained in P, and P is said to be star shaped (see Figure 5.3). In this section we will use function `halfplaneIntersect` in an $O(n \log n)$-time algorithm for constructing the kernel of a polygon.

Our algorithm is based on this theorem:

Theorem 5 (Kernel Construction Theorem) *Suppose P is an n-gon and H is the set of n half-planes determined by the edges of P. Then the kernel of P equals the intersection $I(H)$ of the half-planes.*

Here the half-plane determined by an edge is bounded by the edge and lies to its right.

The theorem follows from this chain of equivalent statements: (1) Point q belongs to the kernel of P, (2) q sees every point of P, (3) no edge of P obstructs q's view, (4) q lies to the left of no edge, (5) q lies in every half-plane determined by an edge of H, and (6) q belongs to $I(H)$ (see Figure 8.3).

Based on the theorem, we can construct the kernel of polygon P by applying function `halfplaneIntersect` to P's edges. Any bounding box containing P suffices since the kernel is contained in P. The following function `kernel` is passed a polygon p. It returns the polygon representing the kernel of p, or an empty polygon if p is not star shaped:

```
Polygon *kernel(Polygon &p)
{
    Edge *edges = new Edge[p.size()];
    for (int i = 0; i < p.size(); i++, p.advance(CLOCKWISE))
        edges[i] = p.edge();
```

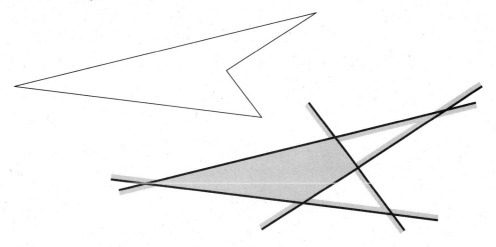

Figure 8.3:   The kernel of polygon P equals the intersection of the half-planes determined by P's edges.

```
    Polygon box;
    box.insert(Point(-DBL_MAX, -DBL_MAX));
    box.insert(Point(-DBL_MAX, DBL_MAX));
    box.insert(Point(DBL_MAX, DBL_MAX));
    box.insert(Point(DBL_MAX, -DBL_MAX));
    Polygon *r = halfplaneIntersect(edges, p.size(), box);
    delete edges;
    return r;
}
```

8.3.1 Analysis

Program `kernel` computes the kernel of an n-gon in $O(n \log n)$ time, its running time dominated by the call to function `halfplaneIntersect`. Interestingly, the program is not optimal—the Chapter Notes cite an optimal kernel-finding algorithm which runs in $O(n)$ time. One might expect there to be a linear-time reduction from the problem of intersecting half-planes to that of finding kernels, thereby transferring the former problem's $\Omega(n \log n)$ lower bound to the latter problem. However, no such reduction exists. The edges of a polygon are not in arbitary position since they connect at vertices; it turns out that it is easier to form the intersection of the half-planes determined by polygon edges than to form the intersection of an arbitrary collection of half-planes.

8.4   Finding Voronoi Regions

Let S be a finite point set in the plane and let p be a point not in S. The *Voronoi region* of p relative to S, denoted $\mathcal{VR}_S(p)$, consists of the locus of points in the plane that are closer to p than to any point of S. For each point $q \in S$, the locus of points lying closer to p than to q equals the half-plane which is bounded by the perpendicular bisector of line segment $\overline{pq}$ and which contains p. The Voronoi region $\mathcal{VR}_S(p)$ equals the intersection of all such half-planes as q ranges over the points of S (see Figure 8.4a). We can express these facts as a theorem:

Theorem 6 (Voronoi Region Theorem)   *Given distinct points p and q, $\mathcal{VR}_{\{q\}}(p)$ equals the half-plane bounded by the perpendicular bisector of $\overline{pq}$, to the side of the perpendicular bisector which contains p. Moreover, given disjoint point sets A and B and point $p \notin A \cup B$, we have $\mathcal{VR}_{A \cup B}(p) = \mathcal{VR}_A(p) \cap \mathcal{VR}_B(p)$.*

The theorem's first assertion follows from the fact that the perpendicular bisector of $\overline{pq}$ consists of all points equidistant from p and q. Regarding the theorem's second assertion, it is not hard to see that $\mathcal{VR}_{A \cup B}(p) \subset \mathcal{VR}_A(p) \cap \mathcal{VR}_B(p)$. To see why $\mathcal{VR}_A(p) \cap \mathcal{VR}_B(p) \subset \mathcal{VR}_{A \cup B}(p)$, suppose that point s lies in $\mathcal{VR}_A(p) \cap \mathcal{VR}_B(p)$. Then s is closer to p than to every point of A, and closer to p than to every point of B. Hence s must be closer to p than to every point of $A \cup B$—that is, $s \in V R_{A \cup B}(p)$.

In light of this theorem, we can compute $\mathcal{VR}_S(p)$ by forming the intersection of the half-planes $\mathcal{VR}_{\{q\}}(p)$ as q ranges over the points of S. The half-plane $\mathcal{VR}_{\{q\}}(p)$ is bounded by the bisector of line segment $\overline{pq}$, which is given by the edge `Edge(p,q).rot()`. The half-plane of interest lies to the right of this edge.

Program `voronoiRegion` is passed a point `p`, an array `s` of `n` points, and a bounding box `box`. It returns the Voronoi region of `p` relative to point set `s`:

```
Polygon *voronoiRegion(Point &p, Point s[], int n, Polygon &box)
{
    Edge *edges = new Edge[n];
    for (int i = 0; i < n; i++) {
        edges[i] = Edge(p, s[i]);
        edges[i].rot();
    }
    Polygon *r = halfplaneIntersect(edges, n, box);
    delete edges;
    return r;
}
```

The bounding box may clip away a portion of the Voronoi region—indeed, if the Voronoi region is unbounded, it does so necessarily. Ideally, the bounding box contains all

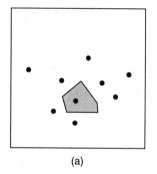 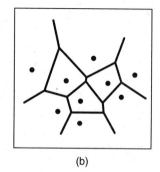 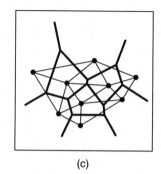

            (a)   (b)   (c)

Figure 8.4:   (a) A Voronoi region, (b) a Voronoi diagram, and (c) the same Voronoi diagram and its dual.

vertices of the Voronoi region so only the uninteresting portion is clipped away. However, given a fixed point p, it is not difficult to devise point sets S such that the vertices of $\mathcal{VR}_S(p)$ lie arbitrarily far from p.

8.4.1 Voronoi Diagrams

Given point set S, the *Voronoi diagram* of S, denoted $\mathcal{VD}(S)$, is the collection of Voronoi regions for each point of S relative to the remaining points of S. That is, the Voronoi regions of $\mathcal{VD}(S)$ are of the form $\mathcal{VR}_{S-\{p\}}(p)$ as p ranges over S. $\mathcal{VD}(S)$ decomposes the plane into convex polytopes (Figures 8.4b and 8.5).

Crystallography provides a pleasing illustration. Imagine the points of S to be crystal seeds which grow in all directions at the same constant rate. Assume that the crystal outgrowths from two or more seeds stop growing wherever they meet. After sufficient time, each outgrowth represents its seed's Voronoi region (although outgrowths corresponding to unbounded regions continue to grow forever). Taken together, the outgrowths represent the Voronoi diagram of S. (It is enjoyable to imagine the process one dimension higher, in which the seeds are fixed points in space. The three-dimensional Voronoi diagram that emerges consists of bounded and unbounded polyhedral regions.)

For brevity, we will write $\mathcal{VR}(p)$ to stand for $\mathcal{VR}_{S-\{p\}}(p)$. For simplicity, we will assume that no four points of S are cocircular. (Recall from section 6.6 that a set of points is *cocircular* if there exists some circle on whose boundary the points lie, and that if such a circle exists and is unique, it is called the *circumcircle* of the points.)

An edge of $\mathcal{VD}(S)$ shared by Voronoi regions $\mathcal{VR}(p)$ and $\mathcal{VR}(q)$ consists of those points in the plane which are equidistant from p and q, and closer to p and q than to the remaining points of S. A vertex v of $\mathcal{VD}(S)$ is the meeting point of three Voronoi regions $\mathcal{VR}(p)$, $\mathcal{VR}(q)$, and $\mathcal{VR}(r)$. Being equidistant from p, q, and r, vertex v is the center of the circumcircle determined by these three points. Moreover, since v is closer to p, q, and r than to the remaining points of S, the circumcircle is point free (no points of S lie in its interior). It follows that the triangle $\triangle pqr$ is a Delaunay triangle of S. (Delaunay triangulations were discussed in section 6.6.) To every vertex of the Voronoi diagram corresponds a triangle of the Delaunay triangulation, and to every Voronoi region corresponds a vertex of the Delaunay triangulation (a point of S). The Voronoi diagram and the Delaunay triangulation

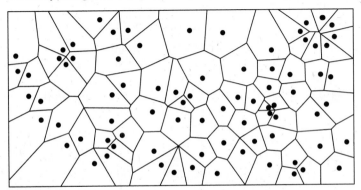

Figure 8.5: The Voronoi diagram for a set of 80 points.

are said to be *dual* to each other. This is illustrated in Figure 8.4c, where the two diagrams are superimposed.

Program `voronoiDiagram` constructs the Voronoi diagram for array s of n points. It returns the list of Voronoi regions that comprise the diagram:

```
List<Polygon*> *voronoiDiagram(Point s[], int n, Polygon &box)
{
    List<Polygon*> *regions = new List<Polygon*>;
    for (int i = 0; i < n; i++) {
        Point p = s[i];
        s[i] = s[n-1];
        regions->append(voronoiRegion(p, s, n-1, box));
        s[i] = p;
    }
    return regions;
}
```

8.4.2 Analysis

Program `voronoiRegion` is dominated by the call to `halfplaneIntersect` and so runs in $O(n \log n)$ time. Indeed, this is optimal. To see that the problem of finding Voronoi regions has lower bound $\Omega(n \log n)$, consider the following linear-time reduction from sorting. Given numbers $x_1, x_2, \ldots, x_n$ to be sorted, map these x_i to points $p(x_i)$ on the circumference of a circle such that the points $p(x_i)$ are ordered around the circle by increasing x_i. Then construct the Voronoi region of the circle's center point relative to these n points. This Voronoi region is a convex n-gon, each edge of which separates the circle's center from one of the points $p(x_i)$ on the circle's circumference. Finally, report the points $p(x_i)$ in edge order around the Voronoi region.

Although $\Omega(n \log n)$ time is necessary to compute a Voronoi region relative to a set S of n points, much more can be accomplished within the same time bound. Indeed, the Chapter Notes cite an algorithm for finding the entire Voronoi diagram of S in $O(n \log n)$ time. This outperforms program `voronoiDiagram` by a factor of n.

8.5   Merge Hull

In this section we present a divide-and-conquer algorithm for computing the convex hull $\mathcal{CH}(S)$ of a point set S. The idea is to partition S by an imaginary vertical line into two equal-size sets S_L and S_R, and then recursively construct $\mathcal{CH}(S_L)$ and $\mathcal{CH}(S_R)$ and merge them to form $\mathcal{CH}(S)$. In the base case ($|S| = 1$), we simply return the 1-gon whose sole vertex is contained in S: This point is its own convex hull.

The algorithm is asymptotically efficient because convex hulls $\mathcal{CH}(S_L)$ and $\mathcal{CH}(S_R)$ can be merged efficiently, in $O(|S|)$ time. To perform the merge, we remove the *right chain* of $\mathcal{CH}(S_L)$ and the *left chain* of $\mathcal{CH}(S_R)$ and replace them by an *upper bridge* and a *lower bridge* (Figure 8.6). Such bridges exist because $\mathcal{CH}(S_L)$ and $\mathcal{CH}(S_R)$ are disjoint—they lie

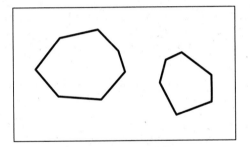 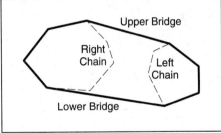

Figure 8.6:   Merging two disjoint convex hulls.

to either side of the imaginary vertical line. This merge step forms the crux of the algorithm, and we shall discuss it shortly.

8.5.1 The Top-Level Program

Program `mergeHull` is passed an array `pts` of n points and returns a polygon representing their convex hull:

```
Polygon *mergeHull(Point pts[], int n)
{
    Point **p = new (Point*)[n];
    for (int i = 0; i < n; i++)
        p[i] = &pts[i];
    mergeSort(p, n, leftToRightCmp);
    return mHull(p, n);
}
```

Program `mergeHull` presorts the points from left to right so point sets can later be partitioned quickly into left and right subsets.

Function `mHull` implements the recursive part of the algorithm:

```
Polygon *mHull(Point *p[], int n)
{
    if (n == 1) {
        Polygon *q = new Polygon;
        q->insert(*p[0]);
        return q;
    } else {
        int m = n / 2;
        Polygon *L = mHull(p, m);
        Polygon *R = mHull(p+m, n-m);
        return merge(L, R);
    }
}
```

In the base case (n==1), function mHull returns a 1-gon. In the general case, it partitions the point set into left and right point sets p[0..m-1] and p[m..n-1] and then constructs their convex hulls L and R and merges them.

8.5.2 Merging Two Convex Hulls

The function call merge(L,R), which combines the two convex hulls L and R, depends on the notion of a *bridge*. Recall from section 5.3 the definition of supporting line: A line ℓ is a *supporting line* of convex polygon P if ℓ passes through a vertex of P and the interior of P lies entirely to one side of ℓ. Line ℓ is a *bridge* of convex polygons P and Q if ℓ is a supporting line of both P and Q. Line ℓ is an *upper bridge* if both polygons lie below ℓ, and a *lower bridge* if they both lie above ℓ.

To merge polygons L and R, we find the upper bridge which connects some vertex $l_1 \in L$ to some vertex $r_1 \in R$, and the lower bridge which connects vertices $l_2 \in L$ and $r_2 \in R$. Vertices l_1 and l_2 divide the boundary of polygon L into a left chain and a right chain; similarly, vertices r_1 and r_2 divide the boundary of R into left and right chains. To merge L and R into $\mathcal{CH}(S)$, we replace L's right chain and R's left chain by the upper and lower bridges.

Function merge combines convex polygons L and R into their convex hull, which it returns. Polygon L is assumed to lie to the left of polygon R. UPPER and LOWER are enumeration values:

```
Polygon *merge(Polygon *L, Polygon *R)
{
    Vertex *l1, *r1, *l2, *r2;
    Vertex *vl = leastVertex(*L, rightToLeftCmp);
    Vertex *vr = leastVertex(*R, leftToRightCmp);
    bridge(L, R, l1, r1, UPPER);
    L->setV(vl);
    R->setV(vr);
    bridge(L, R, l2, r2, LOWER);
    L->setV(l1);
    L->split(r1);
    R->setV(r2);
    delete R->split(l2);
    return R;
}
```

The calls to leastVertex find the rightmost vertex of L and the leftmost vertex of R. Function leastVertex was defined in subsection 4.3.6.

The two split operations in function merge replace the right chain of L and the left chain of R by the upper and lower bridges. Figure 8.7 illustrates how they do this.

Let us look at how function bridge finds the upper bridge of L and R. The function finds a supporting line of L, then of R, and alternates in this manner until finding a supporting line of both—that is, the upper bridge (Figure 8.8a). To accomplish this, function bridge initially positions window vl over the rightmost vertex of L and window vr over the leftmost

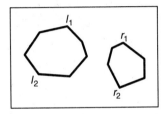 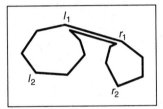 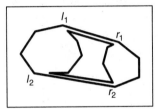

Figure 8.7:   Merging convex hulls L and R through two `split` operations.

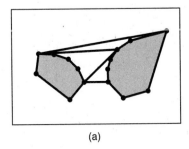 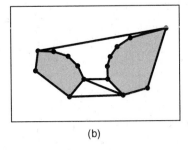

            (a)   (b)

Figure 8.8:   Finding the upper and lower bridge of two disjoint convex polygons.

vertex of R. Then it iteratively performs this block of instructions until neither vl nor vr can be advanced:

1. Find the supporting line ℓ_1 to R such that ℓ_1 lies above R and passes through vertex vl.

2. Set vr equal to the vertex of R that ℓ_1 touches.

3. Find the supporting line ℓ_2 to L such that ℓ_2 lies above L and passes through vertex vr.

4. Set vl equal to the vertex of L that ℓ_2 touches.

    The lower bridge of polygons L and R is found similarly, where *below* replaces *above*. Figure 8.8 shows the sequence of supporting lines discovered during the course of finding the upper and lower bridge.

    Function `bridge` finds a bridge between convex polygons L and R. The vertices where the bridge touches L and R are passed back through reference parameters vl and vr, respectively. Parameter `type` specifies the type of bridge sought (UPPER or LOWER). The function assumes that polygon L lies to the left of polygon R and that vl is initially positioned over some vertex of L's right chain, and vr over some vertex of R's left chain:

```
void bridge(Polygon *L, Polygon *R,
            Vertex* &vl, Vertex* &vr, int type)
{
    int sides[2] = { LEFT, RIGHT };
    int indx = (type == UPPER) ? 0 : 1;
    do {
        vl = L->v();
        vr = R->v();
```

```
        supportingLine(L->point(), R, sides[indx]);
        supportingLine(R->point(), L, sides[1-indx]);
    } while ((vl != L->v()) || (vr != R->v()));
}
```

Function `supportingLine` was defined as part of the insertion hull algorithm of section 5.3.

8.5.3 Analysis

It is not hard to see that polygons L and R are merged in time proportional to $|L| + |R|$. To find each bridge, function `bridge` alternately advances past vertices in L and R. Once a vertex is passed, it is not visited again. Hence each of the two bridges is found in $O(|L|+|R|)$ time, so function `merge`'s two calls to `bridge` take linear time. Moreover, `merge` spends linear time in its call to `leastVertex`, and constant time for its other operations. Thus `merge` runs in linear time.

It follows that the top-level call `mHull(p,n)` runs in $T(n)$ time, where

$$T(n) = \begin{cases} 2T(\frac{n}{2}) + an & \text{if } n > 1 \\ b & \text{otherwise } (n = 1) \end{cases}$$

This is solved by $T(n) \in O(n \log n)$.

The algorithm is not dominated by the initial sorting of points since this too takes $O(n \log n)$ time. Hence merge hull has worst-case running time $O(n \log n)$.

8.6   Closest Points

In this section we consider the *closest pair problem*: Given a set S of n points, find two points in S such that the distance separating them is less than or equal to the distance separating any other pair of points. We will call the two points a *closest pair* in S, and the distance separating them the *closest pair distance* in S. If $n = 1$, the closest pair distance in S equals infinity.

The brute-force solution to this problem is to compute the distance for every pair of points while keeping track of the minimum distance (for brevity, we will use *distance* to mean "distance that separates some pair of points"). Since there are $\frac{n(n-1)}{2}$ pairs, this runs in $\Theta(n^2)$ time. In this section we present a solution based on divide and conquer whose running time is $O(n \log n)$.

The general case of our algorithm works as follows. Given point set S of size $|S| > 1$, we partition S by an imaginary vertical line ℓ into two sets S_L and S_R of approximately equal size, such that the points in S_L lie to the left of ℓ and those of S_R lie to the right of ℓ. Then we apply the algorithm recursively to S_L and to S_R, in order to find a closest pair in S_L and a closest pair in S_R. Either one of these two pairs is also a closest pair in S, or else every closest pair in S must *straddle* S_L and S_R (consist of one point in S_L and the other in S_R). It is the goal of the merge stage to determine which is the case.

Let δ_L and δ_R denote the closest pair distances in S_L and S_R, respectively, and let $\delta = \min(\delta_L, \delta_R)$. If every closest pair in S straddles S_L and S_R, then the distance separating each such pair of points must be strictly less than δ. Thus we can restrict our attention to the points that lie within the vertical strip of width 2δ centered along line ℓ. This is because any point of S_L that lies outside (to the left of) this strip is at least distance δ from line ℓ, hence at least this far from any point of S_R. Similarly, any point of S_R that lies outside this strip need not be considered (see Figure 8.9a).

To process the points in the strip, we maintain a current closest pair distance D, initialized to δ. We update D whenever we discover within the strip a pair of points whose distance is strictly less than D. Interestingly, it is not necessary to compute the distance for every pair of points in the strip. For if the *vertical* distance between two points exceeds D, the distance between them must also exceed D.

Let us relabel the points in the strip as $p_1, p_2, \ldots, p_m$ by increasing y-coordinates. For each p_i, we compute the distance separating p_i and each p_j for $j = i+1, i+1, \ldots, k$, until either (1) $k = m$ or (2) the y-coordinates of p_i and p_{k+1} differ by D or greater. In this manner, only those pairs of points whose vertical distance is less than D are considered.

8.6.1 The Top-Level Program

Program `closestPoints` is passed an array s of n points. It returns the closest pair distance of s and passes back some closest pair through reference parameter c:

```
double closestPoints(Point s[], int n, Edge &c)
{
    Point **x = new (Point*)[n];
    Point **y = new (Point*)[n];
    for (int i = 0; i < n; i++)
        x[i] = y[i] = &s[i];
    mergeSort(x, n, leftToRightCmp);
    mergeSort(y, n, bottomToTopCmp);
    return cPoints(x, y, n, c);
}
```

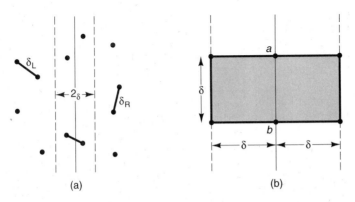

(a)   (b)

Figure 8.9:   (a) The strip of width 2δ, where $\delta = \min(\delta_L, \delta_R)$. (b) No more than eight points of S lie in a $2\delta \times \delta$ band (here two points—one from S_L and one from S_R—coincide at point a, and two others at point b).

Program `closestPoints` presorts the points by *x*-coordinates to expedite the partitioning of point sets, and by *y*-coordinates to expedite the processing of points within vertical strips. Sorting by increasing *y*-coordinates is done using the following comparison function:

```
int bottomToTopCmp(Point *a, Point *b)
{
   if ((a->y<b->y) || ((a->y==b->y) && (a->x<b->x)))
      return -1;
   else if ((a->y>b->y) || ((a->y==b->y) && (a->x>b->x)))
      return 1;
   return 0;
}
```

Function `cPoints` is passed array x of n points sorted by *x*-coordinates, and array y *of the same points* sorted by *y*-coordinates. It returns the closest pair distance for the n points and passes back some closest pair through reference parameter c:

```
double cPoints(Point *x[], Point *y[], int n, Edge &c)
{
   if (n == 1)
      return DBL_MAX;
   else {
      int m = n / 2;
      Point **yL = new (Point*)[m];
      Point **yR = new (Point*)[n-m];
      splitY(y, n, x[m], yL, yR);
      Edge a, b;
      double deltaL = cPoints(x, yL, m, a);
      double deltaR = cPoints(x+m, yR, n-m, b);
      delete yL;
      delete yR;
      double delta;
      if (deltaL < deltaR) {
         delta = deltaL;
         c = a;
      } else {
         delta = deltaR;
         c = b;
      }
      return checkStrip(y, n, x[m], delta, c);
   }
}
```

The vertical dividing line ℓ passes through point x[m], the median of the point set with respect to *x*-coordinates. Function `splitY` partitions the point set with respect to line ℓ, in preparation for the two recursive calls to function `cPoints`.

8.6.2 Processing the Points in the Strip

Function `splitY` partitions array y into two arrays yL and yR. Point p is the dividing point: After the operation, array yL contains those points of y which are less than p—loosely speaking, they lie to the left of point p—sorted by *y*-coordinates; and array yR contains those points of y which are greater than or equal to p, also sorted by *y*-coordinates. The function performs the reverse of the merge operation of merge sort:

```
void splitY(Point *y[], int n, Point *p,
            Point *yL[], Point *yR[])
{
   int i, lindx, rindx;
   i = lindx = rindx = 0;
   while (i < n)
      if (*y[i] < *p)
         yL[lindx++] = y[i++];
      else
         yR[rindx++] = y[i++];
}
```

Function `checkStrip` checks those points of array y that lie within the strip of width `2*delta` centered along the vertical line passing through point p. If the best pair it finds within the strip is separated by distance less than `delta`, the function returns this distance and passes back the pair of points through reference parameter c. Otherwise the function returns `delta` without modifying c:

```
double checkStrip(Point *y[], int n, Point *p,
                  double delta, Edge &c)
{
   int i, striplen;
   Point *s = new Point[n];
   for (i = striplen = 0; i < n; i++)
      if ((p->x - delta < y[i]->x) && (y[i]->x < p->x + delta))
         s[striplen++] = *y[i];
   for (i = 0; i < striplen; i++)
      for (int j = i+1; j < striplen; j++) {
         if (s[j].y - s[i].y > delta)
            break;
         if ((s[i] - s[j]).length() < delta) {
            delta = (s[i] - s[j]).length();
            c = Edge(s[i], s[j]);
         }
      }
   delete s;
   return delta;
}
```

8.6.3 Analysis

We will show that function cPoints runs in $O(n \log n)$ time when called with n points. Since the presorting performed by program closestPoints also takes $O(n \log n)$ time, it will follow that the program as a whole runs in $O(n \log n)$ time.

The running time $T(n)$ of cPoints is expressed by the familiar recurrence $T(n) = 2T(\frac{n}{2}) + an$, hence $T(n) \in O(n \log n)$. The term an represents the time required to merge results, which is dominated by the calls to splitY and checkStrip. Function splitY clearly runs in linear time.

Consider function checkStrip. The body of this function consists of two successive outer for loops. The first for loop accumulates in array s the points that lie within the strip, and clearly runs in $O(n)$ time. The second outer for loop performs one iteration for each point in the strip, for a total of no more than n iterations. How much time is spent executing the inner for loop? Consider the strip in the vicinity of point s_i—specifically, the $2\delta \times \delta$ band extending from $s_i.y$ up to $s_i.y + \delta$ (Figure 8.9b). This band is divided by line ℓ into a left square B_L and a right square B_R, each of size $\delta \times \delta$. Since no two points to the left of ℓ are closer to each other than δ, B_L can contain no more than four points of S. Similarly, B_R also can contain no more than four points of S. Hence the band contains at most eight points of S, one of which is point s_i itself. Since at most seven points in the strip lie within vertical distance δ above s_i, the number of iterations performed by the inner for loop is bounded above by a constant. It follows that the second outer for loop runs in linear time, and hence so does function checkStrip.

The algorithm as a whole works its magic in the vicinity of the dividing line ℓ. By recursing first, before considering pairs of points that straddle ℓ, it obtains an upper bound δ on the closest pair distance. It then uses δ to bound above by $O(n)$ the number of pairs that straddle ℓ, whose distance must be computed.

8.7   Polygon Triangulation

In this section we use divide and conquer to triangulate an arbitrary polygon P. The idea is first to split P along some chord and then recursively triangulate the two subpolygons which result. The base case occurs when the polygon to be triangulated is a triangle. The algorithm is less efficient, but much easier to program, than the method of section 7.4, which splits the polygon into monotone pieces and triangulates each piece in turn. The algorithm is based on a straightforward proof of the following theorem:

Theorem 7 (Polygon Triangulation Theorem)   *An n-gon can be triangulated by $n - 3$ chords into $n - 2$ triangles.*

You might wish to get a feel for the theorem by triangulating some polygons of your own design. Convex polygons are the easiest to triangulate: Choose any one of the polygon's n vertices and then connect the vertex with a chord to each of the $n - 3$ nonadjacent vertices, thereby producing $n - 2$ triangles. A second method for triangulating a convex polygon relies on the fact that every diagonal of a convex polygon is a chord: Split the polygon along any diagonal and then recursively triangulate the two convex subpolygons that result.

Triangulating nonconvex polygons is not as easy; indeed, the assertion that every polygon can be triangulated is not so obvious when nonconvex polygons are considered. We will prove the triangulation theorem both to convince ourselves of the theorem's truth and to motivate the triangulation algorithm to follow.

The proof of the theorem is by induction on n, the number of polygon sides. The theorem is trivially true for $n = 3$, the basis for the induction. So let P be a polygon with $n \geq 4$ sides, and suppose (as the induction hypothesis) that the theorem holds for all polygons with fewer than n sides. We seek a chord of P.

Let b be any convex vertex, and let a and c be its neighbors. Two cases can occur (Figure 8.10). In the first case, diagonal $\overline{ac}$ is a chord of P. Let P' be the $n-1$-sided polygon that results from splitting off triangle $\triangle abc$. By the induction hypothesis, there exists a set of $n-4$ chords that partitions P' into $n-3$ triangles. Adding to this chord $\overline{ac}$ and triangle $\triangle abc$, we are left with a set of $n-3$ chords which partition the original polygon P into $n-2$ triangles.

In the second case, diagonal $\overline{ac}$ is not a chord of P, implying that the interior of triangle $\triangle abc$ must contain at least one vertex of P. Of those vertices inside $\triangle abc$, let d by one furthest from the line $\overleftrightarrow{ca}$. We will call d an *intruding vertex*. By our choice of vertex d, the diagonal $\overline{bd}$ must lie in P—for were some polygon edge to intrude between b and d, at least one of its endpoints must lie inside $\triangle abc$ at greater distance from $\overleftrightarrow{ca}$ than d, contradicting our choice of d. Hence $\overline{bd}$ must be a chord. Now chord $\overline{bd}$ partitions P into two smaller polygons P_1 and P_2 with n_1 and n_2 sides, respectively. Since $n_1 + n_2 = n + 2$ and $n_1, n_2 \geq 3$, it follows that n_1 and n_2 are each less than n. Thus we can apply the induction hypothesis to P_1 and to P_2. Counting chords yields a total of $(n_1 - 3) + (n_2 - 3) + 1 = n - 3$ chords, and counting triangles a total of $(n_1 - 2) + (n_2 - 2) = n - 2$ triangles. The triangulation theorem is proved.

8.7.1 The Top-Level Program

This proof leads directly to the following program for triangulating a polygon. The program is passed a polygon p and returns a list of triangles representing its triangulation. The triangles are accumulated in the list `triangles`:

```
List<Polygon*> *triangulate(Polygon &p)
{
    List<Polygon*> *triangles = new List<Polygon*>;
    if (p.size() == 3)
```

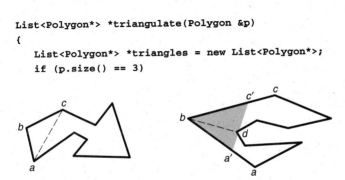

Figure 8.10:   The two cases covered in the proof of the triangulation theorem.

```
        triangles->append(&p);
    else {
        findConvexVertex(p);
        Vertex *d = findIntrudingVertex(p);
        if (d == NULL) { // no intruding vertex exists
            Vertex *c = p.neighbor(CLOCKWISE);
            p.advance(COUNTER_CLOCKWISE);
            Polygon *q = p.split(c);
            triangles->append(triangulate(p));
            triangles->append(q);
        } else {    // d is the intruding vertex
            Polygon *q = p.split(d);
            triangles->append(triangulate(*q));
            triangles->append(triangulate(p));
        }
    }
    return triangles;
}
```

8.7.2 Finding an Intruding Vertex

The program uses the functions findConvexVertex and findIntrudingVertex. When handed polygon p, function findConvexVertex moves p's window over some convex vertex. It does this by sliding windows a, b, and c, positioned over three successive vertices, clockwise around the polygon until detecting a right turn at vertex b:

```
void findConvexVertex(Polygon &p)
{
    Vertex *a = p.neighbor(COUNTER_CLOCKWISE);
    Vertex *b = p.v();
    Vertex *c = p.neighbor(CLOCKWISE);
    while (c->classify(*a, *b) != RIGHT) {
        a = b;
        b = p.advance(CLOCKWISE);
        c = p.neighbor(CLOCKWISE);
    }
}
```

Function findIntrudingVertex is passed polygon p, whose current vertex is assumed to be convex. It returns a pointer to an intruding vertex if one exists, and NULL otherwise:

```
Vertex *findIntrudingVertex(Polygon &p)
{
    Vertex *a = p.neighbor(COUNTER_CLOCKWISE);
    Vertex *b = p.v();
    Vertex *c = p.advance(CLOCKWISE);
    Vertex *d = NULL;        // best candidate so far
```

```
    double bestD = -1.0;    // distance to best candidate
    Edge ca(c->point(), a->point());
    Vertex *v = p.advance(CLOCKWISE);
    while (v != a) {
        if (pointInTriangle(*v, *a, *b, *c)) {
            double dist = v->distance(ca);
            if (dist > bestD) {
                d = v;
                bestD = dist;
            }
        }
        v = p.advance(CLOCKWISE);
    }
    p.setV(b);
    return d;
}
```

Function `pointInTriangle` tests for point-triangle inclusion: The function returns TRUE if point p lies in the triangle with vertices a, b, and c, and it returns FALSE otherwise:

```
bool pointInTriangle(Point p, Point a, Point b, Point c)
{
    return ((p.classify(a, b) != LEFT) &&
            (p.classify(b, c) != LEFT) &&
            (p.classify(c, a) != LEFT));
}
```

Observe that the triangulation produced by the program `triangulate` depends on both the polygon it is passed as well as that polygon's initial current vertex. Figure 8.11 depicts three different triangulations of the same polygon obtained by varying its initial current vertex. You might wish to compare these triangulations to that shown in Figure 7.13.

8.7.3 Analysis

When applied to an n-gon, `findConvexVertex` and `findIntrudingVertex` each take $O(n)$ time. If no intruding vertex is found, a single triangle is extracted from the n-gon

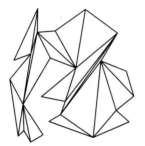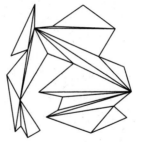

Figure 8.11: Three triangulations produced by program `triangulate`.

and the resulting $n-1$-gon is recursively triangulated. In the worst case, an intruding vertex is *never* found as the program proceeds, and the size of the polygon is reduced by one in each successive stage. This leads to a worst-case running time of $T(n) = n + (n-1) + \cdots + 1$, which is $O(n^2)$. This worst-case performance is achieved when triangulating a convex polygon.

The program is likely to run fastest if intruding vertices are found, since the problem then reduces to two subproblems potentially of roughly equal size. Since only reflex vertices can intrude, the program potentially runs fastest if the polygon possesses many reflex vertices. However, it is not hard to devise a polygon possessing $\Omega(n)$ reflex vertices whose triangulation still requires $\Omega(n^2)$ time—although intruding vertices exist, the algorithm fails to find them or finds only "bad" ones resulting in subproblems of very different size, one large and the other small.

8.8 Chapter Notes

An optimal $\Theta(n)$-time algorithm for computing the kernel of a polygon was devised by Lee and Preparata [53]; the algorithm also appears in [67]. While traversing the polygon boundary, their algorithm incrementally constructs the intersection of the half-planes determined by the polygon's edges. It takes advantage of the polygon's structure to achieve the linear-time performance.

Divide and conquer can be used to construct the Voronoi diagram of a point set S in $O(n \log n)$ time, where $|S| = n$. The idea is to partition S by an imaginary vertical line into point sets S_L and S_R and then recursively construct the Voronoi diagrams $\mathcal{VD}(S_L)$ and $\mathcal{VD}(S_R)$ and merge these to form $\mathcal{VD}(S_R)$. It is the linear-time merge that makes the algorithm both interesting and efficient [51, 66, 74]. To support the merge, Voronoi diagrams are represented by a data structure more sophisticated than the simple list of polygons used by our program `voronoiDiagram`.

The illustration of Voronoi diagrams based on crystallography is noted in [61], which in turn cites [72].

Another divide-and-conquer algorithm for constructing the convex hull of a planar point set S works like this: S is first partitioned into two sets S_1 and S_2—the partition is arbitrary, except that S_1 and S_2 are of roughly equal size. Then convex hulls $\mathcal{CH}(S_1)$ and $\mathcal{CH}(S_2)$ are constructed recursively and merged to form $\mathcal{CH}(S)$ [67]. Since convex hulls $\mathcal{CH}(S_1)$ and $\mathcal{CH}(S_2)$ generally intersect, the merge step is quite different from the one described in this chapter. Yet because this merge step too runs in linear time, the algorithm—like the one in this chapter—runs in $O(n \log n)$ time.

The solution to the closest pair problem presented in this chapter first appeared in [74]. The solution was extended to d-dimensional space in [10], where it was shown that the problem can be solved in $O(n \log n)$ time, where n equals the number of points. These solutions also appear in [67].

The proof on which the triangulation algorithm is based is from [60]. Chazelle [18] presents a linear-time method for finding good chords [it requires $O(n \log n)$ time for preprocessing]. If polygon P is subdivided by such a chord, the two subpolygons that result have size at least $\frac{|P|}{3}$. This chapter's triangulation algorithm runs in $O(n \log n)$ time if Chazelle's chord finding method replaces our method for finding intruding vertices.

8.9 Exercises

1. In proving the polygon triangulation theorem, we assumed that every polygon possesses at least some convex vertex. Show that this is the case.

2. Show that any polygon can be formed by combining suitably chosen half-planes by intersection and union operations.

3. Define a new class for representing bounded and unbounded two-dimensional convex polytopes. What are the advantages of representing convex polytopes using this class instead of class `Polygon`, as in this book?

4. The *farthest pair problem* is defined as follows: Given a point set S in the plane, find some pair whose distance is greater than or equal to the distance between all other pairs. Show that the farthest pair distance is realized by two extreme points [vertices of $CH(S)$].

5. Given planar point set S of n points, devise an $O(n \log n)$ time algorithm to solve the farthest pair problem in S. [Hint: First construct the convex hull $CH(S)$. Next maintain two windows over *antipodal* vertices of S, moving them around the polygon until all antipodal pairs have been considered. Two vertices of a convex polygon are antipodal if they admit parallel supporting lines between which the polygon lies.]

6. Devise an n-gon possessing $\Omega(n)$ reflex vertices, for which the triangulation algorithm of section 8.7 runs in $\Omega(n^2)$ time.

7. Suppose we had defined *intruding vertex* like this: Given convex vertex b and neighbors a and c, vertex d intrudes if (1) d lies inside triangle $\triangle abc$ and (2) d lies closer to vertex b than does any other vertex lying inside $\triangle abc$. Under this revised definition, would the triangulation algorithm be correct? Prove your answer.

8. Devise an $O(n \log n)$-time divide-and-conquer algorithm to report all maxima in a point set. (The *maxima* of a point set was defined in section 7.5.)

9. Design a divide-and-conquer algorithm to report all intersection points given a set of n horizontal and vertical line segments in the plane. The algorithm should run in $O(n \log n + r)$ time, where r intersections are reported.

10. Devise an incremental algorithm for computing the kernel of an n-gon in $O(n)$ time.

11. Let S be a point set in the plane.

    (a) Show that if $p \in S$ and q is the closest point in S to p, then $VR(p)$ and $VR(q)$ share an edge in Voronoi diagram $VD(S)$.

    (b) Given $VD(S)$, design an algorithm to solve the closest pair problem in S. What is the running time of your algorithm?

12. Design a plane-sweep algorithm that solves the closest pair problem. (Hint: When the sweepline reaches a point p, determine whether there exists some point to the left of the sweepline with which p forms a closest pair.)

9

Spatial Subdivision Methods

A *spatial subdivision* is a decomposition of some spatial domain into smaller pieces. Known also as *partitions* or simply *subdivisions*, they permit a problem involving the domain, or geometric objects lying in the domain, to be reduced to simpler or smaller subproblems. For instance, the area of a triangulated polygon can be computed easily by summing the areas of its triangles.

Spatial subdivisions vary widely with respect to shape and structure. *Hierarchical* subdivisions, which are constructed by recursively partitioning the domain into smaller and smaller pieces, are among the most powerful since they readily support recursive methods. A familiar example in one dimension is the binary search tree over a set of real numbers. Each level of the tree corresponds to a partition of the real number line: the root level to the unpartitioned real number line, and each remaining level to a refinement of the partition corresponding to the next-higher level. The tree's lowest level corresponds to the finest subdivision of all (see Figure 9.1).

In this chapter we will examine three hierarchical subdivisions. Two of them—the *quadtree* and the *two-dimensional tree*—will be applied to the *planar range searching problem*. We will also attack this problem using a *grid*, a nonhierarchical subdivision of the domain into small squares.

The last hierarchical subdivision we will look at is the *binary space partition tree*, which we will use to solve a practical problem in computer graphics: Given a static scene of triangles in space and a moving viewpoint, compute a visibility ordering for the triangles for each successive position of the viewpoint. The solution we present can be used to generate successive images in near real time, even for scenes of considerable complexity.

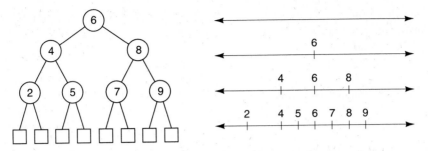

Figure 9.1:   A binary search tree represents a hierarchical subdivision of the real number line.

9.1   The Range Searching Problem

Given a set of points, we sometimes wish to determine which of them lie within a given region. For instance, we might ask which cities lie between given lines of longitude and latitude. Or we might ask for the name of every star that lies within some given distance from some given star or point in space. Such questions are called *region queries*.

If the points lie in the plane and the region is an axes-parallel rectangle, the region query is called a *two-dimensional range query*, and the rectangle is called a *range*. Figure 9.2 illustrates a range query in the plane. To solve the query, we use the fact that a point is contained in a range if and only if the point simultaneously lies within the range's x-extent and its y-extent. In the figure, the points e, f, g, and h lie in the range's x-extent, but of these only f and h also lie in its y-extent.

The strategy is easy to implement. Function `pointInRectangle` returns TRUE if and only if point p lies in rectangle R:

```
bool pointInRectangle(Point &p, Rectangle &R)
{
    return ((R.sw.x <= p.x) && (p.x <= R.ne.x) &&
            (R.sw.y <= p.y) && (p.y <= R.ne.y));
}
```

Range queries frequently arise in settings which are not intrinsically geometrical, but which can be treated as such. In these cases, the components of the "points" represent

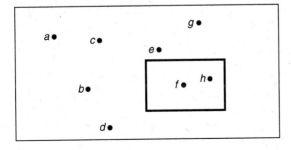

Figure 9.2:   A planar range query.

quantifiable attributes. For example, we might ask for the names of all stars whose brightness and temperature fall within given intervals; the range is an axes-parallel rectangle in the brightness-temperature plane. Database systems support queries of this sort, in which the points are records and their components are fields.

So far we have focused on the range query as a "one-shot" problem: Given a point set S and a range R, report the points of S that lie in R. However, in many situations it is necessary to perform a *series* of range queries for some fixed point set S. In such cases it is generally better first to organize the points of S in a data structure which supports the series of range queries to follow, rather than answer each query independently. This "multishot" version is known as the *range searching* problem. The two-dimensional range searching problem is specified by a static set S of points in the plane. The problem is to organize the points of S into a *spatial data structure* which efficiently supports repeated range queries. Spatial data structures are typically used to support a series of operations; in other words, they are typically used to implement geometrical abstract data types (ADTs). Thus the cost of their construction, which may be considerable, can be amortized over many operations.

The naive approach to range searching is to organize the points S in a list. Then, to query with range R, we test every point in the list for inclusion in R. This takes time proportional to $|S|$, the size of S, which is inefficient when the number of points reported is small compared to $|S|$. The problem is that no attempt is made to confine the search to the vicinity of the range, so even points far from the range are considered.

In the next three sections, we present more efficient solutions which employ spatial data structures to localize search. To simplify our presentation, we will assume that the points of S lie in the positive quadrant of the plane, so they can be enclosed by a square domain $\mathcal{D}$ whose southwest (lower-left) corner coincides with the origin. It is actually domain $\mathcal{D}$ which shall be subdivided, rather than the entire plane.

Although we will concentrate on the range searching problem, it is important to realize that the spatial data structures we will examine can also be used to solve many other kinds of problems. The exercises at the end of this chapter will address some of these.

9.2   The Grid Method

9.2.1 Representation

The simplest subdivision of square domain $\mathcal{D}$ divides it into a grid of small squares or *cells*. To initialize the grid for range searching in point set S, we "drop" each point of S into its appropriate cell—for each cell we build a list of the points that lie in the cell (Figure 9.3). Then, to query with range R, we consider only those cells which intersect R, and for each such cell we test each of its points for inclusion in R.

An $m \times m$ grid is represented by a class containing an $m \times m$ array of lists, one list per cell. Each list contains those points of S that lie in the corresponding cell:

```
class Grid {
 private:
   int m;              // nbr of cells along side of domain
   double cellSize;    // length of a cell side
```

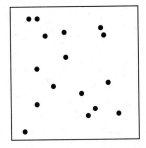 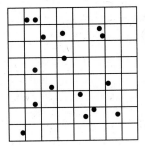

Figure 9.3:   A grid.

```
   List<Point*> ***g;    // mxm grid
   void _Grid(double domainSize, Point s[], int n);
 public:
   Grid(double domainSize, Point s[], int n, int m = 10);
   Grid(double domainSize, Point s[], int n, double M =
1.0);
   ~Grid(void);
   List<Point*> *rangeQuery(Rectangle &range);
   friend class Quadtree;
};
```

9.2.2 Constructors and Destructors

The first constructor is passed an array s of n points, the length domainSize of a side of square domain $\mathcal{D}$, and the grid size _m:

```
Grid::Grid(double domainSize, Point s[], int n, int _m) :
   m(_m)
{
   _Grid(domainSize, s, n);
}
```

The constructor's real work is performed by private member function _Grid:

```
void Grid::_Grid(double domainSize, Point s[], int n)
{
   cellSize = domainSize / m;
   g = new (List<Point*>**)[m];
   for (int i = 0; i < m; i++) {
      g[i] = new (List<Point*>*)[m];
      for (int j = 0; j < m; j++)
         g[i][j] = new List<Point*>;
   }
   for (i = 0; i < n; i++) {
      int a = int(s[i].x / cellSize);
      int b = int(s[i].y / cellSize);
```

```
    g[a][b]->append(new Point(s[i]));
    }
}
```

The grid is stored in the $m \times m$ array g of pointer-to-lists. We implement g as an array of arrays so we can use standard indexing notation. Thus g[i][j] points to the list at row i, column j of the grid. After initializing a new list for each cell of the grid, the constructor loops through the n points, appending each to its proper list.

The grid size m affects efficiency. If m is chosen too large, then the cells will be so small that many will be devoid of points. If m is chosen too small, then the cells will be so large that many will be overfull, containing an excessive number of points. One way to control the size of the grid is to specify a *cell occupancy target M*, a real number representing the desired average number of points per cell. Where set S contains n points, we have $M = \frac{n}{m^2}$. To express m as a function of M, we rewrite this as $m = \lceil \sqrt{\frac{n}{M}} \rceil$. This leads us to the second constructor Grid, which, when passed a cell occupancy target M, uses this formula to derive grid size:

```
Grid::Grid(double domainSize, Point s[], int n, double M) :
   m(int(ceil(sqrt(n / M))))
{
   _Grid(domainSize, s, n);
}
```

The destructor ~Grid deletes the points in the grid, the lists that contain them, and the arrays that make up the grid itself:

```
Grid::~Grid(void)
{
   for (int i = 0; i < m; i++) {
      for (int j = 0; j < m; j++) {
         g[i][j]->last();
         while (g[i][j]->length() > 0)
            delete g[i][j]->remove();
         delete g[i][j];
      }
      delete g[i]
   }
   delete g;
}
```

9.2.3 Performing Range Queries

To query with range R, member function rangeQuery converts the coordinates of R's corners into integer grid indices, which it uses to delimit the search along the grid's rows and columns. For instance, the x-extent of R extends from column int(R.sw.x/cellSize) of the grid through column int(R.ne.x/cellSize). For each cell that function rangeQuery visits, the function tests each point in the cell's list for inclusion in range R.

The points to be reported are accumulated in list `result`:

```
List<Point*> *Grid::rangeQuery(Rectangle &R)
{
    List<Point*> *result = new List<Point*>;
    int ilimit = int(R.ne.x / cellSize);
    int jlimit = int(R.ne.y / cellSize);
    for (int i = int(R.sw.x/cellSize); i <= ilimit; i++)
        for (int j = int(R.sw.y/cellSize); j <= jlimit; j++) {
            List<Point*> *pts = g[i][j];
            for (pts->first(); !pts->isHead(); pts->next()) {
                Point *p = pts->val();
                if (pointInRectangle(*p, R))
                    result->append(p);
            }
        }
    return result;
}
```

9.2.4 Analysis

The constructors build an $m \times m$ grid over n points in $O(m^2 + n)$ time. Moreover, a single range query takes $O(m^2 + n)$ time in the worst case. Indeed, it is not difficult to devise a range query which examines all m^2 cells and all n points without reporting a single point.

Nonetheless, range queries are much more efficient than this on average: A range query which reports r points runs in $O(r)$ time on average when the points are uniformly distributed. To see why, observe that the average-case running time is proportional to the expected number of cells examined plus the expected number of points examined. Each examined cell yields, on average, a small constant number of those points reported; hence the expected number of cells examined is $O(r)$. Furthermore, on average, a fixed fraction of the points in an examined cell are reported; hence the expected number of points examined is also $O(r)$.

Grids perform less well if the points of S are nonuniformly distributed. If too many cells are empty, the expected number of cells examined during a range query is no longer bounded above by $O(r)$. This is because many empty cells may need to be examined, yet they will not contribute any reported points. Alternatively, if too many cells are overfull and the range under consideration happens to be long and thin, slipping as it were between points of S, then the expected number of points examined is not bounded above by $O(r)$. For if cells contain arbitrarily many points of S, it is no longer to be expected that a fixed fraction of the points in each examined cell are reported.

9.3   Quadtrees

Grids are relatively inefficient when the points of S are distributed nonuniformly, dense in some regions of domain $\mathcal{D}$ and scarce in others. In such cases, no choice of grid size can guarantee the ideal—that every cell contains a small number of points of S. The *quadtree subdivision* solves this difficulty by varying cell size in response to the distribution of points, providing a subdivision that is fine where points are dense and coarse where points are scarce.

A quadtree subdivision is obtained by recursively subdividing square domain $\mathcal{D}$ into quadrants. A given quadrant is subdivided by two *cut lines*, one vertical and the other horizontal, which cross at the quadrant's center, thereby dividing it into four equal-size square *subquadrants*. In Figure 9.4a, domain $\mathcal{D}$ has been subdivided into northeast, southeast, southwest, and northwest subquadrants. The northeast and southwest subquadrants, quadrants in their own right, have been subdivided further.

We represent a quadtree subdivision with a *quadtree*, a four-way branching tree (Figure 9.4b). Each node n of the quadtree is associated with a region $\mathcal{R}(n)$, which the node is said to *span*: The root node spans the entire square domain $\mathcal{D}$, and each nonroot node spans one of the four subquadrants of its parent's region. The internal nodes of the quadtree span quadrants that have been subdivided further, and the external nodes span quadrants that have not been subdivided further. Accordingly, we refer to a quadrant as *internal* if it has been subdivided further, and *external* if it has not.

In Figure 9.4b, the branches which descend from each internal node of the quadtree are labeled 0, 1, 2, and 3, corresponding to the node's northeast, southeast, southwest, and northwest subquadrants, respectively. The branch labels can be used in a simple scheme for labeling the nodes of the quadtree; hence also the quadrants of the corresponding quadtree subdivision. The label of the root node is 0. The label of a nonroot node that is entered by a branch labeled i is obtained by appending i to the label of its parent. Equivalently, to obtain the label of a node, we start with 0 and then successively append the branch labels along the unique path which descends from the root down to the node. The labels of some of the quadrants in Figure 9.4a are shown.

What is the proper depth of a quadtree? More to the point, while building a quadtree, how do we control the process of subdividing quadrants? The quadtree is based on the idea of *adaptive subdivision*—quadrants are subdivided until some criterion is met. For the range searching problem, we are interested in controlling the number of points of S which fall in a quadrant. Specifically, we employ this subdivision criterion: A quadrant is subdivided further only if it contains more than M points of S. Here integer M, the cell occupancy target, is supplied when the quadtree is constructed.

If the quadtrees we build are too deep, range queries will be costly. Unfortunately, our subdivision criterion alone is not enough to guarantee reasonably shallow quadtrees.

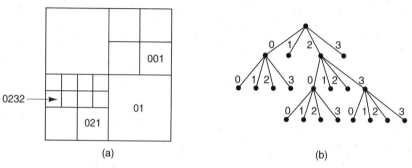

(a)   (b)

Figure 9.4:   (a) A quadtree subdivision and (b) its quadtree representation.

For if $M + 1$ points of S are clustered arbitrarily close together, the quadtree that results must be arbitrarily deep in order to separate the points. To limit the depth of the quadtree, we specify a *cutoff depth* D below which the quadtree is not permitted to grow.

The cell occupancy target M and the cutoff depth D are used together to produce quadtrees satisfying the following properties: For each external node n,

1. n lies no deeper than D;
2. if the depth of n is strictly less than D, then n spans no more than M points of S; and
3. if n is not the root, n's parent spans more than M points of S.

These properties jointly determine a unique quadtree for any given point set S contained in domain $\mathcal{D}$. Informally, they say that we are to continue subdividing quadrants until they contain no more than M points or depth D is reached. Figure 9.5 is an example.

9.3.1 Representation

Let us implement quadtrees for solving the range searching problem. Class `Quadtree` is defined like this:

```
class Quadtree {
 private:
    QuadtreeNode *root;
    Rectangle domain;
    QuadtreeNode *buildQuadtree(Grid &G, int M, int D, int level,
                                int, int, int, int);
 public:
    Quadtree(Grid &G, int M, int D);
    ~Quadtree();
    List<Point*> *rangeQuery(Rectangle &range);
};
```

The nodes of a quadtree are represented by `QuadtreeNode` objects:

```
class QuadtreeNode {
 private:
    QuadtreeNode *child[4];
```

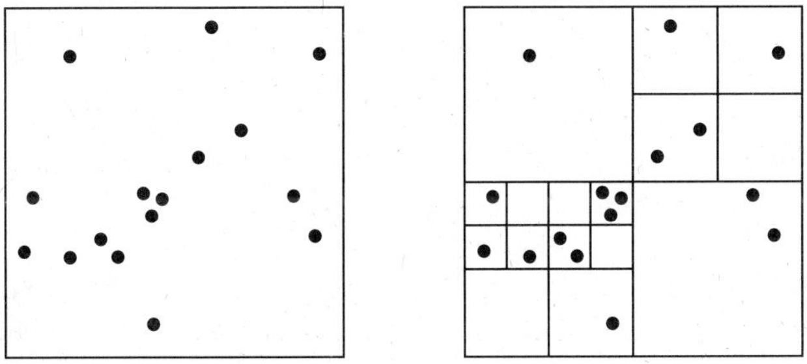

Figure 9.5: (a) A set of 16 points and (b) a quadtree over the points, where $M = 2$ and $D = 3$.

```
    List<Point*> *pts;   // points of S if node is external
                         // NULL if node is internal
    int size;     // nbr of points of S spanned by node
    List<Point*> *rangeQuery(Rectangle &range,
                             Rectangle &quadrant);
    Rectangle quadrant(Rectangle&, int);
    int isExternal();
  public:
    QuadtreeNode(List<Point*>*);
    QuadtreeNode(void);
    ~QuadtreeNode(void);
    friend class Quadtree;
};
```

If this quadtree node is external, data member `pts` is the list of points the node spans (i.e., the points which lie in the quadrant spanned by the node). Alternatively, if this node is internal, then data member `child` points to its four children, and `pts` equals NULL. Note that there is no need to store points in internal nodes since the same points will be stored in the node's descendants—every internal node spans the quadrants of its descendants.

9.3.2 Constructors and Destructors

The constructor `Quadtree` is passed a grid G, a cell occupancy target M, and a cutoff depth D. It constructs a quadtree over the points of grid G subject to the constraints implied by M and D, and it removes the points from grid G in the process. We assume that the number of cells along each side of grid G is a power of 2; that is, $G.m = 2^k$ for some integer k.

```
Quadtree::Quadtree(Grid &G, int M, int D)
{
    root = buildQuadtree(G, M, D, 0, 0, G.m-1, 0, G.m-1);
    domain = Rectangle(Point(0,0),
                       Point(G.m*G.cellSize, G.m*G.cellSize));
}
```

Member function `Quadtree::buildQuadtree` builds a quadtree over grid G from the bottom up, from the level of individual grid cells up to level zero where domain $\mathcal{D}$ is viewed as a single cell. At the lowest level—level k, where the grid is $2^k \times 2^k$—each cell of the grid is represented by its own one-node quadtree. The node contains a list of those points of S that lie in the cell. To construct the quadtrees whose roots lie at level ℓ, we combine groups of four quadtrees whose roots lie at next-lower level $\ell + 1$. When we reach level 0, the topmost level, we will have constructed a single quadtree which spans the entire domain $\mathcal{D}$. Each of the quadtree's external nodes will contain a list of those points of S it spans.

Given four quadtree with roots n_0, n_1, n_2, and n_3 at level $\ell + 1$, we need a way to combine them into a single quadtree with root n at level ℓ. We do this with one of these two actions:

- *Link quadtrees to common parent:* Make n_0, n_1, n_2, and n_3 the children of node n.
- *Merge quadtrees into single node:* Combine the points of S spanned by n_0, n_1, n_2, and n_3 into a single list of points, and associate this list with node n. Then delete nodes n_0, n_1, n_2, and n_3.

How do we decide which of the two actions to perform? The goal is to build a quadtree satisfying the three properties noted earlier. To do this, we *merge* quadtrees n_0, n_1, n_2, and n_3 into a single node n if either (1) the region spanned by node n contains no more than M points of S, or (2) node n lies at level D or greater. Otherwise we *link* n_0, n_1, n_2, and n_3 to node n.

The process of constructing a quadtree over a grid can be viewed this way: Starting with the finest possible quadtree subdivision of grid G wherein each grid cell is a separate quadrant, we proceed, level by level, to merge groups of four quadrants whenever the cell occupancy target M or the cutoff depth D makes this necessary. Figure 9.6 illustrates the process. The quadtree in the figure is finest at level 4, when processing begins. Level 3 results from merging *all* groups of four quadrants—since the cutoff depth is 3, all nodes at level 4 must be merged. The remaining levels (2, 1, and 0) result from merging only those groups of four quadrants which, combined, contain no more than M points of S.

Member function `Quadtree::buildQuadtree` is passed grid G, cell occupancy target M, and cutoff depth D. It constructs a quadtree over the subgrid `G[imin..imax, jmin..jmax]` and returns its root node. Parameter `level` indicates the level at which the root node occurs within the top-level quadtree.

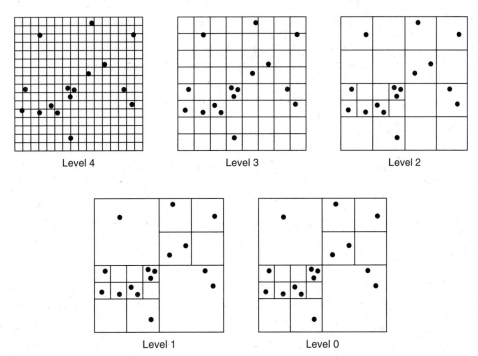

Figure 9.6: Building a quadtree over a grid. Here $M = 2$ and $D = 3$.

```
QuadtreeNode *Quadtree::buildQuadtree(Grid &G,int M, int D,
            int level, int imin, int imax, int jmin, int jmax)
{
   if (imin == imax) {
      QuadtreeNode *q = new QuadtreeNode(G.g[imin][jmin]);
      G.g[imin][jmin] = new List<Point*>;
      return q;
   } else {
      QuadtreeNode *p = new QuadtreeNode;
      int imid = (imin + imax) / 2;
      int jmid = (jmin + jmax) / 2;
      p->child[0] =      // NorthEast
        buildQuadtree(G,M,D,level+1,imid+1,imax,jmid+1,jmax);
      p->child[1] =      // SouthEast
        buildQuadtree(G,M,D,level+1,imid+1,imax,jmin,jmid);
      p->child[2] =      // SouthWest
        buildQuadtree(G,M,D,level+1,imin,imid,jmin,jmid);
      p->child[3] =      // NorthWest
        buildQuadtree(G,M,D,level+1,imin,imid,jmid+1,jmax);
      for (int i = 0; i < 4; i++)
         p->size += p->child[i]->size;
      if ((p->size <= M) || (level >= D)) { // merge children
         p->pts = new List<Point*>;
         for (i = 0; i < 4; i++) {
            p->pts->append(p->child[i]->pts);
            delete p->child[i];
            p->child[i] = NULL;
         }
      }   // end merge children
      return p;
   }
}
```

In the general case, function buildQuadtree recursively constructs root p's four children and links them to p. If necessary, it then merges the four children into p and deletes them. Note that in the base case (imin==imax), the function "steals" lists of points from grid G, leaving the grid empty yet in such a state that it can be safely deleted.

Destructor ~Quadtree is trivial:

```
Quadtree::~Quadtree()
{
   delete root;
}
```

The first constructor QuadtreeNode initializes its class's data members when passed a list of points:

```
QuadtreeNode::QuadtreeNode(List<Point*> *_pts) :
   pts(_pts), size(_pts->length())
{
   for (int i = 0; i < 4; i++)
      child[i] = NULL;
}
```

The constructor `QuadtreeNode`, taking no arguments, is used when an internal node's list of points is constructed within member function `buildQuadtree`:

```
QuadtreeNode::QuadtreeNode(void) :
   pts(NULL), size(0)
{
   for (int i = 0; i < 4; i++)
      child[i] = NULL;
}
```

The destructor `~QuadtreeNode` deallocates this node's list of points if this node is external, or recursively deletes this node's children if this node is internal:

```
QuadtreeNode::~QuadtreeNode()
{
   if (isExternal()) {    // node is external
      pts->last();
      while (pts->length() > 0)
         delete pts->remove();
      delete pts;
   } else                 // node is internal
      for (int i = 0; i < 4; i++)
         delete child[i];
}
```

9.3.3 Performing Range Queries

To query with range R, we apply the query to the quadtree's root node:

```
List<Point*> *Quadtree::rangeQuery(Rectangle &R)
{
   return root->rangeQuery(R, domain);
}
```

To query with range R starting from node n, we first check whether range R intersects region $\mathcal{R}(n)$. If it does not, we return. If n is an external node, we test each of the points in its list for inclusion in R. Otherwise (n is an internal node) we recursively apply the range query to each of n's four children, appending together the reported points into a single list, which is returned:

```
List<Point*> *QuadtreeNode::rangeQuery(Rectangle &R,
                                       Rectangle &span)
{
   List<Point*> *result = new List<Point*>;
   if (!intersect(R, span))
      return result;
   else if (isExternal())    // node is external
      for (pts->first(); !pts->isHead(); pts->next()) {
         Point *p = pts->val();
         if (pointInRectangle(*p, R))
            result->append(p);
      }
   else
      for (int i = 0; i < 4; i++) {
         List<Point*> *l =
               child[i]->rangeQuery( R,quadrant(span,i));
         result->append(l);
      }
   return result;
}
```

Parameter span is the quadrant spanned by this node. Rather than store each node's quadrant explicitly, as a data member of class QuadtreeNode, we compute quadrants on the fly: when a node queries each of its children, it provides the child with the child's subquadrant. Subquadrants are computed with member function quadrant, defined in the next subsection.

9.3.4 Support Functions

Member function QuadtreeNode::quadrant is used during the course of a range query to compute the quadrant spanned by each node. The function returns the quadrant spanned by child i of this node, where we assume that this node spans quadrant s:

```
Rectangle QuadtreeNode::quadrant(Rectangle &s, int i)
{
   Point c = 0.5 * (s.sw + s.ne);
   switch (i) {
    case 0:
     return Rectangle(c, s.ne);
    case 1:
     return Rectangle(Point(c.x,s.sw.y), Point(s.ne.x, c.y));
    case 2:
     return Rectangle(s.sw, c);
    case 3:
     return Rectangle(Point(s.sw.x, c.y), Point(c.x,s.ne.y));
   }
}
```

   Function `intersect` determines whether two rectangles a and b intersect. They do so only if their x-extents overlap and their y-extents overlap:

```
bool intersect(Rectangle &a, Rectangle &b)
{
    return (overlappingExtent(a, b, X) &&
            overlappingExtent(a, b, Y));
}
```

   Two intervals overlap if and only if the left endpoint of one of the intervals lies in the other interval. Function `overlappingExtent` returns TRUE if and only if the extents of rectangles a and b overlap in coordinate i:

```
bool overlappingExtent(Rectangle &a, Rectangle &b, int i)
{
    return ((a.sw[i] <= b.sw[i]) && (b.sw[i] <= a.ne[i])) ||
           ((b.sw[i] <= a.sw[i]) && (a.sw[i] <= b.ne[i]));
}
```

   One other support function requiring mention is `QuadtreeNode::isExternal`, which returns TRUE if this node is an external node:

```
int QuadtreeNode::isExternal()
{
    return (pts != NULL);
}
```

9.3.5 Analysis

Let us consider the running time of constructor `Quadtree` when passed an $m \times m$ grid. The running time $T(m)$ is expressed by the recurrence

$$T(m) = \begin{cases} 4T(\frac{m}{2}) + a & \text{if } m > 1 \\ b & \text{if } m = 1 \end{cases}$$

for constants a and b. It is not hard to show that $T(m) \in O(m^2)$. Note that $T(m)$ is independent of the size of point set S. This is because function `buildQuadtree` takes only constant time, not counting the recursive calls. Whenever the function merges four nodes into their common parent node, four lists of points are merged in constant time with function `List::append`. Whenever the recursion bottoms out, the function "steals" a list of points from the grid in constant time.

   Let us consider the cost of a range query. A query with range R takes time proportional to the number of points examined plus the number of nodes visited. In the worst-case query, all n points of S are examined yet none are reported. This occurs, for instance, when all the points of S happen to fall in the same external quadrant, and R intersects this quadrant yet does not contain any of its points. Thus a range query takes $O(n)$ time at worst, which is no better than the brute-force approach to range searching. However, quadtrees are superior to the brute-force approach in the average-case sense. We will not consider the expected performance of the quadtree for range searching; the question is difficult, and its answer depends largely on what is meant by an expected distribution of points in the plane.

It is, however, worthwhile to question how many quadtree nodes are visited during the course of a range query. Given range R, each node n of the quadtree falls into one of three categories, based on the relationship between R and the node's region $\mathcal{R}(n)$:

- *Disjoint nodes* are characterized by the relation $R \cap \mathcal{R}(n) = \emptyset$. Here $\mathcal{R}(n)$ lies completely outside range R.

- *Surrounded nodes* are characterized by $R \cap \mathcal{R}(n) = \mathcal{R}(n)$. Here $\mathcal{R}(n)$ lies completely inside R.

- *Intersecting nodes* are characterized by $\emptyset \subset R \cap \mathcal{R}(n) \subset \mathcal{R}(n)$. Here $\mathcal{R}(n)$ and R partially intersect.

It turns out that we can ignore disjoint nodes and surrounded nodes. The search does not proceed beyond disjoint nodes: When a disjoint node is visited, its descendants are not visited. On the other hand, when a *surrounded* node is visited, *all* its descendants must be visited. This is because every point of S belonging to a descendant of a surrounded node necessarily lies in range R. Nonetheless, we can easily modify our quadtree implementation so the points of S are stored in internal nodes as well as external nodes: We let every node n—whether internal or external—contain the list of points that lie in region $\mathcal{R}(n)$. Then, whenever a surrounded node is visited during a range query, its list of points is reported directly, making unnecessary a traversal of the node's descendants.

In this way we are free to assume that the search does not proceed to the descendants of either surrounding nodes or disjoint nodes. We must still count the surrounding or disjoint node n itself, but this is easy. If node n is the root, then no other node in the quadtree is visited. Alternatively, if node n is not the root, then the cost of visiting n can be charged to n's parent, which must be an intersecting node. Since this parent node has only four children, at most four such charges can be applied to it. Hence the total number of nodes visited during a range query is proportional to the total number of intersecting nodes visited.

We are left with the problem of counting the number of intersecting nodes visited during the course of a range query. Figure 9.7 illustrates the five types of intersecting nodes that occur. Node n's type is based on how range R and region $\mathcal{R}(n)$ intersect.

For an intersecting node n of each type (0 through 4), range R can intersect the four subquadrants of $\mathcal{R}(n)$ in only a small number of ways, shown in Figure 9.8. Beneath

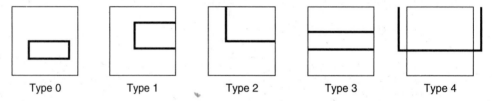

Type 0   Type 1   Type 2   Type 3   Type 4

Figure 9.7:   Given intersecting node n, the five possible relationships between range R and region $\mathcal{R}(n)$.

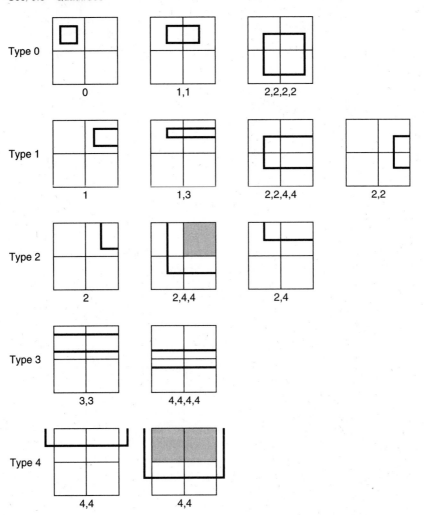

Figure 9.8: For node types 0 through 4, the ways in which range R can intersect.

each diagram is indicated the node types that result from the intersection, one level lower. Shaded subquadrants are enclosed by the range and so correspond to surrounded nodes. Whenever a node of type i is visited, the search proceeds to one or more of its children. Yet in all cases, at most two of the visited children are also of type i, and the remaining visited children are of type greater than i. If the node is type 4, only two-way branching is possible. The node type corresponds to the potential for three-way or four-way branching during the range query. When a three-way or four-way branch occurs, the potential for subsequent three-way or four-way branches decreases in all but at most two of the children. The search proceeds down what is essentially a binary tree embedded within the quadtree—the number of nodes visited is proportional to 2^D, where the quadtree has depth D.

This can be shown more formally. Each row of Figure 9.8 gives rise to a recurrence relation characterizing $T_i(D)$, the number of nodes visited in a quadtree of depth D whose root is of type i. For example, we have

$$T_3(D) = \begin{cases} 2T_3(D-1) & \text{if the first case of row 3 occurs} \\ 4T_4(D-1) & \text{if the second case of row 3 occurs} \end{cases}$$

Since the recurrence for T_i contains terms T_j for $j \geq i$, we solve these recurrences in the order $T_4, T_3, \cdots, T_0$. Specifically, induction can be used to show that

$$T_4(D) \leq 2^{D+1}$$
$$T_3(D) \leq 2^{D+2}$$
$$T_2(D) \leq 2^{D+2}$$
$$T_1(D) \leq 2^{D+3}$$
$$T_0(D) \leq 2^{D+3}$$

It follows that, regardless of the root node's type, at most $2^{D+3} = 8(2^D) \in O(2^D)$ intersecting nodes are visited during the course of a range query.

In light of this analysis, what is a good choice for cutoff depth D? We want D large enough such that few external quadrants contain more than M points, and small enough such that the quadtree is not too deep. The finest possible quadtree subdivision of depth D consists of 4^D external quadrants. For each external quadrant to contain an average of M points would require $\frac{n}{M}$ quadrants, hence $4^D = \frac{n}{M}$. Solving for D yields $D = \lceil \log_4 \frac{n}{M} \rceil$. Using this value of D, the number of nodes visited during a range query is proportional to $2^{\log_4 \frac{n}{M}}$, which is $O(\sqrt{\frac{n}{M}})$.

We have shown that a range query visits no more than $O(\sqrt{n})$ nodes, under the assumption that every node—whether internal or external—stores a list of those points it spans. Unfortunately, as we have seen, in the worst case as many as $\Omega(n)$ points are examined, and this may happen even if none of the points lie in the given range. The snag is that the quadtree subdivision is *space based*: The position and orientation of cut lines depend on the spatial domain $\mathcal{D}$, but not on the points of S. Although the number of nodes visited during a region query is bounded above by $O(\sqrt{n})$, visiting these nodes may be costly—they may contain many points of S, few or none of which are reported. In the next section we will attack the range searching problem with two-dimensional trees, which are *object based*: The position and orientation of cut lines are sensitive to point set S as well as to domain $\mathcal{D}$. Hence we can choose cut lines deliberately to separate points of S, thereby ensuring that visiting a node is inexpensive—in fact, costing only constant time. What results is a spatial data structure that supports range queries in $O(r + \sqrt{n})$ time in the worst-case sense, where r equals the number of points reported.

9.4 Two-Dimensional Search Trees

A *two-dimensional binary search tree*, or *2-d tree*, is a binary tree which recursively subdivides the plane by vertical and horizontal cut lines. The cut lines alternate in direction as we descend down the tree: Even levels (starting at the root) contain vertical cut lines, and odd levels contain horizontal cut lines. For the purpose of range searching in point set S, each node corresponds to a point of S and to a cut line that passes through the point.

Figure 9.9 shows a planar subdivision and its corresponding 2-d tree. The vertical cut line through point a, at the the root of the tree, separates point set S into two sets S_L and S_R, to the left and right of the cut line, respectively. The horizontal cut line through point b, the left child of a, partitions S_L into two sets, above and below the cut line. The horizontal cut line through point c, the right child of a, partitions S_R similarly. Additional cut lines refine the subdivision further. Observe that each cut line separates the remaining points into two sets of approximately the same size.

As with quadtrees, it is helpful to consider the region associated with each node. In 2-d trees, the root spans the entire domain $\mathcal{D}$, and each nonroot node spans the region of its parent, but restricted to one or the other side of its parent's cut line. In Figure 9.9b, node a spans the entire domain, node b spans the half-domain to the left of the vertical cut line through point a, and node d spans that portion of b's region which lies below the horizontal cut line through b.

Figure 9.10 illustrates the 2-d tree over a set of 200 points. For comparison, the quadtree over the same set of points is also pictured.

9.4.1 Representation

We will represent a 2-d tree by an object of class `TwoDTree`:

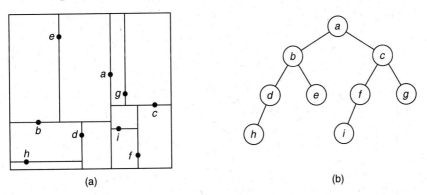

(a)   (b)

Figure 9.9:   (a) Subdivision of the plane by cut lines and (b) the corresponding 2-d tree.

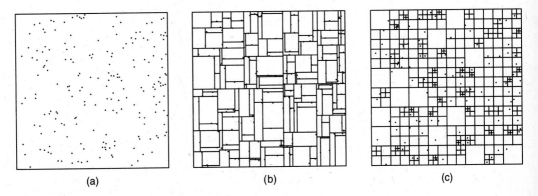

(a)   (b)   (c)

Figure 9.10:   (a) A set S of 200 points, (b) the 2-d tree over S, and (c) the quadtree over S.

```
class TwoDTree {
 private:
   TwoDTreeNode *root;
   TwoDTreeNode *buildTwoDTree(Point *x[], Point *y[],
                               int n, int cutType);
 public:
   TwoDTree(Point p[], int n);
   ~TwoDTree(void);
   List<Point*> *rangeQuery(Rectangle &range);
};
```

Nodes are represented by TwoDTreeNode objects:

```
class TwoDTreeNode {
 private:
   Point *pnt;                 // point associated with node
   TwoDTreeNode *lchild;       // left of or below cutline
   TwoDTreeNode *rchild;       // right of or above cutline
   List<Point*> *rangeQuery(Rectangle &range, int cutType);
 public:
   TwoDTreeNode(Point*);
   ~TwoDTreeNode(void);
   friend class TwoDTree;
};
```

If this node's cut line is vertical, the node pointed to by lchild (rchild) spans the region to the left (right) of the cut line; if the cut line is horizontal, lchild (rchild) spans the region below (above) the cut line. Data member pnt is this node's point.

9.4.2 Constructors and Destructors

The constructor TwoDTree builds a 2-d tree over an array p of n *distinct* points. The constructor presorts the points independently by x-coordinates and by y-coordinates and then calls member function buildTwoDTree:

```
TwoDTree::TwoDTree(Point p[], int n)
{
   Point **x = new (Point*)[n];
   Point **y = new (Point*)[n];
   for (int i = 0; i < n; i++)
      x[i] = y[i] = new Point(p[i]);
   mergeSort(x, n, leftToRightCmp);
   mergeSort(y, n, bottomToTopCmp);
   root = buildTwoDTree(x, y, n, VERTICAL);
}
```

Comparison functions leftToRightCmp and bottomToTopCmp order points in the plane by increasing x-coordinates and increasing y-coordinates, respectively. The former function was defined in subsection 4.3.6, and the latter function in subsection 8.6.1.

To assemble a 2-d tree, member function `buildTwoDTree` (defined later) initializes the tree's root node and then recursively assembles the root's two subtrees, one to either side of the root's cut line. Where $m = n/2$, the root node is associated with the point $x[m]$ and with the vertical cut line through this point. Because array x has been presorted, point $x[m]$ is the median point by x-coordinate, and the vertical cut line through $x[m]$ separates the remaining $n - 1$ points of S into left and right subsets of roughly equal size.

Before recursively constructing the root's two subtrees, function `buildTwoDTree` partitions both array x and array y into two sorted subarrays, one to either side of the vertical cut line. Array x partitions into $x[0..m - 1]$ and $x[m + 1..n - 1]$. Array y is partitioned by function `splitPointSet`, to be defined shortly. Having partitioned the two arrays, the function then constructs the root's left (right) subtree by applying itself recursively to the sorted subarrays of x and y of points to the left (right) of the cut line.

To obtain a *horizontal* cut line at the next lower level, we swap the roles of arrays x and y. In general, as we descend the tree by level, we swap the roles of x and y to alternate between vertical and horizontal cut lines.

Function `buildTwoDTree` is passed arrays `x` and `y` of n points, sorted by x-coordinates and y-coordinates, respectively. Parameter `cutType` indicates the type of cut line with the enumeration value `VERTICAL` or `HORIZONTAL`. The function returns a pointer to the root of the 2-d tree it constructs:

```
enum { VERTICAL = 0, HORIZONTAL = 1 };

TwoDTreeNode *TwoDTree::buildTwoDTree(Point *x[], Point *y[],
                                      int n, int cutType)
{
    if (n == 0)
        return NULL;
    else if (n == 1)
        return new TwoDTreeNode(x[0]);
    int m = n / 2;
    int (*cmp)(Point*, Point*);
    if (cutType == VERTICAL) cmp = leftToRightCmp;
    else cmp = bottomToTopCmp;
    TwoDTreeNode *p = new TwoDTreeNode(x[m]);
    Point **yL = new (Point*)[m];
    Point **yR = new (Point*)[n-m];
    splitPointSet(y, n, x[m], yL, yR, cmp);
    p->lchild = buildTwoDTree(yL, x, m, 1-cutType);
    p->rchild = buildTwoDTree(yR, x+m+1, n-m-1, 1-cutType);
    delete yL;
    delete yR;
    return p;
}
```

The destructor `~TwoDTree` is trivial:

```
TwoDTree::~TwoDTree()
{
```

```
    delete root;
}
```

The constructor `TwoDTreeNode` initializes a node's data members:

```
TwoDTreeNode::TwoDTreeNode(Point *_pnt)
    : pnt(_pnt), lchild(NULL), rchild(NULL)
{
}
```

The destructor `~TwoDTreeNode` recursively deletes this node's two children and then deletes this node's point:

```
TwoDTreeNode::~TwoDTreeNode()
{
    if (lchild) delete lchild;
    if (rchild) delete rchild;
    delete pnt;
}
```

9.4.3 Performing Range Queries

Let us consider how to query with range R, starting from some node of the 2-d tree. First, we check whether the point associated with the node lies in R—if so, we report the point. Second, if part of R lies to the left of (below) the node's vertical (horizontal) cut line, we recursively query from the node's left child. Symmetrically, if part of R lies to the right of (above) the vertical (horizontal) cut line, we recursively query from the node's right child. The objective is to restrict the query to one side of the node's cut line whenever possible—that is, whenever range R does not straddle the cut line.

The top-level query with range R is applied to the 2-d tree's root:

```
List<Point*> *TwoDTree::rangeQuery(Rectangle &R)
{
    return root->rangeQuery(R, VERTICAL);
}
```

Function `TwoDTreeNode::rangeQuery` performs a query with range R, starting from this node. The cut line through this node is assumed to be of type `cutType`, either `VERTICAL` or `HORIZONTAL`. The function returns a list of those points which lie in range R:

```
List<Point*> *TwoDTreeNode::rangeQuery(Rectangle &R,
                                       int cutType)
{
    List<Point*> *result = new List<Point*>;
    if (pointInRectangle(*pnt, R))
        result->append(pnt);
    int (*cmp)(Point*, Point*);
```

```
cmp = (cutType==VERTICAL) ? leftToRightCmp : bottomToTopCmp;
if (lchild && ((*cmp)(&R.sw, pnt) < 0))
   result->append(lchild->rangeQuery(R, 1-cutType));
if (rchild && ((*cmp)(&R.ne, pnt) > 0))
   result->append(rchild->rangeQuery(R, 1-cutType));
return result;
}
```

The function accumulates the points it finds in list `result`. Note how the function uses the corners of range R to determine R's relationship with the cut line. For instance, part of R lies to the left of (below) the vertical (horizontal) cut line only if R's southwest corner is less than `pnt`. Here the meaning of *less than* depends on the cut line's orientation and is determined by the comparison function `leftToRightCmp` or `bottomToTopCmp`.

9.4.4 Support Functions

Function `splitPointSet` is used to separate points by a cut line. Suppose that the cut line is vertical. When passed point p and an array y of points sorted by increasing y-coordinates, the function produces two arrays: yL contains those points of y that lie to the left of p, sorted by y-coordinates; and array yR contains those points of y that lie to the right of p, also sorted by y-coordinates:

```
void splitPointSet(Point *y[], int n, Point *p,
                   Point *yL[], Point *yR[],
                   int (*cmp)(Point*,Point*))
{
   int lindx = 0, rindx = 0;
   for (int i = 0; i < n; i++) {
      if ((*cmp)(y[i], p) < 0)
         yL[lindx++] = y[i];
      else if ((*cmp)(y[i], p) > 0)
         yR[rindx++] = y[i];
   }
}
```

The function performs the reverse of the merge operation of merge sort and differs from function `splitY` of section 8.6 in only two ways. First, point p is included in neither yL nor yR, even if p occurs in array y. Second, function `splitPointSet` separates points according to the comparison function cmp it is passed. We pass the comparison function `leftToRightCmp` to separate points by a vertical cut line through point p, and `bottomToTopCmp` to separate points by a horizontal cut line through p.

9.4.5 Analysis

The recursive function `TwoDTree::buildTwoDTree` constructs a 2-d tree over a set of n points in $T(n)$ time, where $T(n)$ is expressed by the recurrence

$$T(n) = \begin{cases} 2T(\frac{n}{2}) + an & \text{if } n > 1 \\ b & \text{if } n = 1 \end{cases}$$

for suitable constants a and b. Hence $T(n) \in O(n \log n)$. Since the presorting performed by constructor TwoDTree also runs in $O(n \log n)$ time, 2-d tree construction takes $O(n \log n)$ time.

A range query which reports r points runs in $O(r + \sqrt{n})$ time in the worst-case sense. This can be shown by an argument similar to the one used in the previous section to analyze quadtrees. Each node of a 2-d tree can be classified as disjoint, surrounded, or intersecting, based on its relationship to the given range R. It can then be shown that the number of intersecting nodes visited during the course of the range query is bounded above by $O(\sqrt{n})$, and the number of surrounded nodes visited is bounded above by $O(r)$.

9.5 Removing Hidden Surfaces: Binary Space Partition Trees

In this section we turn to a problem closely related to the hidden surface removal problem of section 6.4. Our goal is to devise a spatial data structure over a static collection of triangles in space, to support the following operation: Given any viewpoint p in space, compute a visibility ordering of the triangles with respect to p. (Recall from section 6.4 the significance of a visibility ordering: If triangle P precedes triangle Q in this ordering, then P must not obscure Q when viewed from point p—painting the triangles in this order yields the view from p with hidden surfaces eliminated.) This "multishot" solution to the hidden surface removal problem is practical for computer graphics since it accommodates a viewpoint moving around a static scene. For each successive position of the viewpoint, the data structure supports near real-time image generation, with hidden surfaces removed.

Our data structure is based on a binary partition of space. To visualize what is going on, we will consider binary partitions one dimension lower, in the plane. No loss of generality results from focusing on the plane since the ideas involved apply to spaces of any dimension. Indeed, when we turn to the implementation, we will return to three dimensions so the code can be used for computer graphics.

The two-dimensional analogue of our problem is as follows: Given a set of line segments in the plane, organize them in a data structure to compute a visibility ordering of the line segments with respect to any viewpoint p in the plane. Drawing the line segments in visibility order yields the one-dimensional view from point p with hidden lines removed. Here the line segments are considered opaque, and vision is restricted to the plane.

Let us consider the data structure we will use. A two-dimensional *binary space partition tree*, or *BSP tree*, is a binary tree which recursively subdivides the plane by cut lines. Each node of the BSP tree is associated with both a cut line and a region. As with the 2-d tree, the root's region is the entire plane, and each nonroot node's region is that of its parent, but restricted to one or the other side of its parent's cut line. However, unlike the 2-d tree, the cut lines in the BSP tree are of arbitrary orientation and position. Figure 9.11 illustrates a binary space partition and its corresponding BSP tree. Note that the cut lines to the left of a given cut line ℓ lie in ℓ's left subtree, and those to the right of ℓ lie in its right subtree.

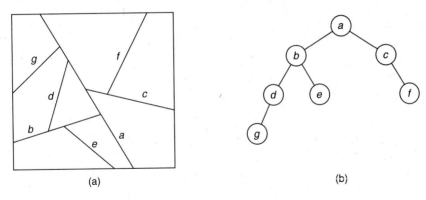

Figure 9.11: (a) A binary space partition and (b) its BSP tree.

Let us consider how to construct a BSP tree to solve our viewing problem in the plane. Given a set S of line segments, we first select an arbitrary line segment from S and associate it with the tree's root node. The root's cut line is the line determined by this line segment, obtained by extending the line segment in both directions. This cut line partitions the remaining line segments into two groups: S_L, to the left of the cut line; and S_R, to the right of the cut line. Any line segment pierced by the cut line is split into two pieces, and the piece to the left of the cut line is added to S_L and the other piece to S_R. Finally, we recursively construct the root's left subtree over S_L and its right subtree over S_R. In Figure 9.12b, the cut line through line segment a splits line segment d into d_1 and d_2. Set S_L contains line segments b, c, and d_1, and set S_R contains d_2, e, and f. Node a's left and right subtrees, BSP trees in their own right, are constructed over S_L and S_R respectively.

Given any viewpoint p in the plane, we use a *modified inorder traversal* of the BSP tree to arrange the line segments in visibility order. Consider how to traverse the BSP tree of Figure 9.13c, starting from the root. Since viewpoint p lies to the right of line segment a, none of the line segments to the left of a can obscure a; nor can they obscure any of the line segments to the right of a. Hence we draw the line segments to the left of a first. Moreover, since a cannot obscure any of the line segments which lie to its right, we next draw a. Finally, we draw the line segments which lie to the right of a. Of course, were viewpoint p

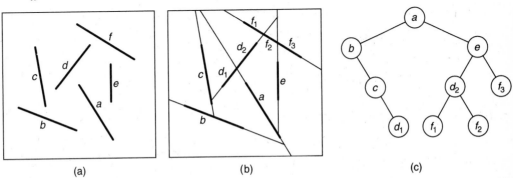

Figure 9.12: (a) A set S of line segments, (b) a binary space partition over S, and (c) the corresponding BSP tree.

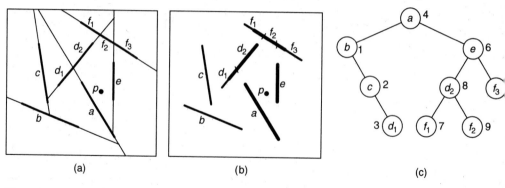

Figure 9.13: (a) A binary space partition and a viewpoint p. (b) The portions of segments visible from p are thicker. (c) The corresponding BSP, where the order in which nodes are visited during traversal is indicated.

to lie to the *left* of line segment a rather than to its right, we would draw in reverse order: first the line segments to the right of a, then a itself, and finally the line segments to the left of a. This modified inorder traversal of the BST tree, starting at node n, is conveyed by the following pseudocode:

```
removeHiddenLines(node n, viewpoint p)
   if p lies to the right of node n's line segment then
      removeHiddenLines(leftchild(n), p)
      draw(n)
      removeHiddenLines(rightChild(n), p)
   else
      removeHiddenLines(rightchild(n), p)
      draw(n)
      removeHiddenLines(leftChild(n), p)
```

Note that the else block is executed if viewpoint p is collinear with line segment a. It would be equally correct to execute the if block in this case, since a would be viewed edge on.

9.5.1 Representation

With these explanations behind us, let us turn to the task of implementing BSP trees. We will consider the problem of visibility sorting for a static collection of triangles in space and a moving viewpoint. Lifting the methods described earlier to three dimensions is straightforward: Line segments become triangles, and cutting lines become cutting planes.

A BSP tree is represented by class BspTree:

```
class BspTree {
 private:
   BspTreeNode *root;
   BspTreeNode *buildBspTree(List<Triangle3D*>*);
 public:
```

```
     BspTree(Triangle3D *t[], int n);
     ~BspTree(void);
     List<Triangle3D*> *visibilitySort(Point3D p);
};
```

Nodes are represented by objects of this class:

```
class BspTreeNode {
 private:
    BspTreeNode *poschild;
    BspTreeNode *negchild;
    Triangle3D *tri;
    BspTreeNode(Triangle3D*);
    ~BspTreeNode(void);
    List<Triangle3D*> *visibilitySort(Point3D);
    friend class BspTree;
};
```

This node's triangle—pointed to by data member `tri`—partitions space into a positive half-space and a negative half-space, as discussed in section 4.5. Data member `poschild` points to this node's child in `tri`'s positive half-space, and `negchild` to its child in `tri`'s negative half-space.

9.5.2 Constructors and Destructors

The constructor `BspTree` creates a new BSP tree for an array t of n triangles. It simply converts t into a list, which it passes to function `buildBspTree`:

```
BspTree::BspTree(Triangle3D *t[], int n)
{
    List<Triangle3D*> *tris = new List<Triangle3D*>;
    for (int i = 0; i < n; i++)
       tris->append(new Triangle3D(*t[i]));
    root = buildBspTree(tris);
    delete tris;
}
```

Member function `buildBspTree` constructs a BSP tree over the list s of triangles it is passed. The function returns a pointer to the tree's root node:

```
BspTreeNode *BspTree::buildBspTree(List<Triangle3D*> *s)
{
    if (s->length() == 0)
       return NULL;
    if (s->length() == 1)
       return new BspTreeNode(s->first());
    List<Triangle3D*> *sP = new List<Triangle3D*>;
```

```
List<Triangle3D*> *sN = new List<Triangle3D*>;
Triangle3D *p = s->first();
for (s->next(); !s->isHead(); s->next()) {
    Triangle3D *q = s->val();
    int cl[3];
    for (int i = 0; i < 3; i++)
        cl[i] =(*q)[i].classify(*p);
    if ((cl[0] != NEGATIVE) &&
        (cl[1] != NEGATIVE) &&
        (cl[2] != NEGATIVE))
        sP->append(q);
    else if ((cl[0] != POSITIVE) &&
             (cl[1] != POSITIVE) &&
             (cl[2] != POSITIVE))
        sN->append(q);
    else
        refineList(s, p);
}
BspTreeNode *n = new BspTreeNode(p);
n->poschild = buildBspTree(sP);
n->negchild = buildBspTree(sN);
delete sP;
delete sN;
return n;
}
```

    In the general case, when list s contains more than one triangle, the first triangle p in list s is stored in the root node, and each remaining triangle q is added to either list sP or list sN, depending on whether q lies in p's positive or negative half-space. If the plane of p intersects triangle q, the call to function `refineList` splits q by the plane of p and, within list s, replaces q by its pieces. Function `refineList` was defined in section 6.4.

    The destructor `~BspTree` deletes the root of the tree:

```
BspTree::~BspTree()
{
    delete root;
}
```

    The constructor `BspTreeNode` initializes data members:

```
BspTreeNode::BspTreeNode(Triangle3D *_tri) :
    tri(_tri), poschild(NULL), negchild(NULL)
{
}
```

    The class destructor recursively deletes this node's two children and then deletes its triangle:

```
BspTreeNode::~BspTreeNode()
{
   if (poschild) delete poschild;
   if (negchild) delete negchild;
   delete tri;
}
```

9.5.3 Performing Hidden Surface Removal

Member function `BspTree::visibilitySort` is passed a viewpoint p, and returns a visibility-ordered list of triangles:

```
List<Triangle3D*> *BspTree::visibilitySort(Point3D p)
{
   return root->visibilitySort(p);
}
```

Member function `BspTreeNode::visibilitySort` implements the modified inorder traversal described earlier, for the BSP tree rooted at this node and for viewpoint p. The function returns a visibility-ordered list of triangles:

```
List<Triangle3D*> *BspTreeNode::visibilitySort(Point3D p)
{
   List<Triangle3D*> *s = new List<Triangle3D*>;
   if (p.classify(*tri) == POSITIVE) {
      if (negchild) s->append(negchild->visibilitySort(p));
      s->append(tri);
      if (poschild) s->append(poschild->visibilitySort(p));
   } else {
      if (poschild) s->append(poschild->visibilitySort(p));
      s->append(tri);
      if (negchild) s->append(negchild->visibilitySort(p));
   }
   return s;
}
```

9.5.4 Analysis

We will only state some results; the analysis itself is beyond the level of this text. Constructing a BSP tree over n non-intersecting line segments in the plane takes $O(n^2 \log n)$ time on average. The expected size of the BSP tree is $O(n \log n)$, implying that a visibility ordering is computed in $O(n \log n)$ time on average.

For the three-dimensional case, assume that the n triangles in space are non-intersecting. Then the expected size of the BSP tree is $O(n^2)$, and the expected time for its construction is $O(n^3 \log n)$.

9.6   Chapter Notes

A wide range of spatial data structures, as well as their many variants and uses, is covered by Hanan Samet in [69, 70, 71]. A survey of data structures for the range searching problem can be found in [8]. The uses of multidimensional search trees are explored in [7].

The term *quadtree* is sometimes used to refer to any spatial data structure based on the recursive decomposition of space. Such data structures may vary with respect to both the type of data they represent and the principle guiding decomposition. In light of so broad a definition, quadtrees have been around for a long time. Some of their earliest uses include hidden surface elimination [86], statistical analysis [47], range searching [27], and image processing and feature detection [42, 81]. The *octree*, the three-dimensional analogue of the quadtree, recursively partitions a cube into eight octants. Octrees are used in computer graphics to represent solids in space and to speed up rendering [28].

The articles [29, 30] treat the use of BSP trees for removing hidden surfaces, given a static scene and moving viewpoint. Our randomized algorithm for building BSP trees is described and analyzed in [58, 63]; the latter reference also explains how to improve the worst-case performance of BSP trees at the expense of simplicity (the methods are made deterministic). BSP trees are also used to represent and manipulate polyhedra in space [64, 85].

9.7   Exercises

1. Implement *octrees*, the three-dimensional analogue of quadtrees, to solve the three-dimensional range searching problem.

2. Implement *3-d trees*, the three-dimensional analogue of 2-d trees, to solve the three-dimensional range searching problem.

3. The constructor we have defined for quadtrees is passed a grid and builds the quadtree from the bottom up. Define a new constructor which is passed a list of points in the plane and builds the quadtree for the points from the top down. The quadtree should possess the same three properties discussed at the start of section 9.3. What are the advantages and disadvantages of building a quadtree from the top down?

4. Modify our implementation of grids so initialization of an $m \times m$ grid over n points takes $O(m + n)$ time.

5. Implement a constructor `Quadtree` like the one defined in this chapter, but which does not clear the grid it is passed.

6. For range searching a planar point set S, implement quadtrees such that each node—whether internal or external—contains a list of the points of S spanned by the node. How much more memory does this data structure require than the quadtree as implemented in this chapter?

7. Complete the proof that no more than $O(2^D)$ nodes of a quadtree of depth D are visited during a range query, assuming points are stored in both internal and external nodes.

8. Why does the constructor `TwoDTree` for 2-d trees fail if passed a list of points containing duplicates? Modify the constructor to handle this. Do our implementions of quadtrees and grids work for duplicate points?

9. Implement a version of range query in 2-d trees which checks whether a node is a surrounding node and, if so, avoids testing its descendants for inclusion in the range.

10. The *disk searching problem* asks us to organize a set S of points in the plane to support *disk queries*: Given any point p and positive real number r, report the points of S whose distance from p does not exceed r. Solve this problem using grids, quadtrees, and 2-d trees.

11. A quadtree can be used to represent a planar region R as follows. Every external node n contains a bit indicating whether quadrant $\mathcal{R}(n)$ is entirely contained in R or is disjoint from R. Region R equals the union of all "in" quadrants, those contained in R.

    (a) Implement this scheme.

    (b) Write a function for classifying a point with respect to a quadtree-represented region R: Given point p, determine whether p lies in R.

    (c) Write a function for forming the union of regions represented by quadtrees: Given two quadtrees representing regions A and B, respectively, construct a third quadtree representing region $A \cup B$.

    (d) Write a function that, when passed two quadtrees representing regions A and B, constructs a third quadtree representing their intersection $A \cap B$.

12. In our implementation of BSP trees, every cut plane is determined by one of the triangles in the scene. Implement a version of BSP trees in which cut planes are determined by some other criterion. What is the advantage of cutting along the planes determined by the triangles?

13. Given an arbitrary n-gon P, devise a data structure that supports point enclosure queries: Given a point p in the plane, report whether p lies in P. In Chapter 5 we explored two techniques for performing this query in $O(n)$ time. Now try to do so in $O(\log n)$ time.

Bibliography

[1] G. M. Adelson-Velskii and E. M. Landis, An algorithm for the organization of information, *Soviet Mathematics Doklady*, 3, 1259–1262 (1962).

[2] A. V. Aho, J. E. Hopcroft, and J. D. Ullman, *The Design and Analysis of Computer Algorithms*, Addison-Wesley, Reading, MA, 1974.

[3] L. Ammeraal, *Programming Principles in Computer Graphics*, John Wiley and Sons, New York, 1992.

[4] F. Aurenhammer, Voronoi diagrams: A survey of a fundamental geometric data structure, *ACM Computing Surveys*, 23(3), 345–405 (1991).

[5] D. Avis and B. K. Bhattacharya, Algorithms for computing d-dimensional Voronoi diagrams and their duals, in *Advances in Computing Research*, edited by F. P. Preparata, JAI Press, 159–180 (1983).

[6] R. Bayer, Symmetric binary B-trees: Data structure and maintenance algorithms, *Acta Informatica*, 1, 290–306 (1972).

[7] J. L. Bentley, Multi-dimensional binary search tree used for associative searching, *Communications of the ACM*, 18(9), 509–517 (1975).

[8] J. L. Bentley and J. H. Friedman, Data structures for range searching, *ACM Computing Surveys*, 11(4), 397–409 (1979).

[9] J. L. Bentley and T. A. Ottmann, Algorithms for reporting and counting geometric intersections, *IEEE Transactions on Computers*, 28, 643–647 (1979).

256

[10] J. L. Bentley and M. I. Shamos, Divide-and-conquer in multidimensional space, *Proceedings of the Eighth ACM Annual Symposium on Theory of Computation*, 220–230 (1976).

[11] G. Booch, *Object-Oriented Design with Applications*, Benjamin Cummings, Redwood City, CA, 1990.

[12] E. Brisson, Representing geometric structures in *d* dimensions: Topology and order, *Proceeding of the 5th Annual ACM Symposium on Computational Geometry*, 218–227 (1989).

[13] T. Budd, *An Introduction to Object-Oriented Programming*, Addison-Wesley, Reading, MA, 1991.

[14] A. Bykat, Convex hull of a finite set of points in two dimensions, *Information Processing Letters*, 7, 296–298 (1978).

[15] T. Cargill, *C++ Programming Style*, Addison-Wesley, Reading, MA, 1992.

[16] E. Catmull, A subdivision algorithm for computer display of curved surfaces, Ph.D. Thesis, University of Utah Dept. of Computer Science, Technical Report UTEC-CSc-74-133 (1974).

[17] D. R. Chand and S. S. Kapur, An algorithm for convex polytopes, *Journal of the ACM*, 17(1), 78–86 (1970).

[18] B. Chazelle, A theorem on polygon cutting with applications, in *Proceedings of the 23th Annual Symposium on Foundations of Computer Science*, IEEE Computer Society, 339–349 (1982).

[19] B. Chazelle, Triangulating a simple polygon in linear time, *Discrete and Computational Geometry*, 6, 485–524 (1991).

[20] T. H. Cormen, C. E. Leiserson, and R. L. Rivest, *Introduction to Algorithms*, The MIT Press, Cambridge, MA, 1990.

[21] M. Cyrus and J. Beck, Generalized two- and three-dimensional clipping, *Computers and Graphics*, 3(1), 23–28 (1978).

[22] L. Deneen and G. Shute, Polygonizations of point sets in the plane, *Discrete and Computational Geometry*, 3, 77–87 (1988).

[23] S. C. Dewhurst and K. T. Stark, *Programming in C++*, Prentice Hall, Englewood Cliffs, NJ, 1989.

[24] D. P. Dobkin and M. J. Laszlo, Primitives for the manipulation of three-dimensional subdivisions, *Algorithmica*, 4, 3–32 (1989).

[25] W. Eddy, A new convex hull algorithm for planar sets, *ACM Transactions on Mathematical Software*, 3(4), 398–403 (1977).

[26] M. A. Ellis and B. Stroustrup, *The Annotated C++ Reference Manual*, Addison-Wesley, Reading, MA, 1990.

[27] R. A. Finkel and J. L. Bentley, Quad trees: A data structure for retrieval on composite keys, *Acta Informatica*, 4, 1–9 (1974).

[28] J. D. Foley, A. van Dam, S. K. Feiner, and J. F. Hughes, *Computer Graphics: Principles and Practice*, Addison-Wesley, Reading, MA, 1990.

[29] H. Fuchs, G. D. Abram, and E. D. Grant, Near real-time shaded display of rigid objects, *Computer Graphics*, 17(3), 65–72 (1983).

[30] H. Fuchs, Z. M. Kedem, and B. F. Naylor, On visible surface generation by a priori tree structures, *Computer Graphics*, 14(3), 124–133 (1980).

[31] M. R. Garey, D. S. Johnson, F. P. Preparata, and R. E. Tarjan, Triangulating a simple polygon, *Information Processing Letters*, 7(4), 175–180 (1978).

[32] K. E. Gorlen, S. M. Orlow, and P. S. Plexico, *Data Abstraction and Object-Oriented Programming in C++*, Wiley, Chichester, England, 1990.

[33] R. L. Graham, An efficient algorithm for determining the convex hull of a finite planar set, *Information Processing Letters*, 1, 132–133 (1972).

[34] P. J. Green and B. W. Silverman, Constructing the convex hull of a finite planar set, *Information Processing Letters*, 22, 262–266 (1979).

[35] L. J. Guibas and R. Sedgewick, A dichromatic framework for balanced trees, in *Proceedings of the 19th Annual Symposium on Foundations of Computer Science*, IEEE Computer Society, 8–21 (1978).

[36] L. Guibas and J. Stolfi, Primitives for the manipulation of general subdivisions and the computation of Voronoi diagrams, *ACM Transactions on Graphics*, 4(2), 74–123 (1985).

[37] R. H. Güting, An optimal contour algorithm for isooriented rectangles, *Journal of Algorithms*, 5(3), 303–326 (1984).

[38] D. Harel, *Algorithmics: The Spirit of Computing*, Addison-Wesley, Reading, MA, 1992.

[39] D. Hearn and M. P. Baker, *Computer Graphics*, Prentice Hall, Englewood Cliffs, NJ, 1994.

[40] S. Hertel and K. Mehlhorn, Fast triangulation of simple polygons, *Proceedings of the Conference on Foundations of Computing Theory*, Springer-Verlag, New York, 207–218 (1983).

[41] J. A. Hummel, *Introduction to Vector Functions*, Addison-Wesley, Reading, MA, 1967.

[42] G. M. Hunter and K. Steiglitz, Operations on images using quad trees, *IEEE Transactions on Pattern Analysis and Machine Intelligence*, 11(2), 125–153 (1979).

[43] R. A. Jarvis, On the identification of the convex hull of a finite set of points in the plane, *Information Processing Letters*, 2, 18–21 (1973).

[44] P. J. Kahn, *Introduction to Linear Algebra*, Harper & Row, New York, 1967.

[45] M. Kallay, Convex hull algorithms in higher dimensions, unpublished manuscript, Dept. of Mathematics, Univ. of Oklahoma, Norman, Oklahoma, 1981.

[46] D. G. Kirkpatrick and R. Seidel, The ultimate planar convex hull algorithm? Tech. Rep. 83-577, Dept. of Computer Science, Cornell University, 1983.

[47] A. Klinger, Patterns and search statistics, in *Optimizing Methods in Statistics*, edited by J. S. Rustagi, Academic Press, New York, 303–337 (1971).

[48] D. E. Knuth, *Fundamental Algorithms*, Vol. 1 of *The Art of Computer Programming*, 2nd edition, Addison-Wesley, Reading, MA, 1973.

[49] D. E. Knuth, Big omicron and big omega and big theta, *ACM SIGACT News*, 8(2), 18–23 (1976).

[50] J. M. Lane, L. C. Carpenter, T. Whitted, and J. F. Blinn, Scan line methods for displaying parametrically defined surfaces, *Communications of the ACM*, 23, 23–34 (1980).

[51] D. T. Lee, Proximity and reachability in the plane, Report R-831, Coordinated Science Laboratory, University of Illinois at Urbana, 1978.

[52] D. T. Lee and F. P. Preparata, Location of a point in a planar subdivision and its applications, *SIAM Journal of Computing*, 6, 594–606 (1977).

[53] D. T. Lee and F. P. Preparata, An optimal algorithm for finding the kernel of a polygon, *Journal of the ACM*, 26, 415–421 (1979).

[54] W. Lipski, Jr. and F. P. Preparata, Finding the contour of a union of iso-oriented rectangles, *Journal of Algorithms*, 1, 235–246 (1980).

[55] D. T. Lee and B. Schachter, Two algorithms for constructing Delaunay triangulations, *International Journal of Computers and Information Science*, 9(3), 219–242 (1980).

[56] U. Manber, *Introduction to Algorithms: A Creative Approach*, Addison-Wesley, Reading, MA, 1989.

[57] S. B. Maurer and A. Ralston, *Discrete Algorithmic Mathematics*, Addison-Wesley, Reading, MA, 1991.

[58] K. Mulmuley, *Computational Geometry: An Introduction Through Randomized Algorithms*, Prentice Hall, Englewood Cliffs, NJ, 1994.

[59] M. E. Newell, R. G. Newell, and T. L. Sancha, A solution to the hidden surface problem, in *Proceedings of the ACM National Conference 1972*, 443–450 (1972).

[60] J. O'Rourke, *Art Gallery Theorems and Algorithms*, Oxford University Press, 1987.

[61] J. O'Rourke, *Computational Geometry in C*, Cambridge University Press, 1994.

[62] J. O'Rourke, C.-B Chien, T. Olson, and D. Naddor, A new linear algorithm for intersecting convex polygons, *Computer Graphics and Image Processing*, 19, 384–391 (1982).

[63] M. S. Paterson and F. F. Yao, Efficient binary span partitions for hidden surface removal and solid modelling, *Discrete and Computational Geometry*, 5, 485–503 (1990).

[64] D. Peterson, Halfspace representations of extrusions, solids of revolution, and pyramids, SANDIA Report 84-0572, Sandia National Laboratory, 1984.

[65] F. P. Preparata and S. J. Hong, Convex hulls of finite sets of points in two and three dimensions, *Communications of the ACM*, 2(20), 87–93 (1977).

[66] F. P. Preparata and M. I. Shamos, *Computational Geometry: An Introduction*, Springer-Verlag, New York, 1985.

[67] F. P. Preparata and K. J. Supowit, Testing a simple polygon for monotonicity, *Information Processing Letters*, 12(4), 161–164 (1981).

[68] D. F. Rogers, *Procedural Elements for Computer Graphics*, McGraw-Hill, New York, New York, 1985.

[69] H. Samet, The quadtree and related hierarchical data structures, *ACM Computing Surveys*, 16(2), 187–260 (1984).

[70] H. Samet, *Applications of Spatial Data Structures*, Addison-Wesley, MA, 1990.

[71] H. Samet, *Design and Analysis of Spatial Data Structures*, Addison-Wesley, MA, 1990.

[72] B. Schaudt and R. L. Drysdale, Multiplicatively weighted crystal growth Voronoi diagrams, *Proceedings of the 7th Annual ACM Symposium on Computational Geometry*, 214–223 (1991).

[73] R. Sedgewick, *Algorithms in C++*, Addison-Wesley, Reading, MA, 1992.

[74] M. I. Shamos and D. Hoey, Closest-point problems, *Sixteenth Annual IEEE Symposium on Foundations of Computer Science*, 151–162 (1975).

[75] M. I. Shamos and D. Hoey, Geometric intersection problems, *Seventeenth Annual IEEE Symposium on Foundations of Computer Science*, 208–215 (1976).

[76] J. S. Shapiro, *A C++ Toolkit*, Prentice Hall, Englewood Cliffs, New Jersey, 1991.

[77] R. F. Sproull and I. E. Sutherland, A clipping divider, *AFIPS Fall Joint Computer Conference*, Thompson Books, Washington, DC, 765–775 (1968).

[78] T. A. Standish, *Data Structure Techniques*, Addison-Wesley, Reading, MA, 1980.

[79] B. Stroustrup, *The C++ Programming Language*, Addison-Wesley, Reading, MA, 1991.

[80] I. E. Sutherland and G. W. Hodgman, Reentrant polygon clipping, *Communications of the ACM*, 17(1), 32–42 (1974).

[81] S. Tanimoto and T. Pavlidis, A hierarchical data structure for picture processing, *Computer Graphics and Image Processing*, 4(2), 104–119 (1975).

[82] R. E. Tarjan, Amortized computational complexity, *SIAM Journal on Algebraic and Discrete Methods*, 6(2), 306–318 (1985).

[83] R. E. Tarjan, *Data Structures and Network Algorithms*, Volume 44 of *BMS-NSF Regional Conference Series in Applied Mathematics*, Society for Industrial and Applied Mathematics, Philadelphia, PA, 1983.

[84] R. E. Tarjan and C. J. van Wyk, An $O(n \log \log n)$-time algorithm for triangulating a simple polygon, *SIAM Journal of Computing*, 17(1), 143–178 (1988).

[85] W. C. Thibult and B. F. Naylor, Set operations on polyhedra using binary space partitioning trees, *Computer Graphics*, 8(7), 153–162.

[86] J. Warnock, A hidden-surface algorithm for computer generated half-tone pictures, University of Utah Computer Science Dept. Technical Report TR 4-15, NTIS AD 753 671 (1968).

[87] G. S. Watkins, A real-time visible surface algorithm, University of Utah Computer Science Dept. Technical Report TR UTEC-CSc-70-101, NTIS AD 762 004 (1970).

[88] K. Weiler and P. Atherton, Hidden surface removal using polygon area sorting, *Computer Graphics*, 11, 214–222 (1977).

[89] M. A. Weiss, *Data Structures and Algorithm Analysis*, Benjamin Cummings, Redwood City, CA, 1992.

[90] D. Wood, *Data Structures, Algorithms, and Performance*, Addison-Wesley, Reading, MA, 1993.

Index